Technology, Education—Connections
The TEC Series

Series Editor: Marcia C. Linn
Advisory Board: Robert Bjork, Chris Dede, BatSheva Eylon,
Carol Lee, Jim Minstrell, Mitch Resnick

WISE Science

Web-Based Inquiry in the Classroom

James D. Slotta
Marcia C. Linn

Foreword by Carol D. Lee

Teachers College, Columbia University
New York and London

We dedicate this book to the middle- and high-school
students, classroom teachers, school administrators,
undergraduate students, graduate students, postdoctoral
fellows, and staff members who participated as learners,
critics, designers, programmers, investigators, professional
developers, evaluators, and instructors.

Published by Teachers College Press, 1234 Amsterdam Avenue, New York, NY
10027

Library of Congress Cataloging-in-Publication Data
Slotta, James D.
  WISE science : web-based inquiry in the classroom / James D. Slotta, Marcia
C. Linn.
     p. cm.
  Includes bibliographical references and index.
  ISBN 978-0-8077-4949-4 (pbk. : alk. paper)
  ISBN 978-0-8077-4950-0 (hardcover : alk. paper)
  1. Science—Computer-assisted instruction. 2. Science—Study and teach-
ing (Elementary) 3. Science—Study and teaching (Secondary) 4. Web-based
instruction. I. Linn, Marcia C. II. Title.
  LB1585.7.S57 2009
  507.8′54678—dc22   2009005899

ISBN 978-0-8077-4949-4 (paper)
ISBN 978-0-8077-4950-0 (cloth)

Printed on acid-free paper
Manufactured in the United States of America

16   15   14   13   12   11   10   09   8   7   6   5   4   3   2   1

Contents

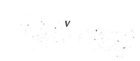

Foreword

Among the most persistent challenges in education is how theory informs practice. This challenge is further complicated by the assumptions we (i.e., the public, researchers, policymakers) entertain about what is entailed in good teaching and the capacity of those drawn into teaching to develop real mastery. Influenced in large part by behaviorist theories of learning, a generation of what was called process–product research assumed that if we could document the methods of teachers whose students have good test scores, we could then define what good teaching looks like for most students and, as a consequence, could design what would essentially be a teacher-proof curriculum. In this era of high-stakes accountability, even though our science of learning has moved beyond behaviorism (i.e., the idea that we can generate behaviors with the appropriate stimulus) toward a constructivist orientation (i.e., the idea that by active and conscious engagement with experience we construct models of how phenomena work), direct-instruction curriculum models are alive and well, indeed a growth industry, in many states and districts. Direct instruction works from the assumption that explicit teaching (usually of declarative knowledge such as facts and straightforward procedures) through repetition will facilitate learning, especially among students who are struggling as learners. And proponents of direct instruction have also invested, with good monetary returns, in low-level technology that offers on screen versions of what one finds in the worksheets that abound in direct instruction curriculum. It should be noted that, in fact, direct instruction is quite good at teaching students learning that requires memorization.

And yet, despite this popular hold-over of behaviorism, there has been an explosion in theory building about what is entailed in learning to engage in complex problem solving. Resnick has defined complex problem solving as involving strategies and modes of reasoning that cannot be fully specified in advance. Problem solving in domains of scientific reasoning is made all the more complex because the phenomenon of interest can often only be indirectly observed in the natural world. Or it may be the case that while the phenomena is observable, the tools we would use to examine the phenomena are not a part of most folks' everyday practice. And in many instances, what we are able to observe with our senses belies underlying explanatory principles. Testing hypotheses about the natural world can often be quite costly and require mathematical modeling that can be difficult for novices. Further, unless youth, for example, live close to the natural world (i.e., on farms, in rural areas, etc.), they have little cause in their everyday experiences to have practical reasons to hypothesize, indeed to test hypotheses, about how phenomena in the natural world work.

However, we live in a world where digital technologies make possible visualizations, modeling, simulations, access to manipulatable databases that can tremendously expand students' opportunities to engage in complex scientific reasoning, often using tools that have heretofore been accessible only to professionals. Over the past two decades, the National Science Foundation and others, such as the McDonnell Foundation, have invested heavily into the development of rich technologies to support complex scientific investigations by K–12 students. With these new technologies have come many challenges in terms of how individual teachers and schools have implemented these innovative technologies and curricula. However, in that broad family of science curricular supports, WISE has excelled and achieved against the odds in terms of outcomes and scope of usage. It is immensely laudatory that access to its online toolkit has remained free. Other examples of fine technology-based tools in science education have been restricted to school sites where the designers have been able to negotiate access and sustain external funding for their work in the schools. Others have been transformed into commercial products which can be challenging for schools in districts with limited resources. WISE, by contrast, has found institutional partners who have not only helped in the development of the tools and curricular content, but who also facilitate dissemination by virtue of their own institutional activities.

The WISE team has built a conceptual model for the work that is sufficiently generative and robust to allow it to be adapted by local actors in ways that minimize what we have come to refer to as lethal mutations. Part of the beauty and elegance of that model, indeed part of its generativity, is that it actually supports teacher learning and self-reflection without dictating simplistic strategies. It thus respects the professionalism of teachers while simultaneously stimulating new thinking about how to make visible what are often the invisible processes of the natural world. The underlying model includes opportunities for teacher learning by creating tools for teachers to communicate, for classrooms in different schools virtually across the globe to collaborate, for teachers to create lessons—all using exciting digital resources that are free. In addition, the resources are user-friendly and practical, with support for assessment and aligning learning objectives with local standards. Thus this suite of resources represents a way of thinking about teacher and student learning in tandem.

This book is important for several reasons. First, it offers a historical overview of evolution of the project. This is important both intellectually and practically. The challenges of coordinating with multiple partners and sustaining institutional infrastructure over time are important to understand. Second, the analysis of the varied patterns of uptake of the resources available through WISE is equally important for both the research community and the world of educational practice. Understanding such variability is crucial to how we address the persistent problem of how new reforms are deployed on the ground. These patterns of uptake are also important because they illustrate how intellectual community in K–12 schools can develop both from the bottom up and across time and space. Finally, discussions of the design principles for the tools and for the dissemination are important to inform new generations of technologies to support K–12 STEM learning.

A major task of education in a democracy is to make available to youth who face significant life challenges (due to poverty, racism, structural inequalities) the most robust opportunities to learn that our sciences make available. I am delighted to see these opportunities to visualize, model, and simulate in order to test hypotheses available to schools serving the rich and the poor. The approach to science topics in the WISE suite helps to situate scientific investigations to real world problems, helping students to understand not only the beauty but also the utility of science. With these opportunities comes the hope that more of our youngsters will learn to appreciate the wonder of science, including the organisms that inhabit the natural world and its universe, and the excitement of systematic efforts to understand the mysteries of this universe, as well as to protect this great Mother we call Earth.

—Carol D. Lee
School of Education and Social Policy,
Northwestern University

Acknowledgments

The WISE project would not have become such a wonderful success story, worthy of a book like this one, without the contributions of a great many people. We begin by acknowledging the support of the U.S. National Science Foundation. In addition to their important grant programs that support such a wide range of educational research, we are grateful to the many NSF officers who offered feedback and guidance over the years, including Spud Bradley, Janice Earle, Ray Hannapel, Mike Haney, Eammon Kelly, Andrew Molnar, Nora Sabelli, Bob Sherwood, and others.

Next, such a large and diverse project could not have succeeded without staff support for the many layers of our work that are often hidden but tremendously important, such as project management, business and human resource management, preparation of manuscript and research materials, coordination of events, and much more. We want to especially acknowledge Freda Husic, who was the project manager from 2003 to 2007 and guided the strategic planning of the work. She enabled us to create new, powerful inquiry projects and to expand the usage of WISE to hundreds of teachers across the United States. For their excellent and vital assistance in all aspects of WISE, we gratefully acknowledge the help of Jon Breitbart, David Crowell, Christy Kinnison-Dixon, and Barbara Nakakihara.

In regard to the preparation of this volume, we give heartfelt thanks to Meg Lemke, our fearless editor from Teachers College Press, who provided helpful comments on every aspect of our writing and our ideas. We also thank Cheryl Madeira for her careful reading and assistance in the preparation of the manuscript.

WISE has succeeded in part because it was such an excellent vehicle for research and thus allowed a number of different individuals and research labs to participate. These researchers have used WISE throughout its history in order to investigate their own questions about learning, instruction, or teacher professional development. We wish to acknowledge the following educational researchers from around the world—all of whom have collaborated in studies that employed WISE in science classrooms: Bob Bjork, Rick Duschl, Frank Fischer, Janice

Gobert, Doris Jorde, Yael Kali, Ingo Kollar, Marsha Matyas, Jim Monaghan, Amy Pallant, Lindsey Richland, Janet Russell, Roel Scheepens, Greg Schultz, Tammy Schellens, and Hilde Van Keer.

Our project has also depended on the direct participation of natural scientists and science disciplinary specialists. These are individuals or groups, described in later chapters, who have a distinct interest in creating rich inquiry curriculum within their respective domains. Because we are educational researchers, we required the participation of science experts in our design of curriculum. We could not have created accurate and engaging WISE curriculum projects on chemical reactions, deformed frogs, global climate change, or wolf management without the help of these wonderful colleagues: Rita Bell, Francesca Cava, Karen Dodson, Laura Duffy, Laura Frances, Paul Horwitz, Amy Kay Kerber, Randy Kochevar, Marsha Matyas, Tony Murphy, Duncan Parks, Stan Sessions, Henry Spliethoff, Kim Swan, and Bob Tinker.

WISE owes a special debt to all of the graduate students and postdoctoral researchers who conducted their own research studies using WISE and contributed directly to the design of new technology or curriculum features. We wish to gratefully acknowledge the contributions of the following graduate students: Tom Azwell, Philip Bell, Kathy Benemann, Hsin Yi Chang, Britte Cheng, Jennie Chiu, Alex Cuthbert, Betsy Davis, Jason Finley, Matt Fishbach, Brian Foley, Tara Higgins, Chris Hoadley, Amy Hollowell, Sherry Hsi, Brian Levey, Alan Li, Lydia Liu, Jacquie Madhok, Kevin McElhaney, Katrina Rotter, Beat Schwendimann, Sherry Seethaler, Linda Shear, Stephanie Sisk-Hilton, Elisa Stone, Ricky Tang, Erika Tate, Michelle Williams, Helen Zhang, and Tim Zimmerman. We also wish to acknowledge the distinguished contributions of the following postdoctoral scholars who have been leaders within the WISE community: Eric Baumgartner, Stephanie Corliss, Doug Clark, Jeff Holmes, Hee Sun Lee, Ji Shen, Michelle Spitulnik, Keisha Varma, and Michelle Williams.

Another important group that we must acknowledge in the WISE endeavor are the technologists. Over the past 12 years or so, there have been a number of insightful and hard-working individuals who brought WISE to life and helped it evolve into its current form. We wish to acknowledge the contributions of the following individuals, including full-time and part-time programmers, designers, and undergraduate students from the University of California, Berkeley: Jeff Morrow (1996–1999), Greg Pitter (1999–2002), and Turadg Aleahmad (2002–2005), who respectively led the design team through several major versions of software; Hiroki Terashima, Tony Perritano, and Geoffrey Kwan, our masterful technology team at the time of this writing; and a number of others who have helped along the way, including Sean Harris, Dustin Masterson, and Jeff Schoner. This is a neverending process of design and development, and these technology specialists have been more than programmers; they have been advisors, designers, and vital collaborators in the research.

The project also owes its success to a host of classroom teachers, principals, and superintendents who have adopted WISE curriculum in their schools and shared their insights with us. The instructional materials, research findings, and technology environment benefitted immeasurably from these contributions. While many of the teachers and administrators prefer to remain anonymous, we want to acknowledge the following participants who have made our work possible: Sara Backowski, Carolyn Berzin, Lucy Bryndza, Tom Castro, Ryan Chinn, Robin Cooper, Greg Corpuz, Margaret Elliot, Bryan Flaig, Corrie Garner, Jefferson Hartman, Debra Hill, Theresa Hoppe, Vana James, Bob Johnson, Moon Kim, Diana Lamson, Susan Lee, Kelly Miller, Crystal Mosteiro, Lauren Nourse, Meg O'Mahony, Ariel Owen, Joanna Pace, Jeff Parrish, Marty Place, Priscilla Robinson, Laine Smith, Stacey Uyeda, Janice Vinco, and Earl Walls.

We wish to thank the leaders in learning sciences and natural sciences who have served as advisory board members for the projects that supported this work. We give special thanks to Roy Pea, who has served on all advisory boards and as chair of the board most recently. Other board members include George Araya, John Bransford, Ian Carmichael, Micki Chi, Michael Clancy, Jere Confrey, Harvey Feinberg, Susan Goldman, Louis Gomez, Paul Holland, Lee Hood, Sheila Jasanoff, Eamonn Kelly, Don Kennedy, Catherine Lewis, Barbara Means, Jim Minstrell, Patricia Morse, Anne Peterson, Brian Reiser, Elliot Soloway, Nancy Songer, Eugene Stanley, Neil Stillings, and Mark Wilson.

While these acknowledgments make some attempt at being comprehensive, there are so many students, teachers, staff, and collaborators who have participated in WISE that we cannot list everyone. Please know that we are grateful for every contribution.

Finally, we wish to acknowledge the immeasurable contribution of Mr. Doug Kirkpatrick: an extraordinary science teacher who has been a continuous source of insight and support for all of our efforts. His special style and energetic participation are clearly founded in his success as a teacher, his care for students, and his deep understanding about how they learn. We began developing WISE in Mr. K's classroom, building on previous environments (described below) that were also developed in his classroom. Throughout all of these efforts, he has been our most important councilor, co-designer, and friend. We could not and would not have come to this point in our work without his steady presence and conscientious participation. After he retired from teaching in 2000, he joined the WISE group as a full-time project coordinator who focused on supporting teacher professional development. There is no book that we could ever write, now or for the remainder of our careers, that would not owe a deep debt of acknowledgment to Doug Kirkpatrick.

Introduction

This book captures the accomplishments and lessons learned within a large community of educational researchers as they designed, developed, and investigated a new technology-enhanced learning environment known as WISE: the Web-based Inquiry Science Environment. WISE was developed to capitalize on the exciting new features of the Internet in order to bring new kinds of learning and instruction into the science classroom. The project takes advantage of advances in the learning sciences that provide insight into how students learn and how instruction succeeds. The project began in 1996 at the University of California, Berkeley, and has grown over more than a decade with contributions from researchers, teachers, and scientists from across North America, Europe, Israel, and Asia. Throughout this time period, we have improved WISE by incorporating the latest results from science education research, including from the findings from our own studies of curriculum and instruction carried out in numerous science classrooms where we have studied WISE in action and continuously refined its design.

WISE has enjoyed great success in both the research and practitioner communities, largely as a result of its capacity to bring so many expert voices together to develop powerful inquiry activities within a technology-enhanced learning environment. This endeavor has attracted a large community of participants from a variety of disciplinary backgrounds. For example, WISE has provided a technology platform as well as a curriculum framework for educational researchers from many different institutions. WISE has also partnered with science organizations such as the American Physiology Society, the International Wolf Center, the Thousand Friends of Frogs, NASA, and the U.S. National Oceanic and Atmospheric Association (NOAA) to co-design inquiry projects that met the needs of those organizations while also capturing the WISE pedagogical principles. We partnered with computer scientists from the University of California, Berkeley and other institutions to create a state-of-the-art technology environment for teachers, researchers, and students.

WISE has provided a valuable infrastructure for educational researchers from across the United States and around the world, supporting their investigations of different aspects of science inquiry. For example, Janice Gobert was investigating the use of visualizations and models to help students develop a deeper understanding of Earth science concepts. Her approach had been successful in laboratory studies, but lacked the rich curricular context that would help the models be effective in a classroom setting. Gobert was able to embed her approach, including the visual simulations, within a WISE inquiry project called "Plate Tectonics: What's on Your Plate?" Thus, WISE provided Gobert with a research platform in which she could develop materials, deliver them to classrooms, and collect student assessments with great levels of control. The WISE technology benefited from Gobert's studies, which helped in the design of new functionality for peer exchange and collaboration. Such partnerships have resulted in a wealth of new research, including scholarly publications (e.g., Gobert, Slotta, & Pallant, 2002; Gobert, 2005), presentations (e.g., Gobert, 2004), and funded projects. In addition, the WISE technology environment and materials have been translated into many other languages, including Norwegian, Dutch, German, Hebrew, Japanese, Chinese, and Korean.

WISE has also proven its worth for students and teachers in classrooms around the world. This project can be judged a success based solely on the number of teachers who have adopted WISE in their science courses for all topics from grades 6 to 12 (ages 11 to 17). More than 200,000 students have now participated in a WISE inquiry project, and more than a thousand teachers. WISE is one of the very few products of educational research that has been able to cross over into the world of schools, teachers, and students who were not affiliated in any way with the originating research group. This viability of WISE has offered new research opportunities relating to the scaling of innovations within schools and districts, and models of professional development for science teachers.

What makes WISE unique is its ease of implementation for teachers from such a wide range of school settings. Previous research projects—including some of our own discussed in this book—have produced exciting new technology environments, curriculum materials, and assessments. But these research-oriented materials were not typically intended for wide use by teachers, and would not have succeeded in the classroom without additional support. WISE is different because it was developed with the explicit goal of providing a technology-enhanced learning environment for a wide community of science teachers and educational researchers.

Our initial design of WISE was informed by a synthesis of the research literature, including more than 2 decades of our own prior research. Since then, WISE has been the focus of our ongoing research as well as that of our collaborators. From these efforts, we have developed the knowledge integration framework (Linn, 1995; Linn & Hsi, 2000) and design principles (Linn, Davis, & Bell, 2004) to guide future designs.

Currently, there are new funded projects under way. In addition, we have recently released a new open source version of the software that will enable researchers and other developers to adopt and adapt the WISE technology and curriculum materials for their own purposes.

This book offers a comprehensive narrative about our experience in WISE, recounting the history of the ideas, the theoretical foundation of our designs, the challenges we have confronted, and the implications for science education. In Chapter 1, we introduce the challenges and opportunities related to technology in education. Chapter 2 presents an overview of the WISE learning environment, including its various tools and features, the curriculum library, and how it has been used by various teachers and research collaborators. Chapter 3 describes the theoretical framework, called Scaffolded Knowledge Integration, that has guided the design of all WISE technologies, curriculum, and assessments. Chapter 4 outlines how we have developed curriculum patterns that build on the theoretical framework. Chapter 5 reviews some of the research that has demonstrated the effectiveness of WISE. Chapter 6 describes our partnership method of creating WISE curriculum and assessments, which has resulted in a fascinating range of inquiry projects and some ongoing research collaborations. Chapter 7 provides details about how teachers have succeeded with WISE, and Chapter 8 follows with a review of our efforts in teacher professional development. In Chapter 9, we begin looking forward to the legacy of WISE, in terms of the communities of sharing and exchange that it has fostered. We conclude the book by suggesting some important policy implications for science curriculum, educational technologies, and teacher professional development, as well as some specific ways that educators can get involved.

Throughout the book, we limit our use of academic citations mainly to cases where specific projects or researchers are being addressed. All citations are referenced to a bibliography, presented at the end of the book. In addition, at the end of each chapter we provide an annotated set of recommended readings that make specific connections to the research literature.

This book presents a narrative that is directly relevant to some of the most important issues facing educators today: How can teachers help students achieve a deep understanding of science when they are confronted by standards and expectations that require a breadth of coverage approach? How can we deliver on the promise of technology to enhance learning, engage students, and enable new forms of assessment? How can teachers respond to the challenge of helping every student in their class? We hope that such a volume will be useful within graduate training programs, pre-service courses for teacher preparation, in-service programs for teacher professional development, school leadership, or any individual teacher, parent, or developer who is concerned with these issues.

CHAPTER 1

Teaching and Learning Science in the 21st Century

The Internet is one of the defining characteristics of our transition into the new millennium. The World Wide Web emerged in the late 1990s, as if on cue to usher in the 21st century. Almost overnight, it seems that every aspect of our lives developed an online component: communications, shopping, reading the news, finding directions, searching for apartments, sharing videos and photos, paying our bills, and trading stocks. Never has a new medium enjoyed such a swift uptake and made such an enormous impact in the world. Within a decade there were Internet cafés in every city around the world, and most sectors of society were embracing new forms of workflow, communication, and exchange.

Science itself has been profoundly transformed by the emergence of the Internet. At the most basic level, scientists now routinely exchange emails, drafts of manuscripts, and analyses in progress, with vastly greater rates of turnaround than in any previous era. At an organizational level, scientists now coordinate workshops, conferences, and even online journals using Internet technologies. At an even deeper infrastructural level, there are now open access datasets where the latest genomic sequences or astronomical images are published by scientists for purposes of review and outright sharing with their peers—within hours of their initial collection. In addition, new Internet-based functionality, such as graphical information systems (GIS) and agent-based simulations, are profoundly altering the analytic processes within scientific communities, ranging from geology to physics to social psychology.

Students must develop a fluency with information technologies to succeed in almost any walk of life. Yet K–12 education has only just begun to show any signs of transformation in the age of the Internet, and most of those signs are at the administrative level rather than in the classroom. Internet technologies are indeed revolutionizing the collection and management of student information, offering powerful new mechanisms to track performance and attendance, coordinate special education programs, and communicate with parents. In higher education, we are now witnessing a slow but steady growth in the use of learning management systems, where student activities and student-teacher exchanges are coordinated through online environments. Some instructors are even using these environments in new ways to change the structure of their courses, including collaborative projects, online discussions, and peer review. Instructors are also developing online resources for their courses that can be reused and improved with each new course offering.

In K–12 classrooms, however, Internet technology has yet to make any meaningful impact. Several prominent analyses of teachers' use of technology (e.g., Becker & Ravitz, 1999; Cuban, 2001; National Research Council, 2002) have revealed that there has been little to no transformation of U.S. classrooms by computers and information technology. These reports and surveys have documented teachers' preference for conservative, rather than revolutionary, applications of technology, primarily related to skills acquisition using word processors or spreadsheets, or as a source for independent research projects.

Educators understand that the Internet presents many wonderful new opportunities for learning and teaching, and some teachers have indeed begun to experiment with new curriculum designs that engage students with online resources and activities. But the integration of technology into science classrooms has been a slow process, as teachers remain focused predominantly on lectures and textbooks, using the Internet primarily as a supplemental resource for Web searches or multimedia materials. In part, this reluctance to deeply integrate technologies is related to the issue of access and reliability: In order to truly integrate Internet technologies into the science curriculum, all students must have constant, reliable access to Web-enabled computers. Still, even with increasing levels of access to technologies (see Figure 1.1), teachers find it challenging to redesign their approach to instruction in order to integrate new materials, new functionality, or new patterns of exchange between students.

For several reasons, teachers have been reluctant to incorporate new methods that integrate technology, even when they have access to computers and the Internet. In addition to the technical challenges of access and reliability, there are substantial challenges relating to pedagogical design. While it is true that the Internet offers powerful new interactive materials, for example, it is not clear how to design science lessons that integrate those materials effectively so that all students learn. Online collaborations between students, which could provide a heightened level of interactivity and exchange within a

Figure 1.1. Percentage of U.S. public school classrooms connected to the Internet from 1994–2005. Figures obtained from the U.S. National Center for Educational Statistics (http://nces.ed.gov/)

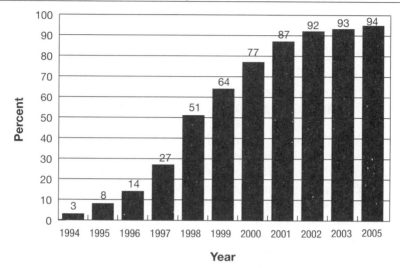

classroom setting, are not a straightforward matter in terms of curriculum design. What should students collaborate about? How should teachers monitor or assess students' progress?

Thus, while teachers might try out some interactive learning materials or online adventures as supplemental or occasional resources, they are perhaps rightfully hesitant to undertake a major overhaul of their instruction. Given the current climate of standards-based instruction and high-stakes accountability for teachers, such caution would be warranted. It is challenging to deeply integrate technology within an instructional design, coordinating the flow of people, activities, and materials so that all participants are rewarded with a rich learning experience.

K–12 teachers look to educational research to provide good examples of Internet environments and technology-enhanced learning—including evidence of student achievement. And indeed, WISE was developed in order to test and refine such a framework, as well as to provide a rich example for teachers and researchers of how technology can support new forms of learning and instruction. One of the most important goals of WISE is to provide a solid technology platform that will allow teachers to adopt new forms of inquiry-based instruction with confidence and support. Particularly in science education, such approaches offer promise, as instructors are challenged to communicate vexing topics such as natural selection, chemical bonding, DNA replication, or geophysical processes. Clearly, there is an opportunity for technology to play a meaningful, even central, role in science instruction. But before this can happen, projects such as WISE must investigate new models and make successful approaches easy for teachers to adopt.

RESEARCHING THE INTEGRATION OF INQUIRY AND TECHNOLOGY IN SCIENCE CLASSROOMS

In order for teachers, principals, or school boards to change the nature of science curriculum, instruction, or assessments, they need substantial evidence from educational research. Teachers may wish to increase the emphasis on inquiry in their classes but lack confidence in the materials they find on the Web. Often, these materials require a level of teacher support that is unrealistic or access to equipment that is unavailable. Teachers may find appealing materials such as dynamic, interactive visualizations on the Web, but have no way of knowing how students will engage with these materials. Materials on the Internet are often complex, and not originally prepared for purposes of K–12 instruction. For example, many sophisticated scientific visualizations on the Web were produced by scientists for use by their peers or graduate students. It is difficult to predict how precollege students will engage with such materials, or what they will learn. Particularly in science, it is essential to address the issues of accuracy, reliability, and age-appropriateness of instructional materials. Educational research is needed to investigate coherent approaches to the design of curriculum that takes into account how students learn. Teachers need materials that guide students through inquiry activities and support their interactions with peers and instructors in the classroom.

In the past 2 decades, educational research has made some progress in defining productive roles for technology within the classroom. Much of this research has focused on defining pedagogical patterns where technology helps students and teachers interact with instructional materials in new ways, with greater levels of collaboration, peer review, and reflection that lead students to a deep conceptual understanding of topics. In the following sections of this chapter, we synthesize the research literature into four important principles that have guided our development of WISE. Variations of these principles appear commonly in many research reviews (e.g., Roschelle, Pea, Hoadley, Gordin, & Means, 2001; Quintana et al., 2004; Linn & Eylon, 2006), reflecting consensus among researchers. WISE was first envisioned as a way of capturing these basic themes and extending them to science classrooms in the form of a technology-enhanced learning environment.

1. Support Autonomous Learning

It is widely held by educational research that learners construct their understanding of a topic through active reasoning that connects with their previous views or experiences. Science lectures are not likely to help students build such connections because they do not engage students in active reasoning about topics, but rather in passive efforts to understand a spoken message. Students tend to add these ideas to their set of views but not distinguish them from other ideas. For example, students may learn about how electrical circuits work but still believe that electricity flows out of the wall and gets "used up" by a lamp.

Activities that promote autonomous learning help students make sense of new ideas and develop the ability to evaluate new information. For example, lab-based activities and small-group work are much more likely to give students the opportunities to make connections to their existing ideas, test their own hypotheses, and develop a personal understanding of topics. However, using labs or small groups is not sufficient in itself to ensure that students are reflecting and developing a deep understanding of science topics. Students can still just add new ideas instead of critiquing them and considering how they connect to their existing ideas. When teachers become a "guide on the side," they can enhance learning by listening to students' ideas, suggesting alternative explanations, and prompting students to make deeper reflections. Thus, opportunities to learn autonomously allow students to engage deeply with the science topics and are more successful when teachers interact with students and encourage their reflections.

2. Encourage Collaboration and Peer Exchange

Learning in everyday life is rarely conducted in isolation from our peers. In nearly every place of work in every sector of society, our learning is conducted in close exchange with others. This is fortunate, because psychological theorists such as Vygotsky (1978) have argued that people learn best when they learn with peers who share comparable backgrounds and interests. Classrooms are an ideal setting for such peer exchange, and there is ample evidence from the research literature that students learn effectively in collaboration with peers. For example, when students construct a circuit and discuss how electrical circuits work, they can test ideas, develop criteria for distinguishing ideas, and critique the ideas of their peers. Often, a hint from a peer can be sufficient to help a student compare the observation that the lamp is plugged into the wall with the finding that a wire from the battery to the bulb is not sufficient to power the bulb.

Collaborative learning is most successful when it is carefully designed. Some investigators have explored direct methods such as peer tutoring or peer learning circles. Richard Anderson and his colleagues have developed a method called Collaborative Reasoning, where elementary students develop literacy skills by collaboratively reading and debating literature (Anderson et al., 2001). Marlene Scardamalia (e.g., 2002) and her colleagues have investigated the benefits of collaborative knowledge construction, developing a technology environment where students add written reflections, images, and other media objects to a common database of ideas that helps them in subsequent learning activities. In our own prior research, we have explored the use of online discussions where students debate science topics with peers (Hoadley & Linn, 2000; Linn & Slotta, 2006). Taken together, this research demonstrates the value of collaboration and peer exchange, which should be included in the design of any technology-enhanced approach to learning.

3. Make Ideas Visible to Students and Teachers

The axiom "a picture is worth a thousand words" is widely accepted because it captures the powerful experience that comes from looking at a visible representation of complex ideas. In science, this is particularly true. Who could imagine learning about chemical bonding and orbital shells without some of the rich visualizations employed by textbooks? Of course, with such power comes the capacity to do harm or to interfere with learning. A wealth of research has explored the misconceptions caused by scientific visualizations— particularly when complex or abstract representations are used with students who are encountering these ideas for the first time. Students may focus on the surface features—for example, the red circles and the blue circles in a simulation of ideal gases—mistakenly believing that one of the gases is blue and the other one red! Researchers have found that simplified conceptual models, designed at an intermediate level of complexity, are more effective at helping students develop a conceptual understanding.

Simulations and interactive models are perhaps the most powerful form of scientific visualization, because they represent complex ideas and causal relationships in a temporal, "playable" format. For example, Figure 1.2 shows an interactive model of global warming designed by Bob Tinker and Keisha Varma and implemented in the Netlogo system developed by Uri Wilensky (1999) and his colleagues. In this simulation, students observe a cross-section of the atmosphere with the sun's rays entering through a cloud layer, and a dynamic temperature graph on the side that shows the average temperature of the Earth. Students are asked to click buttons that say "Add CO_2," or "Add Clouds," and observe the effects on global temperature as time moves forward. Of course, this is a highly simplified representation of the global system, but it provides students with an opportunity to make predictions and test their own ideas about the role of these variables, such as increasing the level of CO_2 or the amount of cloud cover.

In order for visualizations to make ideas visible to students, they need to be embedded in an inquiry activity and strengthened with guidance from the teacher. For example, students using the Netlogo global climate simulation above without guidance would probably just play around with the buttons and watch the temperature graph without developing any conjectures about the role of variables such as CO_2 or clouds. Thus, for scientific visualizations to make thinking visible, we must carefully develop supporting materials that help to guide students' explorations and reflections. Even more important, the teacher must pay attention to what students are doing and what they are saying about such visualizations in order to be sure that they are gaining the intended benefits of the experience and not developing misconceptions.

Figure 1.2. Netlogo Model—interactive modeling for global warming. Simulations and interactive models offer a powerful form of scientific visualization (Tinker & Wilensky, 2007).

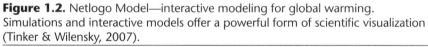
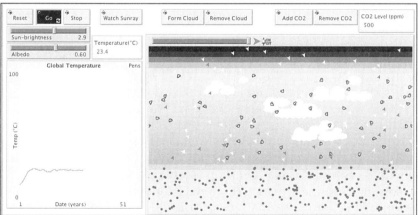

Technology tools or environments can also help make students' emerging scientific ideas visible for themselves and others. For example, students could interact with technology-enhanced visualizations such as the global climate model above to test their ideas or compare with peers, and teachers could gain valuable insight into what students believe about the various processes being represented. Another way of making students' ideas visible is through concept maps, drawings, or graphs—all of which can provide the students with powerful ways of building their own understanding and also give teachers a visual lens into what their students know.

Thus, technology can make scientific ideas visible to students, make student ideas visible to teachers, and support inquiry activities that stimulate constructivist learning in science. Educational researchers have made gains in investigating how such tools can make thinking visible and continue to develop more powerful approaches.

4. Promote the Personal Relevance of Science

Another principle that has emerged from educational research is to focus on the relevance of science to students in their everyday lives. To help every student develop a deep understanding of science that can be used in everyday situations, science instruction must feature activities that offer relevant and meaningful connections to students' own ideas and experiences. Global climate, for example, can be used as an engaging and effective context in which to address chemical reactions and several other aspects of physical science because of its direct personal relevance to students' lives. If the curriculum emphasizes that chemistry and physics are at the heart of global warming, this will foster engagement and a sense of the relevance of school science. Topics such as genetically modified foods, ecology, or the design of familiar things such as houses, cars, and schools can all help students find relevance in science.

Researchers have recognized that students have much more to gain from science than simply an understanding of conceptual topics. Ideally, science class is where students will learn the valuable skills of critical thinking and argumentation that will be important throughout their lives. Citizens today must be able to decipher complex arguments about issues such as stem cell research, global warming, or home electricity usage in order to participate in our democratic society. They need to understand the political debates on such issues so they can vote responsibly and help shape public policy.

The Internet, in particular, offers a valuable source of information for every conceivable topic, but searching for relevant information and distinguishing the validity of sources can be quite challenging. Science class can offer students the opportunity to learn how to search for valid evidence and to distinguish between persuasive messages and evidence-based assertions. These are valuable lifelong learning skills.

When it comes to science topics in class, on the playground, at home, and throughout their lives, students need to engage in critical discussions with peers, evaluate arguments, and respond to feedback. Science class can become a place where students engage in such practices and see the relevance of the course to everyday life.

THE NEED FOR DEPTH OF COVERAGE IN SCIENCE CURRICULUM

Teachers receive mixed messages about assessment from various professional sources. During pre-service instruction, they learn that continuous, formative assessment is essential to allow them to gauge student progress and respond to individual students appropriately. Such assessments provide some measure of student understanding during instruction, to which the teacher can respond in real time. They are not assessments that occur at the end of the curriculum to measure student achievement, but rather, they serve to reveal measures of students' progress at particular points within the curriculum. Ongoing or continuous assessments can provide valuable information that helps teachers make curricular decisions, such as whether students need further clarification about particular topics, or whether they are successfully collaborating with peers.

While teachers learn initially that ongoing assessments are vital to effective practice, but when they arrive in schools they encounter a heavy emphasis on coverage of content standards and high-stakes, summative assessments. For various reasons, the prevailing atmosphere within many schools is one of concern over demonstrating successful performance on examinations that are directly linked to the content standards. In science, the national and local standards are a daunting set of topics that would be challenging for even the most veteran teacher to address with any depth. As a result, science teachers are often pressed to "make it through" their required standards in the limited time given to them within a school term. Teachers have trouble justifying any curriculum approach that demands more than the allocated fraction of time implied by the science standards. This can lead teachers to the belief that "there is no time for inquiry or project-based learning," because of the need to cover all the standards and prepare for the test.

As a result, many students are left behind, feeling that science is a heavy load of facts and relationships that must be endured and mastered for a test. This inevitably leads to a competitive atmosphere, where students strive for a good grade, and not for understanding and fulfillment. Only a fraction of students manage to endure this treatment and go on to discover that science may be more than just a scholastic challenge. The others, many of our brightest and most sensitive students, are left with a negative impression and lowered self-esteem by science courses, and proceed to put all of science behind them.

The four educational research themes discussed in the previous section do not emphasize the coverage of content standards at the expense of students' deep understanding. When teachers are forced to address a great many topics within a single course, they have very little time to devote to any innovative, inquiry-oriented approach. Yet research shows clearly that only by reflecting, applying ideas, and collaborating with peers can students develop a sense of the relevance of science and build a coherent understanding. Many researchers have criticized the traditional form of lecture-based instruction as being too superficial. This is captured by the famous "Bloom's taxonomy" of educational objectives, where the rote learning of knowledge is seen as the most primitive form of learning, subordinate to higher-level objectives such as the application of ideas to new purposes, the analysis of ideas, and the synthesis of ideas (Bloom, 1956). Thus, a breadth-oriented approach might boost students' performance on exams, but it will result in disconnected learning of facts and procedures that students will be unable to apply to other problems, and will quickly forget.

A ROLE FOR
TECHNOLOGY-ENHANCED LEARNING ENVIRONMENTS

Traditional lecture and breadth of coverage methods are familiar to teachers and students alike, and are straightforward for teachers to practice. In contrast, it is much more challenging to adopt depth of coverage methods where students collaborate in pairs or small groups to perform inquiry activities. Teachers are justifiably wary about experimenting with such methods in their own classrooms. In order to support teachers as they adopt innovative approaches, many researchers have developed technology-based tools, such as online scientific notebooks, graphing tools, simulations, concept maps, and reflection notes. Such technologies can serve to capture student ideas in real time, making those ideas available to teachers for purposes of timely feedback and formative assessment.

Indeed, one of our basic motivations in developing WISE and its predecessors, described below, was to support students and teachers as they engaged in a depth of coverage approach to learning science topics. By supporting students as they conduct complex activities, technology-enhanced learning environments also serve to support teachers as they adopt such approaches. With well-designed technology environments helping to guide their students through complex inquiry activities, collect student work, and prompt students for reflections, teachers are free to focus on more meaningful interactions with students. Using such technology environments, teachers can gain confidence that students will remain on-task as they circulate within the classroom, observing students' ideas on the computer monitors and interacting with students when they see good opportunities for relevant discussion.

Technology-enhanced learning environments are software systems that present curriculum materials to students, collect student work for purposes of assessment, and provide helpful user interfaces to guide students and teachers alike as they enact curriculum. The technology environment can deliver a wide range of curriculum, including functionality for the display of webpages, for collaboration between students, and for various tools such as data tables, graphing and drawing, online discussions, and various simulations and modeling tools. Such technology tools can be woven together to support inquiry projects, scaffolding student activities, providing guidance in the form of helpful hints or prompts, and capturing all student work for purposes of assessment.

Many technology-enhanced learning environments have been created by researchers in recent years. For example, the Thinkertools environment, developed by Barbara White and John Frederickson, helps guide students in the use of scientific simulations to address their possible misconceptions of physics topics (White & Fredericksen, 2000). NetLogo, developed by Uri Wilensky and his colleagues, provides students a hands-on modeling and programming environment (Wilensky & Resnick, 1999). BGuILE, the Biology Guided Inquiry Learning Environment, was developed by Brian Reiser, Bill Sandoval, and their colleagues to investigate how students could work with realistic scientific datasets to address classic problems in biology (Reiser et al., 2001).

Before the age of the Internet, and before we ever conceived of WISE, our group conducted 2 decades of research in the domain of technology-enhanced inquiry learning. We developed two different technology environments to support our investigations of inquiry curriculum for middle school science in grades 6 to 8 (ages 11 to 13). First, the Computer as Learning Partner (CLP) project developed technology scaffolds to help students make predictions about heat and temperature phenomena, experiment with simulations, and compare their predictions against data they collected using probeware and graphed in real time. Next, the Knowledge Integration Environment (KIE; see Figure 1.3) expanded on the work of CLP by creating a more sophisticated technology environment, adding links to the World Wide Web and improving our integration of tools such as reflection notes, data tables, and online discussions. Begun in 1994, KIE was perhaps the first comprehensive research effort to incorporate Web materials into science inquiry projects (Bell, Davis, & Linn, 1995).

Research in the KIE project addressed several topics that would become foundational to our efforts in WISE. We investigated the most effective designs for student reflection prompts, the most engaging topics for online discussions, and the best way to introduce complicated webpages. We also began to investigate the designs for different kinds of curriculum projects, such as debate projects, where students used webpages and other evidence to make their own arguments about science controversies such as "How Far Does Light Go?" Many of the

Figure 1.3. The Knowledge Integration Environment was developed to expand on the work of CLP. It was a direct predecessor to WISE.

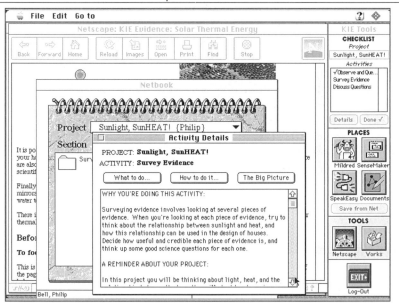

findings of these two projects are reviewed in Chapter 3, as they provide the research basis for our development of WISE curriculum.

All the technology environments mentioned above were designed to support specific lines of educational research, with the aim of extending the field's knowledge about learning and instruction. These systems were not intended for wide adoption by teachers, nor were they suited for that purpose. For example, the KIE environment was rather unwieldy, requiring a substantial effort to install software, with frequent technology bugs. Moreover, KIE curriculum projects consumed several weeks of class time, and generally required the presence of a research assistant in the classroom in order to help respond to student questions and solve technology problems. In most science classrooms, curriculum time is at a premium, and teachers could never spend several weeks on a single inquiry project. Nor could they afford the luxury of an assistant to help them administer the curriculum. KIE was not generally intended as a scalable system that would work well for any science teacher. Rather, it was a research system that was meant to help our group investigate questions about technology-enhanced learning. Thus, KIE was only implemented in a few classrooms, but it provided a foundation for our design of the WISE technology environment, which was designed to survive in the wilds of real science classrooms.

In WISE, we set out to design a new technology environment that would capture the core principles from research as outlined above, that would be easy to use for students and teachers, and that could be used widely in science classrooms. This raised a compelling conundrum: How can researchers develop materials that allow them to conduct their investigation while still being accessible to teachers? The answer requires a new technology environment that applies the research findings while responding to the complexity of classrooms and the diversity of teacher needs. In order to achieve these acrobatic goals, WISE would require a simple user interface, a reliable technology infrastructure (server, database, etc.) and well-designed curriculum and assessments. The next chapter provides an overview of WISE, including several examples of curriculum and detailed descriptions of all the technology components.

RECOMMENDED READINGS

We selected the following readings to serve as a good representation of the wealth of research that has addressed the role of technology in inquiry-oriented learning. Each of these books or papers provides a slightly different perspective.

Bransford, J. D., Brown, A. L., & Cocking, R. (1999). *How people learn: Brain, mind, experience, and school.* Washington, DC: National Academy Press.

> This book presents a deep synthesis of research from across the learning sciences. It is a report sponsored by the U.S. National Research Council (NRC) that captures the results of a workshop, and draws on the expertise of a committee of renowned experts. At the time of printing, the book is available online in multiple formats at the following URL: *www.nap.edu/html/howpeople1/*

diSessa, A. (2000). *Changing minds: Computers, learning, and literacy.* Cambridge, MA: MIT Press.

> This is a thought-provoking book by a respected scholar in the domains of cognitive psychology and education. Professor Andrea diSessa offers a penetrating discussion of the challenges of learning in the 21st century and the opportunities that technology can provide.

Edelson, D. C., Gordin, D. N., & Pea, R. D. (1999). Addressing the challenges of inquiry-based learning through technology and curriculum design. *Journal of the Learning Sciences, 8*(3/4), 391–450.

> This paper reviews the design and development of several technology-based curricula in the geosciences and identifies five significant challenges to inquiry-based learning.

Quintana, C., Reiser, B. J., Davis, E. A., Krajcik, J., Fretz, E., Duncan, R. G., Kyza, E., Edelson, D., & Soloway, E. (2004). A scaffolding design framework for software to support science inquiry. *Journal of the Learning Sciences, 13*(3), 337–386.

> This article reviews the various successful approaches to technology-enhanced learning that have come from educational research and proposes a new framework that synthesizes the most effective design features.

Songer, N. B. (1996). Exploring learning opportunities in coordinated network-enhanced classrooms: A case of kids as global scientists. *The Journal of the Learning Sciences, 5,* 297–327.

> This research paper reports on one of the earliest Internet-enabled science curricula: a 6-week weather unit where middle school students investigated various phenomena using Web resources, and even communicated online with peers.

CHAPTER 2

WISE: The Web-Based Inquiry Science Environment

WISE, the Web-based Inquiry Science Environment, was developed as a "next generation" system that would build upon the research principles described in the previous chapter and allow a continuation of our own research of technology-enhanced inquiry in the science classroom. In designing the WISE technology and curriculum, we set out to develop an accessible resource for science teachers that would function on any Internet-connected computer and would not require a great deal of external support. In responding to this challenge, we began to research interesting new questions relating to patterns of interaction in the classroom. We explored new methodologies, worked with a greater audience of teachers and students, and developed a much wider range of curriculum materials. We also developed a state-of-the-art technology infrastructure that could support our development efforts as well as the scaled use by a large number of teachers and students.

The WISE software operates completely within a Web browser application such as Firefox or Internet Explorer. Figure 2.1 shows a screen capture of the WISE learning environment running the inquiry project called "Deformed Frog Mystery." Teachers can choose from a small library of inquiry projects that were carefully designed by partnerships between science teachers, educational researchers, and science domain experts. WISE curriculum is designed according to a theoretical framework, known as Scaffolded Knowledge Integration, that we have developed over the course of 2 decades of research. This framework, described in detail in Chapter 3, supports the design of curriculum projects where students investigate problems, critique solutions, and debate with their peers. These inquiry projects address key science standards, but they do so in a depth of coverage approach, requiring substantial classroom time for students to work autonomously within the WISE environment, developing a coherent understanding of the science topics.

Students navigate through the sequence of inquiry activities using the inquiry map on the left-hand side of the WISE window. Each

Figure 2.1. Screen capture of a WISE inquiry project called "The Deformed Frog Mystery."

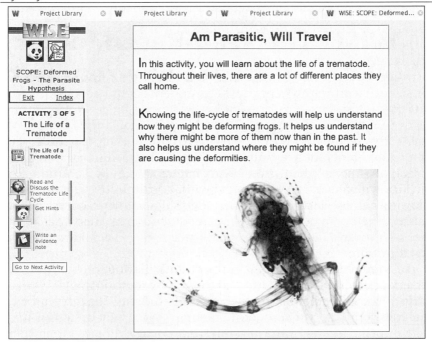

time they click on a new step within the map, some new inquiry tool or material appears in the main portion of the WISE window. For example, one step might call up a webpage that displays photos of deformed frogs from North American waterways, followed by a step that brings up a WISE reflection note to help students focus on the most relevant aspects of the webpage.

Our previous generations of technology in the CLP and KIE projects (described earlier) had required support from researchers in order to maintain software and respond to problems. In WISE, we drew on the power of the Web as a delivery mechanism, with no software to install, since all content and functionality would be accessed through the Web browser. We also sought to develop more streamlined versions of the curriculum that captured our research principles but made more efficient use of class time so that teachers could run a WISE curriculum activity in roughly one week. This chapter will present an overview of the various components of WISE, including examples of several curriculum projects, and a discussion of the technology supports we implemented for teachers, students, and curriculum authors.

THE WISE STUDENT LEARNING ENVIRONMENT

WISE set out to create a new software environment for students, teachers, and curriculum authors, including new software tools for inquiry curriculum and assessments. When we began in 1996, the Web had just appeared on the scene, and we were excited about its capacity to distribute educational content. The Web also offered a natural resource for science learning materials, where students could access the latest data from governmental or nonprofit science agencies or search for pages that were relevant to their arguments. Finally, the Web offered new software functionality, enabling hypertext navigation, browser frames, and tools such as online discussions or concept mapping. The notion of a "portal" had also recently emerged (e.g., MyYahoo), where each individual user has an account with specific security permissions, allowing users to customize the features that appear in their portal and manage their own personal files. In creating our new Web-based learning environment, we sought to capitalize on all of these new technology directions.

In conducting WISE inquiry projects, middle- and high-school students work collaboratively and make use of "evidence" from the World Wide Web. For example, in the "Deformed Frogs Mystery" project, students compare two competing theories about why deformed frogs are appearing in American waterways, surveying evidence provided by practicing scientists and designing their own arguments about what is causing the deformities. In the "Sunlight, SunHEAT" project, students critique and compare energy-efficient homes from the Web, conduct an experiment that converts light energy to heat energy, and participate in online discussions about passive solar architecture. Figure 2.2 shows the WISE "Sunlight, SunHEAT" project, including a WISE note with a reflection prompt and a cognitive hint (delivered by Amanda the Panda).

A WISE project consists of steps that students complete in sequence by clicking one step at a time within the WISE inquiry map (presented in the left-hand frame of the browser window). When a step is clicked, it opens some materials or tools within the main part of the browser window. Steps could simply launch webpages, or they could open the WISE Journal or Reflection Notebook, or any of the WISE inquiry tools, such as the Data Visualizer, which presents tables and graphs; the Sensemaker, where students sort scientific evidence into arguments; or the Causal Map, where students arrange causal factors in an interactive concept map. Table 2.1 lists all the available WISE inquiry tools, with short descriptions for each. These tools have been developed in response to the needs of different research projects

Figure 2.2. Screen capture of the WISE "Sunlight, SunHEAT" project, showing the WISE Reflection Prompts and a Cognitive Hint.

over the past several years. For example, in the initial development of WISE, our research was focused on the critique of scientific evidence and arguments and the use of online discussions as a forum for peer exchanges. Thus, the evidence display, critique, and online discussion tools were the first to be developed. In order to enable subsequent research studies, we developed tools for drawing, graphing, concept mapping, brainstorming, student portfolios, and more.

On a technical note, some of the WISE inquiry tools, such as online discussions, brainstorms, or reflection notes, are implemented using Web-based software such as javascript and PHP. Other, more interactive tools such as the drawing tool or the Causal Map were created using the Java platform and run as "applets" within the Web browser. The result is a seamless user experience where students click successively on the steps within a WISE project, launching a variety of different inquiry tools in a sequence that was designed by the curriculum author. The current status of WISE technology development is discussed in Chapter 9.

THE WISE AUTHORING TOOL

An authoring tool was one of the first software systems developed within the WISE research program, primarily because we needed some way to

Table 2.1. Description of WISE Step Types.

Brainstorm	Students are prompted to write a short response to a question and then evaluate the comments of their classmates.
Branchpoint Selection	Students choose one of several options that you can write (e.g., you can provide the different sides of a debate or a list of geographical locations). Later steps in WISE can then be made into hinging steps so that a different step is shown to students depending on the answer they choose from this step. See *Hinging Steps*, below, for more information on how this works.
Challenge Questions	A small set of multiple-choice questions that are presented at strategic points in the project. If students miss any of the questions, they are automatically redirected to the relevant point in the project and encouraged to try answering the question again.
Causal Mapper	Students create a concept map in which various factors are connected with arrows showing their causal relationship.
Data Grid	A simple Web form in which students enter numerical data into a table.
Discussion Forum	Threaded online discussion forum with many options, such as the "gated" discussion, in which students are asked to respond to an opening topic and then their responses are made visible as the base comments of an open-ended discussion.
Display Page and Evidence Page	Each of these tools displays a page of HTML text, possibly with links to outside webpages. Evidence pages generally are used for providing key information relevant to the project's content. Display pages are used for more operational duties (introduction to the project, explanation of what the next step will entail, etc.), but the user can use either type of page for any purpose.
Form Analysis	A part of the WISE forms engine that allows students to view collected forms of data from their group, their class, or all classes that have already responded to the form.
Form Blank	A part of the WISE forms engine that creates an HTML form for students to fill out. This is used in conjunction with hand-held computers to allow data collection in the field.
Form Review	A part of the WISE forms engine that prompts students to review their own responses to a WISE form.
Hints	Teachers can display cognitive hints for any WISE step in order to help students reflect on the step. Hints are typically in the form of strategic questions.
Notes	Students are presented with a question and starter prompt aimed at encouraging them to reflect upon evidence or other information they have been presented with. The notes section also allows for assessments in the form of multiple-choice responses or brief open-ended responses.

(continued)

Table 2.1. (*continued*)

Outside URL	Students are sent directly to an outside webpage. In many cases, it's preferable to set up an evidence page with a link in order to provide students with some initial content before they visit the outside webpage.
Problem Set	The students are presented with a set of questions, either for assessment purposes or surveys. Numerous question formats are available, and they can be arranged on multiple pages with some advanced options (such as multiple versions, restricted times of availability, etc.).
Self-Test	Students answer a series of questions that will then let them know how they did. Students are given an explanation of why certain answers were right or wrong.
Sensemaker	A Java applet that prompts students to visually make sense (thus the name) out of assorted bits of data and evidence by sorting them based on what viewpoints or arguments they support.
Show-n-Tell	Prompts students to create a presentation out of their work-to-date in the project. Students can select their step work, add comments, share their presentation, and comment on other presentations.
Show Alert	Pops up a simple alert box with a short instruction for the student. Often, a display page works better for this, but alerts do tend to grab the user's attention.
Show All Work	Displays a page that presents all of the student's work. This page can also be accessed at any time via an icon in the upper left of the WISE display.
Student Assessment	Similar to a problem set, the assessment is generally used as a non-revisable option—meaning that once students click the "I'm done" button, they cannot return to revise their responses.
Student Journal	Similar to the notes section (described earlier), but with a focus on encouraging students to add to the journal over the course of a project. A journal icon is available in the student interface (in the upper left), allowing students to immediately bring up the journal and add to it.
WISE Data	Students can draw a graph from a given set of data points. Different kinds of graphs can be drawn, and students can modify them by changing the parameters, such as the ranges on the axes or the item plotted on each axis.
WISE Draw	A full-featured drawing program that lets students create and manipulate shapes and drawings, including text boxes and labels.

actually create the curriculum that would run in the WISE student environment. We sought to design an authoring system that would allow any member of our research team or any collaborating teacher or scientist to participate in authoring. Over time, we found that the best approach was for a small team of researchers, teachers, and science content experts to collaborate in the development of a WISE curriculum project. This is because each member of such an authoring team contributes a different form of expertise. The teachers bring a deep knowledge of their students and the broader curriculum in their course. The science specialist brings a deep knowledge of the disciplinary content that will be emphasized within the inquiry project. And the researcher, usually a member of the WISE group, brings knowledge of the pedagogical structures and theoretical foundation that leads to successful inquiry designs. This partnership model of authoring is discussed at length in Chapter 5.

Together, the members of a WISE authoring team use an online authoring environment to develop rich, interactive inquiry materials where students debate current science issues, critique evidence and arguments, and design solutions to personally relevant problems. These materials include embedded assessments, such as reflection notes or concept maps, which help students develop a deeper understanding of topics while helping teachers understand how their students are learning about these topics.

The WISE authoring tool is shown in Figure 2.3. It displays the WISE "Sunlight, SunHEAT" Project as it appears when authoring

Figure 2.3. Screen capture showing the WISE Authoring Tool as it appears for the "Sunlight, SunHEAT" project.

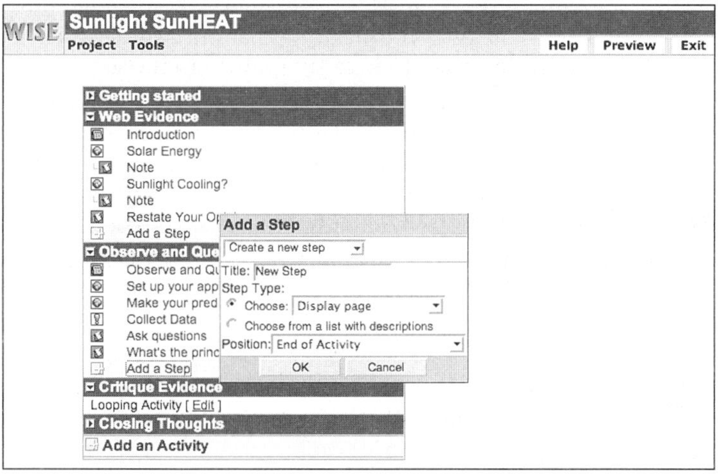

occurs. Notice that each activity in the project, such as "Getting Started" and "Web Evidence," has a set of distinct steps, just as it does in the WISE student software. Authors click on any existing step to open a menu that includes items such as "change step name" or "author step content." Each step type has its own special authoring mode. For example, the authoring mode for Online Discussions allows authors to set the discussion topic, as well as various settings related to the discussion tool. The authoring mode for the Display Page steps simply asks for any HTML code to be pasted into the authoring window.

The WISE authoring tool allows the development of a very broad range of curriculum, including any sequences of inquiry steps that could be envisioned by authors. Thus, we also require guidelines for how to develop that curriculum so that it successfully fosters learning, which is the essence of our research. Chapters 3 and 4 will focus on the research foundations and the resulting design principles that help provide some guidance to help authors develop effective and engaging inquiry projects.

Many inquiry projects have now been created, as a growing community of educators has employed WISE, either as a platform for research or as a curriculum development and delivery environment. To support the diverse groups of authors who collaborate in designing, creating, critiquing, and revising these materials, WISE includes a sophisticated user portal that provides viewing and editing permissions to any curriculum author, and allows that author to share those permissions with other WISE authors or teachers. In this way, WISE allows curriculum authors to host their own work on the WISE server, share that work with other authors, and manage versions of curriculum.

THE WISE STUDENT AND TEACHER PORTALS

Teachers can find a wide variety of WISE curriculum projects that have been carefully authored, tested, and refined by our research group. When they first login to the WISE home page, they are asked to register for an account, which results in their addition to the WISE Teacher's Portal (see Figure 2.4). The Teacher's Portal is a powerful Web site that keeps track of all personal information related to a teacher's account, including his or her student accounts, grades, and any customizations of curriculum that the teacher has created.

As shown in Figure 2.4, the Teacher's Portal includes several distinct sections or menus, which support teachers in different aspects of using WISE. In the Projects menu, teachers find links to the various

Figure 2.4. Screen capture showing the WISE Teacher Portal, where teachers can access curriculum, perform assessments, and manage student accounts.

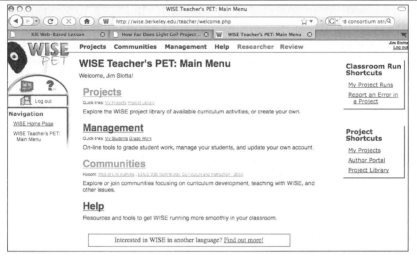

WISE projects in the curriculum library, which is searchable by science topic or grade/age level. Each project includes a link to the student materials, a detailed lesson plan, pre- and post-assessments, connections to national (U.S.) science standards from the American Association for the Advancement of Science, and tools for setting up a custom grading scheme. When teachers select a WISE curriculum project to run in their classroom, that project becomes visible to students when they login to their portal.

The Management menu is where most of the important activities and interactions occur within the Teacher's Portal. Teachers can create new passwords for students, assign them to working groups, and examine student work within a WISE project. Using the WISE Feedback tool, they can send comments to students concerning their progress or ideas within a project that is under way. In the WISE Assessment tool, they can view all student work, set up custom grading schemes, and assign grades and annotations to every student note, drawing, concept map, or other artifact created during the course of the project. Teachers can also set up custom assessments and even coordinate "share project runs" where their class joins another teacher's class during the WISE project's online discussions or peer exchanges.

In the Community menu, teachers may join special groups consisting of teachers, researchers, and science content specialists. For example, the "WISE Wolf Community" is a special-purpose webpage designed to support all the teachers who are interested in the WISE "Wolves in Your Backyard" project. WISE online communities provide exclusive features for their members, including supplemental resources, online discussions among teachers, links to different versions of the curriculum, and organizational tools, such as calendars and whiteboards. Several distinct types of communities have been created, including the "topic community" (e.g., the Wolves community); "authoring communities," which support teams that are co-authoring a WISE curriculum project; "professional development communities," which support teachers who are participants within a common professional development program; and "school district communities," which support the teachers who are working within a common school board or district.

The goal of the WISE Student Portal (see Figure 2.5) is to make the student's experience using WISE as simple as possible. When students login to WISE, they find a selection of materials that were placed there by the teacher. For example, they may find a new project ready for them to begin, such as "Sunlight, SunHEAT." They click on that project and it brings them into the WISE learning environment. They may also find comments left for them by their teacher from the previous day's efforts, or the results of assessments. Because of the careful

Figure 2.5. WISE Student Portal. The sample student shown here is looking at a list of three curriculum projects that she currently has underway.

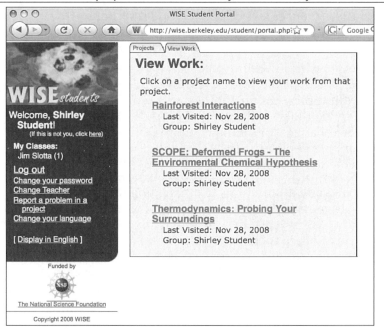

control that is permitted by the WISE database, students never see any information from other teachers or students outside of their class. When they enter a WISE project from the Teacher's Portal, students are always taken to the exact point where they last left that project (for example, "Activity 2, step 3" within the project). All of a student's work is stored in his or her private user account, which enables students to conduct project work from any Internet-connected computer, with no materials stored on any local computer. Thus, students can work on their WISE project between class sessions, either from their home or the school library, and they do not need to return to the same computer in the school computer lab. Only the teacher or other members of the student's working group can see any of that student's work online.

Over the past decade, WISE has matured into a sophisticated, reliable, easy to use technology platform for the design, development, and delivery of interactive curriculum. More than a thousand teachers have implemented WISE projects in their science classrooms, and several school districts have established long-term collaborations with our project. This success with teachers is primarily a result of the library of curriculum projects that target some of the most challenging science topics at all grade levels. Most teachers can find a project within the library that fits within their course, allowing them to add inquiry and technology to their own classroom.

THE WISE CURRICULUM LIBRARY

The technology tools within WISE can help students learn from peers, make their ideas visible, and develop a deep understanding of personally relevant topics, but only if they are used within carefully designed curriculum that takes advantage of opportunities for learning, reflection, and exchange. For example, sending students to a particular Web site might be completely ineffective unless they are encouraged to develop predictions before visiting the page, followed by carefully structured reflections that help them reconcile their predictions with what they observed. Similarly, online discussions can be fruitful opportunities for students to develop their own ideas, express them to peers, and receive feedback, but they could also be superficial and unproductive if not carefully designed.

Indeed, the WISE technology environment was developed by our research group primarily so that we could investigate such curriculum design issues. When we started, there was no guaranteed recipe, nor any theoretical formula for the design of a technology-enhanced inquiry project. Most WISE curriculum projects were originally developed as research materials that served as a basis for a variety of investigations. For example, one line of research was concerned with the use of student-generated visualizations as a means of helping make their ideas visible. To support this research, we created the WISE Draw tool, where students draw their own predictions of a temperature graph or map where they think an invasive species will appear within a geographical region. While a full discussion of such research is provided in later chapters, the sections below present three different forms of WISE curriculum project that have emerged as a result of our research activities.

WISE Critique Projects

In WISE critique projects, students learn to critically evaluate resources in terms of their scientific credibility or relevance. Many educators have expressed a concern about the source credibility of Web sites, which is a common argument against the use of Internet resources in science instruction. WISE critique projects respond to this challenge, recognizing that the science students of today will be the discerning citizens of tomorrow who will be making meaningful decisions throughout their lives based on scientific arguments and evidence from a variety of sources. Discussions about the energy efficiency of certain kinds of heating may be more suspect, for example, if they are found on a Web site managed by an energy corporation, than if they are found on a governmental science agency Web site. However, the Web has become an invaluable source of information in part because it represents a range of sources. Rather than trying to narrow the range of sources that students encounter, science instruction should help them learn to critique the full spectrum of sources in terms of motivation, credibility, and scientific content.

In WISE critique projects, students are engaged with a range of scientific evidence relating to a specific inquiry topic. The curriculum is carefully designed so that students first encounter a personally relevant science problem, and reflect on that problem. They are then presented with a set of "evidence items"—typically in the form of Web sites that were found by the curriculum authors for purposes of the project—that they must consider in relation to the science problem. For each evidence item, students are asked to rate it in terms of its relevant science content, its source credibility, and its usefulness to the current problem. The WISE learning environment guides students through these various steps in sequence, providing them with a set of evidence items to be critiqued, together with Web forms to collect their critiques and reflection notes to capture their detailed ideas. WISE critique projects typically culminate with an online discussion of the science problem where students are encouraged to comment on different aspects of the various evidence items.

In the "SunLight, SunHEAT" project, for example, students are presented with the scientific problem of passive solar energy, beginning with a hands-on lab where they investigate the effect of light on black and white surfaces. They are then presented with the notion that some houses are designed to capitalize on this scientific phenomenon, followed by a set of evidence items consisting of specific houses that were found on the Web. These are house designs that vary in the degree to which they capitalize on passive solar energy, and also vary in terms of who authored the webpage and what the author's motivation was for producing that page. For example, one evidence item called the Earthship (see Figure 2.6) documents an innovative house that relies on passive solar heating and cooling and makes use of recycled materials such as old tires for exterior walls and soda cans for interior walls. This is a good example of the kind of interesting resource that

Figure 2.6. WISE Reflection Notes provide students with guidance and instructional context—in this case prompting them to consider two questions about the source credibility and other questions about the passive solar design of the home (image from http://www.earthship.net).

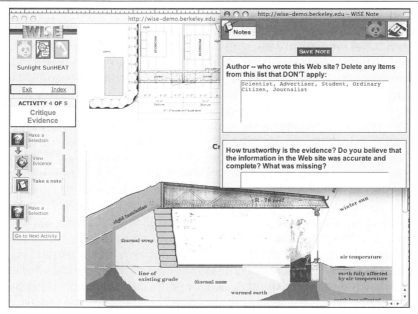

the Web offers to science education, but that requires some guidance and instructional context in order to be used effectively.

When encountering the Earthship evidence in WISE, students are asked questions such as: Who do you think wrote this webpage? How reliable is the scientific argument presented? Finally, students are prompted to ask two questions about the passive solar design of the home. The "Sunlight, SunHEAT" Project includes six different house designs that vary in terms of source credibility (some pages are actually advertisements that market specific house designs), as well as relevant science (some homes make little or no use of passive solar architecture). The project is structured so that students critique all six designs, then perform a culminating discussion in which they share their questions about the evidence and discuss the need for critical reflection about evidence (Slotta & Linn, 2000).

WISE Debate Projects

Another kind of WISE project is the scientific debate, where students learn to make use of evidence in constructing or evaluating scientific arguments. WISE researchers have investigated the best design for such curriculum: Should students be asked to take their own position in the debate before considering any evidence? What kinds of reflection prompts would be most helpful as they evaluate evidence? When should they debate with peers, and what should be the format of such debates? What should the teacher's role be, as students are engaged in the online activities? The researchers employed WISE to investigate successful structures and content for such debate projects, ultimately resulting in several effective projects such as the WISE "Deformed Frogs Mystery," where students evaluate and compare various arguments about why malformed frogs are appearing in North American waterways (Bell, 2004).

Another debate project is "What's in a House?", where students critique, compare, and debate different features of houses that make them energy-efficient, particularly for hot, desert climates. This project was developed as part of a sequence, building on the critiquing skills that students gained in "Sunlight, SunHEAT." In the debate project, students consider evidence for a wide variety of windows, walls, and roofing materials, critique that evidence in terms of its scientific content, and debate the most suitable components for house designs. Figure 2.7 shows "What's in a House?" with an evidence item related to tinted windows, which is one of the kinds of windows they critique in this project. Students critique many different architectural Web sites and then perform a comparison activity in which they are asked to debate the various strategies for windows, walls, and roofs in terms of their de-

Figure 2.7. The WISE "What's in a House?" project. The screen capture shows an Evidence Page providing students with some contextual information about a website before they visit the site and explore its relevant information.

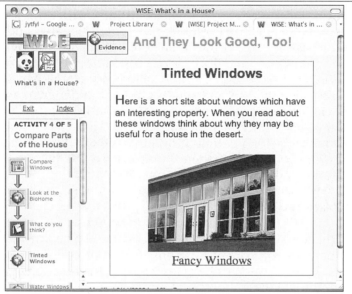

sirability for the construction of houses located in desert climates. The students who originally participated in this research lived in a desert region of California, making this a very relevant and engaging task.

WISE Design Projects

In design projects, a third form of WISE inquiry curriculum, students are guided by the WISE learning environment and the teacher to complete a sequence of activities in which they apply scientific ideas to the task of designing a solution to a personally relevant problem. Design-oriented curriculum has been advocated by many educational researchers as a powerful, engaging form of inquiry (e.g., Kolodner et al., 2003). WISE researchers recognized that design curriculum would be well suited to technology-enhanced learning environments, as the technology could scaffold a wide range of online and offline activities, collect student ideas, enable peer exchange, and encourage deep reflection about the science underlying students' designs.

For example, in extending the curriculum sequence of "Sunlight, SunHEAT" and "What's in a House?", we added a culminating design project where students apply their critique and comparison skills. If critique processes are seen as an important cognitive precursor to debate or comparison, then comparisons might likewise be interpreted as an important aspect of design. Designing a house for the desert will involve comparing different approaches to windows, such as tinting, gas-filled, glass block, reflective blinds, or awnings, which is exactly the kind of activity supported by "What's in a House?" In order to complete the sequence of WISE desert house projects and allow students to apply their critiquing and comparison skills, we created a final design project, known as "Houses in the Desert" (see Figure 2.8).

In WISE design projects, the technology-based learning environment supports students in a complex design project that consists of many subprocesses involving critique, comparison, and reflection (Cuthbert & Slotta, 2004). Activities include journals and reflection notes, discussions with peers, drawing and sketching, searching the Web, completing science worksheets, and even performing offline experiments or observations. In the "Houses in the Desert" project, for example, students were asked to specialize in one aspect of house design—windows, walls, or roofs—then serve as expert consultants for peers who were not spe-

Figure 2.8. Screen capture from the WISE "Houses in the Desert" project.

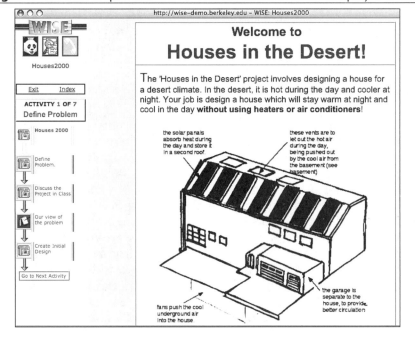

cialists in their area. They created an initial draft of their house design using the WISE Drawing tool, informing their choice of design features with reference to the science of heat and temperature (e.g., passive solar heating and cooling). Students worked in pairs, and consulted with peers who had specialized in aspects of house design other than their own. WISE provided students with design worksheets to help guide their decisions and encourage connections to the science. They submitted their initial designs for peer review, and then revised them based on feedback they received. All project activities were guided by the WISE inquiry map, including the provision of timely hints and prompts.

As a result of many research investigations conducted by members of our research group, the WISE curriculum library has gradually grown to more than 50 inquiry projects, suitable for middle school and high school science. These projects are available on the WISE Web site free of charge, in an easily searchable form, with excellent support materials for teachers. Many of these projects incorporate the general sequence of critique, comparison, and design that was discussed above, although there are also other kinds of projects. For example, several projects have been written to engage students in modeling activities, where they investigate interactive models in order to test and refine their ideas about topics such as global warming or relative velocities. Other recent projects have explored an experimentation pattern, where students are asked to develop predictions of a model, then conduct experiments to test those predictions. Table 2.2 shows titles and short descriptions of a portion of the projects from the WISE curriculum library. The full library can be found on the WISE project Web site (http://wise.berkeley.edu).

MAINTAINING THE WISE CURRICULUM LIBRARY

All of the projects in the WISE library have been created in partnership with teachers and science experts from universities or governmental agencies. They have all been tested in several classroom trials and refined based on our analyses of where students might have been confused or overly challenged.

As a volunteer, collaborative effort, the projects in the WISE library are a work in progress. They are not a commercial product, and thus lack the highly polished and refined aspect that is present in most published texts. Indeed, there is no form of published or commercial product that is anything like WISE. These curriculum projects are highly advanced research materials that have been iteratively refined until they are suitable for use by the wider community of teachers.

Table 2.2. Short descriptions for some of the many WISE curriculum projects that have been developed for middle and high school science. A complete list including detailed descriptions, lesson plans, and connections to science standards can be found on the WISE project Web page: http://wise.berkeley.edu.

Life Science	
Antibiotics: Will They Work?	This project was created to help students understand antibiotic resistance—both the science behind it and how our use of antibiotics can affect resistance development.
Creek Detectives	Students learn about watersheds, what is carried in them, and how to make careful observations. They examine the creek at different points along the water path and compare their observations from different seasons.
How Do Earth and Space Plants Grow?	Students investigate different conditions for growing plants in space and on the Earth. Then, they compare regular Earth plants with NASA space plants, observing plant growth and development and graphing their observations.
Mitosis and Cell Processes	Students understand the stages of mitosis and associated cell structures within the context of cancer. They investigate three hypothetical plant-based medicines, each of which interferes with mitosis in a different way.
Genetically Modified Foods	Students develop an understanding of genetically modified foods and debate what agricultural practices should be used in their area.
HIV Prevention	Students investigate the transmission of HIV and learn how they can protect themselves from HIV infection and AIDS.
Malaria Controversy	Students learn about the various cycles that characterize malaria, and debate three different strategies for controlling the spread of malaria worldwide.
DDT-Malaria Controversy	Students critique the scientific evidence related to the productive uses and harmful side effects of DDT. They create an argument about the proposed global ban of DDT and present this argument during a classroom debate.
Deformed Frogs Mystery	Students investigate the nature and cause of frog deformities in North America and debate competing hypotheses about the cause of those malformations.
Wolves in Your Backyard	Students learn about the basic biology of wolves, including their social nature, and critique a wolf management plan from either Minnesota or their own local region.

Physical Sciences	
Life on Mars Debate	Students explore a contemporary scientific controversy related to the presence of life on Mars, debating evidence and creating their own argument.
Friends: Velocity Style	Through scenarios about friends and their adventures around town, students practice calculating velocity and interpreting multiple representations of velocity.
How Far Does Light Go?	Can light travel forever, or does it eventually die out? Students explore "evidence" of different aspects of light and create their own argument to support their position.

	Physical Sciences (*cont'd*)
Probing Your Surroundings	Students explore the temperature of objects around them, making predictions, gathering data and discussing principles to explain why objects feel hot or cold.
Sunlight, SunHEAT!	Students learn about passive solar energy, developing criteria for critiquing information from Web. They evaluate the source credibility and validity of evidence.
Houses in the Desert	Students design a house that would be energy efficient in a desert environment, drawing on skills in critique and comparison learned during previous projects.
Modeling Static Electricity	Students investigate incidents of refueling fires caused by static electricity and use different levels of models (charge, atomic, energy) to explain their observations.
How Can We Recycle Old Tires?	Students investigate solutions to the problem of how to recycle scrap tires, connecting the chemical structures and chemical bonding exhibited by metals, ceramics, and polymers to methods of recycling those materials.
Gas-Powered Vehicles: A Thing of the Past?	Using interactive simulations and models, students gain a conceptual understanding of energy released during chemical reactions and apply those concepts to critique hydrogen fuel cells as an alternative.

	Earth Sciences
Climate Change: Who's to Blame	Students investigate evidence for global warming and debate whether human activities or natural processes are the main cause for global climate change.
Rainforest Interactions	Students consider species interactions, make a food web using the WISE causal mapper, play a simulation game offline, and predict relative numbers of organisms.
Global Warming: Virtual Earth	Students learn about the greenhouse effect and global warming using an interactive model that represents heat flow on the Earth.
The Next Shake	Can we predict earthquakes, or how much damage they will cause when they do occur? Students explore these questions using evidence from the Web.
Rock Cycle: Igneous Rocks	Students learn about rock formation and the importance of models in science by creating models of the crystalization process and the formation of magma.
Ocean Trawling: What a Drag!	Students collect evidence on the four main principles of evolution: variation, natural selection, change over many generations, and species change. They debate whether clown fish can evolve after bottom trawling destroys their habitat.

The WISE technology and curriculum resources are supported by our research team in a volunteer effort, which means to say that WISE receives no funding for the maintenance of our public Web site or materials. However, we greatly value this aspect of our work, and must maintain the project library for our own research purposes as well. Occasionally, a Web site that is linked from within a WISE project will disappear, which will only be discovered the next time a teacher or researcher tries to use the project. In these cases, or whenever a typo or technical bug is discovered, WISE researchers respond to the problem. Over time, we have maintained this library, expanded it, and watched it grow as new research projects develop materials.

We developed WISE in order to provide ourselves and the wider research community with a flexible platform for classroom-based research in topics related to inquiry and technology. However, we already had a sizeable head start, from a wealth of prior research that preceded WISE. Thus, while WISE was developed in order to promote research of inquiry and technology, it was designed according to a firm foundation of existing research. Furthermore, all the research that we've conducted using WISE over the past 10 years has focused on extending this foundation. The next two chapters of this book present the theoretical foundation that underlies all WISE curriculum, including detailed examples from our prior research in the CLP and KIE projects as well as some further illustrations from WISE.

RECOMMENDED READINGS

Cuthbert, A., & Slotta, J. D. (2004). Fostering lifelong learning skills on the World Wide Web: Critiquing, questioning and searching for evidence. *The International Journal of Science Education, 27*(7) 821–844.

> This research paper describes the WISE "Houses in the Desert" curriculum in terms of its use of the underlying patterns of critique and comparison. It also introduces a new pattern of jigsaw specializations, where students choose one component of house design (windows, walls, or roofs) and become a specialist in that area, providing advice and expertise within their design groups.

Slotta, J. D. (2004). The Web-based Inquiry Science Environment (WISE): Scaffolding knowledge integration in the science classroom. In M. C. Linn, P. Bell, & E. Davis (Eds.), *Internet Environments for Science Education.* (pp. 203–232). Mahwah, NJ: Lawrence Erlbaum.

> This chapter provides a detailed overview of WISE and reviews a research study where all the science teachers in a middle school adopted WISE projects over a period of several years. The chapter reviews the trajectory of the teachers and comments on interesting differences in their classroom practices.

CHAPTER 3

The Knowledge
Integration Approach

How do students learn complex science? How do students make sense of everyday science experiences? How can we take advantage of these everyday activities to build student understanding? These questions have motivated our work for the last 20 years and led to the knowledge integration framework that has guided the design of the WISE learning environment as well as the curriculum materials created in WISE.

WHAT STUDENTS BRING TO CLASS:
EVIDENCE FROM THE COMPUTER AS LEARNING PARTNER PROJECT

What ideas do students have about science, and how do they go about responding to science instruction? We received a Wheels for the Mind grant from Apple Computer to investigate these questions in the Computer as Learning Partner project (CLP). This research, started in the 1980s, led to the development of the knowledge integration framework that forms the basis for all curriculum and assessments used in WISE.

In CLP, our research team collaborated with a middle school to introduce temperature probes in science classrooms and study how students used real-time data collection as part of their experimentation about heat and temperature. Initially, we asked students about the difference between heat and temperature and about phenomena such as the direction of heat flow, insulation, and thermal equilibrium. We were quite frustrated by the glib responses that students gave. For example, the students who considered themselves to be the "science types" would say things like, "Heat is calories. Temperature is degrees." But these answers did not connect to students' other ideas or even to the experiments that they conducted using the temperature-sensitive probes.

To get a better sense of students' ideas, we introduced questions that connected their classroom investigations with familiar problems.

Thus, we asked students to predict what would happen if you were stirring a pot of noodles with a metal spoon or a wooden spoon. We asked them which would be the better spoon for stirring the noodles. The scientifically normative idea here is that heat flows at different rates depending on the material. In addition we hope that the students will learn about the nature of a subset of materials, appreciating that heat flows faster in metals such as aluminum than in wood or Styrofoam.

When we asked students these questions, we found that they had many very interesting and rich ideas about heat flow, based on their observations in their everyday lives. Students said things like, "Metal spoons are bad—they get too hot," or "My mom uses a wooden spoon so she won't burn her hand." We extended this question, asking students, "If you were going to roast marshmallows, would you rather have a wooden stick or a metal stick?" Students were very good at making predictions about which would be most desirable, arguing for a wooden stick. However, students were less able to explain why one choice was better than another. Indeed, in spite of these relatively rich observations about spoons and sticks, many students argued that heat flowed at the same rate in all materials, completely disconnecting their observations of the world from their assertions about the science.

We further extended this approach to questions about insulation. We asked students to predict whether, for example, water would cool faster in a metal cup than in a Styrofoam cup. Here, the normative scientific idea is that materials are insulators when heat flows slowly and are conductors when heat flows more rapidly. This is a relative distinction.

In response to these questions, students were relatively sure that the Styrofoam cup would be better at insulation than a metal cup, based on their experience, but again, they lacked an argument based on rate of heat flow to explain the difference. Eileen Lewis, a graduate student at the time, asked students what was best to wrap a drink in to keep it cool in their lunch, and she gave them choices such as aluminum foil, newspaper, or nothing. The vast majority of students preferred to wrap the drink in aluminum foil. They frequently argued that their mothers used this strategy for wrapping drinks in their lunch to take to school. After studying about these ideas, students were observed to change their behavior and not wrap their drinks as often.

Lewis extended this approach, asking a more intriguing question that caused some confusion for students. She asked whether it would be better to use a sweater or aluminum foil to keep a drink cold. Students frequently responded that a sweater would be a bad choice because sweaters warm you up. Thus, students argued that a sweater has the property of imparting heat rather than its actual capability of slowing the rate of heat flow, which works to both keep a drink cold for lunch and to keep an individual warm on a cold night (Lewis & Linn, 1994).

Lewis then probed students' understanding, asking why they thought aluminum would be a good choice for keeping a drink cold. Many students responded that if you feel metals at home, the metals feel colder than the wool. So they argued that metals have the property of making things cold. Lewis was intrigued to see that students were imputing agency to sweaters for keeping people warm and to aluminum foil and other metals for making things cold. Essentially, students ignored their own body temperature and their role in producing heat. Thus, rather than realizing that a sweater insulated them and, therefore, slowed the flow of heat, they assumed that the sweater actually could make them warm.

Although these ideas that students exhibit in such personally relevant tasks are not scientifically sound, the research team was interested in them because they reflected an effort on the part of students to really make sense of complex phenomena and to try to explain why sweaters or aluminum foil might impact the temperature of an object. These observations further convinced the research team that students possess a lot of intriguing and potentially valuable ideas about science, but that there are some limits in their ability to interconnect these ideas or to apply them to new phenomena or problems.

Other members of the research team extended these investigations to new topics, exploring issues that have to do with thermal equilibrium. Stop and think for a minute about how the students depicted above might describe the temperature of a wooden desk, a metal chair, and a rabbit that are all in the same room. As the reader might predict, many students thought that a thermometer would show that metals have a lower temperature than wood if measured in the classroom, and that sweaters would have a higher temperature than other materials. These predictions were consistent with students' beliefs about the ability of materials to impart heat or cold, and helped the research team understand the reasoning that students go through to make conjectures about scientific phenomena. Students were surprised to find, when they did the experiment, that the desk, chair, sweater, Styrofoam cup, and other objects would not all have different temperatures consistent with the way they feel to the touch. They accurately predicted that the rabbit had a different temperature from the temperature of the room.

In this situation, students most likely will predict that the thermometer would measure temperature as what the object feels like when they touch it. Thus, students tend to forget that their hands have a temperature that is usually different from that of the room—which is consistent with the idea that they are producing heat to maintain their body temperature. When students sort out the difference between the temperature of their hand and the temperature of the objects, they realize that the apparent temperature differences that they were feeling are actually just differences in the rate at which heat is flowing between their hand and the object. In a typical room, a metal chair and wooden desk are cooler than their hand, so the heat energy flows from their hand into those objects. Here, students must use the idea that heat flows at different rates depending on the material, and understand that the heat flows faster from their hand into the metal chair than from their hand into the wooden desk.

Overall, CLP served to reveal the rich ideas that students brought to science class, particularly once we extended questions about heat and temperature beyond simple laboratory experiments and into everyday contexts. Many of these ideas were non-normative, meaning that they would not hold up to scientific scrutiny. Furthermore, many times students appeared to hold self-contradictory ideas. For example, students would combine the idea that heat flows only in one direction, based often on some prior science instruction about heat flowing from hot to cold objects, with their observations about heating and cooling. Thus, when we asked students whether heat flowed from warmer to colder or from colder to warmer objects, many concluded that if you placed an ice cube next to a warm drink, the "cold" would flow into the drink and the "heat" from the drink would flow into the ice cube, thus hypothesizing that two processes would be occurring simultaneously. These complex ideas helped the research team develop a deeper understanding of the nature of student ideas and led us to new ideas about instructional experiences that could help students improve their understanding of heat and temperature.

We realized that science education must capitalize on the views held by students, for two reasons: first, because the ideas represent intellectual contributions of the students, who have thought about the situation and have come up with a conjecture that takes advantage of some of the evidence they have observed, and second, because by connecting science activities to everyday experiences, we can make science more relevant for students and encourage them to consider scientific issues outside of science class. Far too often, students isolate their science learning in the classroom and see no reason to connect science ideas learned in class to their experiences outside of class. By incorporating everyday situations into the instruction materials, CLP was able to address this tendency and encourage students to think about heat and temperature within a broader and more personally relevant context.

Our observations about the diverse and sometimes conflicting ideas that students bring to class were somewhat new to the research literature. Many cognitive and educational researchers argued that students have a single conceptualization about a topic that, if non-normative, can be addressed or corrected by instruction. Instead, our work revealed that students often hold two or more differing and potentially self-contradictory ideas at the same time. It was difficult to reconcile this view of a cacophony of contradictory and incomplete notions with traditional theories of cognitive or conceptual development, such as that of Jean Piaget, who said that students go through a series of stages in their development. However, other researchers were also beginning to argue that students do, in fact, possess a fragmented or incoherent set of conceptualizations that they use selectively. For example, Andrea diSessa (1993) had identified what he called phenomenological primitives as a set of ideas that students hold that emerge from their experience.

Our research group surveyed evidence from across the research literature as well as that from our own studies within CLP, and concluded that calling the ideas students developed in the course of trying to make sense of scientific phenomena "misconceptions" was unfair and misleading. These ideas, although certainly not consistent with scientific norms, were nevertheless grounded in students' observations and experience. Students had noted, for example, that metals feel colder than wood at room temperature, even though they had imputed an inaccurate mechanism to explaining that difference. Based on the CLP research and our ongoing reflections about how student ideas emerge, we formulated the knowledge integration framework, which has guided all of our designs and development over the past 2 decades.

THE KNOWLEDGE INTEGRATION FRAMEWORK

The knowledge integration framework emerged to make sense of the ideas that students bring to science class and to identify ways to make science learning more effective. Knowledge integration starts with the view that students bring a repertoire of rich, confusing, and intriguing ideas to science class. Of course, they need scientifically normative ideas, but they also need specific versions of these ideas that can help them make sense of their observations. In order to understand why metal and wood feel different at room temperature, even though the thermometer says that they are the same temperature, students need to understand two important scientific principles: first, that heat flows at different rates depending on the material, and second, that how hot or cold an object feels to the touch is actually related to the flow of heat into or out of the person's finger.

Metal objects feel cooler than plastic objects at room temperature because the heat energy flows more easily from our fingers or hands into the metal than it does into plastic. For the same reason, metal objects feel much hotter than wood objects when they have been left in a hot car or oven, because the heat energy flows more quickly into the person's hand from the metal than from the wood. If students lack these important ideas—or fail to see their relevance to the situation— then they will have difficulty reconciling their perception that a metal and wood object would feel different with their observation that they have the same temperature measurement.

In addition, students must improve at making inferences from their observations. Many times, students have enough information to reach a valid conclusion but do not realize that the evidence they are utilizing lacks validity. For example, students knew that Styrofoam cups keep drinks at their temperature longer than metal cups, but they fail to consider that information when they choose what to wrap a drink in to keep it cool in their lunch. Similarly, students may often regurgitate isolated "facts" memorized from science instruction, or learn to solve specific kinds of problems, but fail to understand the concepts behind these facts and strategies. They might add new ideas from science class to their existing repertoire, but these would not be integrated with any previous knowledge. This could lead to a phenomenon we had observed frequently during CLP and other studies, where students believe that the ideas they learn in science class hold true in the classroom, but not on the playground or at home.

So students not only need new ideas from science instruction; they also need to improve their capabilities to make inferences from the evidence at their disposal, to develop criteria for what constitutes important evidence, and to draw conclusions based on multiple ideas or observations. The knowledge integration framework emerged to describe this process. Students need to build from the ideas that they hold when they come to class. They need to link their ideas to new ideas. And they need evidence to sort out the alternative ideas they hold. This framework suggests instructional approaches that have the potential to increase students' coherent understanding.

The knowledge integration framework was informed via comparison of two instructional programs that had both succeeded in helping students develop more coherent ideas but were, in fact, designed for very different topics. One of those instructional programs was the CLP project, discussed above. The second one was aimed at computer science instruction and designed to increase the effectiveness of undergraduate computer science courses at the University of California, Berkeley. We had formed a partnership with instructors of a new programming course to help students make sense of computational metaphors. Up until this point, efforts to teach list processing languages such as LISP and Scheme were thwarted by the difficulties that students had faced, and our efforts to improve students' ability to write computer programs in these languages constituted another important source of evidence for our definition of the framework.

By comparing studies of iterative refinement in the two curriculum programs—one in computer science and the other in middle school thermodynamics—we began to identify features of effective instruction. In both cases, researchers conducted iterative refinements of the curriculum, implementing the curriculum with one cohort of students, looking at student progress, diagnosing difficulties in student learning, redesigning the curriculum, and implementing it again with a new cohort. For the purposes of this book, we will confine our discussion to the CLP studies, although it is important to note that two lines of work contributed to the development of the framework (for discussion of the computer science work, see Linn, 1995; Davis, Linn, Mann, & Clancy, 1993; Davis, Linn, & Clancy, 1995).

In the case of the Computer as Learning Partner (CLP) curriculum, eight different versions of the curriculum were tested over a 10-year period, resulting in an overall increase of 400% in student performance, as shown in Figure 3.1. In one important CLP assessment, students were asked a difficult question: "What is the difference between heat and temperature?" They were required to give two everyday examples to illustrate their ideas. The requirement to provide examples helped ensure that students would not simply provide a memorized reply based on their studies.

The initial version of the CLP curriculum, which was essentially the typical middle school science textbook with a few supplemental activities, resulted in only about 12% of the students succeeding fully in this assessment. By the time we arrived at our eighth version of the curriculum, over 50% of the students were able to provide an accurate

Figure 3.1. By gradually improving our CLP curriculum over a span of eight semesters, we were able to improve students' ability to differentiate between the concepts of temperature and heat energy.

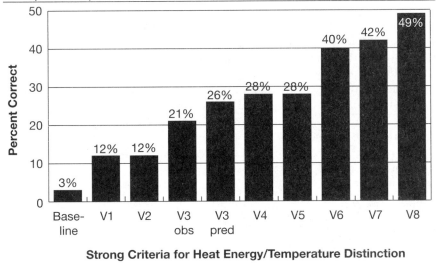

Strong Criteria for Heat Energy/Temperature Distinction

Source: Linn & Songer, 1991.

answer along with two examples, and the other half of the students were providing more sophisticated responses than anything we had observed in our first version of the curriculum. Students used evidence from their investigations and connected their reasoning to everyday experiences. Much more detail about the CLP curriculum is provided in the recommended readings at the end of this chapter.

In developing the knowledge integration framework, we identified common elements of effective instructional materials from the CLP project and the computer science course. These common elements became the tenets of knowledge integration. The remaining sections of this chapter describe the tenets of knowledge integration. We connect the tenets to a curricular example and explain how these tenets have guided the design and development of WISE curriculum.

Make Learning Accessible

The first tenet of knowledge integration is to make science accessible. The tenet responds to our research on the repertoire of ideas that students bring to science class. This tenet calls for curriculum that makes science accessible to students by introducing a broad range of relevant and familiar contexts that serve to broaden students' perspectives on a science topic.

Embedding instructional materials in contexts that are personally familiar to students is one way to accomplish this goal. To help students understand thermal equilibrium, for example, the CLP curriculum asks them to make predictions about the temperature of objects on a hot day at the beach (around 100°F) and in a cold ski cabin before the heat is turned on (around 30°F). In order to contrast these two cases, students must extrapolate from their beliefs, as indicated above. At first, students often make the same predictions for these extreme temperature situations as they made for the case of wood and metal in the classroom: Metal would feel colder than the wood. But when prompted to reflect, they often change their minds, saying that metal would feel really hot on a hot day, much hotter than wood, rather than colder. They also noted that metal might feel much, much colder than wood in a ski cabin, rather than just a little cooler, as they experienced in the classroom. These extreme hot and cold cases became powerful opportunities for instruction when the students learned that, just as they measured in the classroom, all the objects are still at equal temperature, no matter how they feel to the touch.

How could this be so? There must be some explanation. The teacher is able to engage students with this challenging puzzle, which was personally familiar to students, enabling them to reason more deeply about the underlying science. By asking students to extrapolate their predictions to the new contexts of a much warmer surround and a much colder surround, the curriculum helped them make comparisons between their predictions for everyday temperatures and their predictions for more extreme temperatures.

In CLP, we continued developing thermodynamics problems, such as designing a way to keep yourself warm in the wilderness or exploring ways to keep the drink in your lunch cold or the pizza warm. These problems were integrally connected to the science concepts, which is a key factor of making science accessible. Many textbooks, for example, attempt to make science accessible by including a captivating photograph of firefighters in protective clothing or a historical anecdote about phlogiston, but neglect the important task of connecting these materials to the principles taught in the unit. By introducing numerous examples and connecting those examples to the science, designers can enable students to articulate a broad repertoire of ideas, ensuring that all of their ideas are integrated into the learning experience. This sets the stage for students to sort out their ideas, find the most promising ones, and connect ideas to form a coherent understanding of the science.

Consider the WISE "Deformed Frogs" project discussed in Chapter 2, where the science is made accessible by presenting a dilemma that is reported in news accounts: the declining population of frogs and the increase in frog deformities. In general, students find frog malformations to be an extremely interesting topic. Linda Shear, who studied this project in early classroom trials, remarked that "If students say 'Yuck, gross!' you know that they will be paying attention to the curriculum." Because frog deformities were frequently in the news, it was possible to add to the accessibility of this topic by personalizing the scientists themselves. We involved several scientists in this curriculum who were actually working on problems related to amphibian decline and malformation. We introduced those students to the scientists virtually, through "Meet the Scientist" pages within WISE, and even engaged students in asking the scientists questions at different points within the project (Linn, Shear, Bell, & Slotta, 1999).

The make-science-accessible tenet of knowledge integration guides our development of the curriculum in several ways. First, it guides our designs of inquiry activities that connect science principles to relevant scientific problems. Second, it appears in prompts that ask students to explain personally relevant problems using science principles. For example, students might be asked to explain why a cake cools faster in a metal pan than in a pottery pan, using the principles they've already learned about thermal equilibrium and insulation in conduction. Third, make-science-accessible appears in the curriculum in opportunities for students to understand scientific inquiry processes. Making these processes accessible to students can involve guiding them through the process of investigation, such as by asking them to make predictions, to conduct a simple experiment, and to interpret the results of that experiment based on their predictions.

Make Thinking Visible

The second tenet of knowledge integration is to make thinking visible wherever possible within the curriculum. Students must be enabled to make their ideas visible both to themselves and to their teachers. In addition, teachers and curriculum materials have the opportunity to make new ideas visible to students.

In traditional classrooms, students usually make their ideas visible only on homework and tests, with only occasional opportunities to do so during class. Technology-enhanced learning environments such as WISE use embedded assessments to provide teachers with access to student ideas with greater frequency, such as when they write reflection notes or participate in online discussions. By making student ideas visible more regularly and more comprehensibly, technology-enhanced instruction can increase teachers' awareness of the variety, diversity, and complexity of student ideas. Adding more information about student ideas means that teachers have an opportunity to enhance and strengthen their instruction based on how their students are thinking in the moment.

There are many ways that curriculum activities can enable students to make their thinking visible. Students could be asked to make predictions about the outcome of an investigation, or to write reflections on their investigations, both of which would result in a visible representation of their ideas. The make-thinking-visible tenet can be met through the use of online discussions, where students respond to or initiate threads. Students can also reveal their thinking when they work with a partner or small group, providing the teacher with insight into how the students are learning. By moving around the classroom listening to pairs of students discussing a complex scientific dilemma, teachers can observe how students think about scientific experiences in ways that are not readily tapped by whole-class discussion—where only a handful of students typically participate.

Making thinking visible also helps students understand their own ideas. When students make their ideas visible to themselves, they have the opportunity to reflect on their thinking and to keep ideas in mind as they move through the curriculum. Thus, by making their ideas visible, students gain insight into their own learning process, a factor we address below in the section on promoting autonomous learning.

In the CLP project, we worked with a veteran master teacher named Doug Kirkpatrick, known to the students as Mr. K. Even though he had more than 20 years' experience in middle school science classrooms before he even joined our team, Mr. K quickly reported that his own instruction had been transformed by the improved access to students' ideas as they were learning within the CLP curriculum. He was surprised that students held such a variety of views and that they could produce so many varied examples about insulation and conduction. He discovered that some students hypothesized that air was necessary for heating and cooling to occur. Others claimed that there needed to be holes in Styrofoam so that heating and cooling could occur by transporting air between objects. He learned that other students thought it was only possible for heating and cooling to be influenced if objects were touching one another. These students neglected the role of air as a factor in healing and cooling.

Mr. K told our research team that he had not previously obtained such information from traditional classroom activities for two reasons. First, by the time a quiz came along, students had often forgotten or ignored their intuitive ideas, or they may have been reluctant to speculate in the same fashion as the CLP activities encouraged them to do. Second, during class discussion in previous years, only a small fraction of the students had ever participated. Even when he had made efforts to call on other students in order to broaden the participation in the discussion, Mr. K found that many students were reluctant or even unwilling to voice their ideas. The increased opportunity to gather student insights into the learning process while they were still grappling with complex science material strengthened Mr. K's understanding of how his students were learning.

Another important way to make thinking visible is to use visualizations of scientific phenomena. In the CLP research, we investigated the question of how to make important scientific ideas more visible for students. The first area we investigated was concerned with data collection and graphing. We approached this challenging area by allowing students to use computer-based temperature probes to record information about scientific experiments and investigations they were conducting during the CLP curriculum. Using this approach of collecting "real-time data," we were able to free students from the tedium of recording information, provide them with immediate graphs even as the data were being recorded, and emphasize the importance of observing and recording results carefully. Teachers also have the opportunity to make thinking visible by adding new ideas for students to consider. Traditionally, most new ideas have been added by textbook presentations or lectures. Today, it is also possible to use computer-delivered models, simulations, and interactive visualizations.

The CLP project connected the computer to various probes, heat sources, and other devices to make thinking visible. For example, students have difficulty understanding the relationship between the amount of heat, the volume of the water, and the change in temperature. CLP used immersion heaters, temperature probes, and graphs of the temperature over time to illustrate the impact of adding what was referred to as a "dollop of heat" to a cup of water. This experiment keeps the volume of the water constant and allows the student to add fixed amounts of heat. The combination of the immersion heater and the temperature probe allowed students to precisely calibrate the relationship between the amount of heat added and the temperature change of the system. Students could explore this phenomenon by varying the amount of the liquid to which they were adding heat while keeping the amount of heat added constant. In this way, students were able to conduct experiments and to study the relationship between the amount of heat added and the observed temperature of the system.

The use of temperature probes to gather data and computers to display data was controversial. Many teachers were sure that this "shortcut" would undermine students' understanding of temperature graphs. However, we found that the opposite was true. By using temperature probes, students were able to understand graphing more deeply. They interpreted graphs of heating and cooling more effectively when they could watch the graph form as the temperature probe collected information than they could when composing the graph by hand.

This finding was somewhat counterintuitive, as some teachers feel that students benefit more from constructing a graph than from watching the graph develop automatically based on probeware and graphing software. However, our classroom observations in CLP showed that when students constructed a graph by hand, they often lost sight of the purpose of the experiment. Students were distracted by the graphing procedure, since they typically had several jobs to perform, such as holding the thermometer, recording the data, or reading the output, rather than making sense of the experiment. In contrast, when they carefully observed the probe collecting data and watched the graph form automatically on the screen, they were able to notice important qualitative characteristics of the system. For example, in watching a liquid boil, students were able to see that the temperature curve suddenly leveled off once the liquid began boiling. They frequently wanted to conduct another experiment and vary one or another of the conditions. Thus, our experience in CLP showed that when students used the temperature-sensitive probes and real-time data collection, the real-time graphing helped make ideas visible. Through interacting with these resources, students were more able to interpret experimental investigations, and were more inclined to come up with their own investigations.

Another way in which CLP made thinking visible was by using a simulation called "Heat Bars" to help make visible the rate of heat flow in different materials. Using Heat Bars, students could select two materials, each in the form of a long rectangular bar, and observe a simulation of heat flowing through the two bars when they are both placed next to identical heat sources (see Figure 3.2). The heat bar simulation made the rate of heat flow visible, which many students found extremely helpful in reasoning about thermal phenomena. Research conducted by Eileen Lewis showed that the heat bar simulation, more than any other classroom activity, helped students learn to distinguish the rate of heat flow in different materials and to connect their understanding to situations such as cooling curves for water (Lewis, Stern, & Linn, 1993).

Figure 3.2. Heat Bars Simulation from CLP project. Students compared the rate at which heat energy flows through two different materials, in this case copper and stainless steel. Initially, the two bars both appeared as solid white in color and were touched at the end by identical heat sources (the shaded rectangles). Students observe as the heat energy (in the form of shading) progresses through the bars at differing rates.

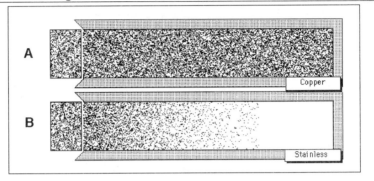

The WISE project drew on our CLP approaches to incorporate ways to make ideas visible, and added some new methods as well. One approach, called the WISE Principle Maker (see Figure 3.3), challenged students to combine phrases to construct scientific principles. This provided an advantage for those students who found writing about science troublesome, as they could articulate their ideas effectively by selecting among choices in drop-down menus. In his Ph.D. research, Doug Clark (2004) found that such a visual principle constructor provided a good source of information for assigning students to small-group discussions in order to ensure that each group was made up of individuals who held diverse viewpoints.

Another way that students can make their thinking visible is by writing a report or keeping a journal. Betsy Davis (1998) explored this approach when she asked students to write a news article to explain Web-based advertisements concerning the nature of insulation and conduction. She found that students expressed very interesting ideas when asked to create a longer narrative and to warrant their assertions with evidence.

How does making thinking visible help students learn? Visualizations can be confusing and misleading. The visualizations in WISE and CLP succeeded for several reasons. First, these visualizations allowed students to analyze controlled experiments. In heat bars, students could compare metal and wood placed next to a heat source of the same intensity. Second, the visualizations helped students build connections to familiar situations. Third, they enabled students to create a narrative about the results. For example, CLP reflections helped

Figure 3.3. WISE Principle Constructor—Making students' ideas visible. In the case displayed here, the students reveal their belief that two objects will never become the same temperature, and they provide some evidence of their reasoning.

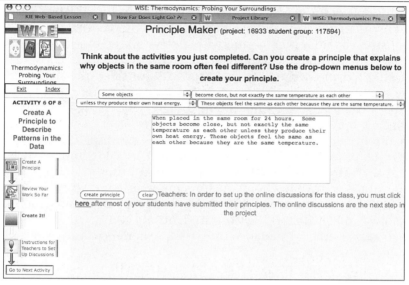

students make their ideas visible about an experiment with immersion heaters, as they could articulate their own narrative, such as, "When you add five dollops of heat to one cup of water, it doesn't get as hot as if you add the same amount to a smaller cup of water." Fourth, visualizations draw students' attention to salient and essential information. In the case of heat bars visualization, students' attention is drawn to the different rates of heat flow in different materials.

Learn from Others

A third tenet of knowledge integration concerns how students learn from one another. Well-designed interactions with peers can improve understanding of complex science. In classrooms, many activities enable students to interact with one another, but the circumstances under which these activities help students learn from one another is more limited. Often, class discussions follow a well-worn pattern where students who already know the answers to the teacher's questions speak up while the other students are left out of the discussion and do not benefit. In this normal form of classroom discussions, there is very little exchange between students and their peers, and there is little opportunity for students who hold non-normative ideas to build connections to their ideas.

What can students learn from their peers? First, when students conduct investigations and discuss topics such as the difference between heat and temperature, they can expand their repertoire of ideas by considering those ideas held by their peers. In the CLP project, students work in pairs and discuss evidence and observations such as their predictions about which container is likely to keep a hot drink warm for the longest time. Listening to these conversations in class, teachers are often pleased to see that students consider alternatives that they might not have considered if they were working by themselves. In such exchanges, students might disagree about their hypotheses, regarding, for example, whether heat will flow faster in wood or metal. When required to write down their reason, one student might argue that "metals feel cold" as a reason that heat will flow more slowly in metal than in wood. Another student might bring in a different example and say, "Well, when you stir soup with a metal spoon, it gets hot faster, so the heat will flow through the spoon faster." Such discussions can be valuable, because students are considering alternative explanations, adding evidence from their experience, and negotiating to reach consensus.

Learning among peers can also be effective when one student models effective ways of articulating ideas for other students. For example, discussions of rate of heat flow can help students develop effective ways to express their ideas. These opportunities to learn from others involve adding ideas that students had not considered, articulating ideas that students had not been able to verbalize, or clarifying ideas by explaining them to a peer.

Research in CLP and WISE explored a number of ways to orchestrate effective classroom and curricular activities that allow students to learn from one another. One effective approach is that of online discussions. Over the years, we have conducted many studies to identify factors that make such discussions effective. Initially, our online discussions were conducted in the back of the classroom on a stand-alone computer where students took turns entering their views and responding to the views of their peers. This was a relatively cumbersome way to participate in a class discussion, but it had the advantage that students thoughtfully responded to ideas contributed by others.

Sherry Hsi (1997) designed this early system, known as the *multimedia forum kiosk,* and then studied its impact on students' understanding of science topics. She found several factors that increased the effectiveness of learning under these circumstances. First, it was helpful to require students to first make an assertion about a situation before they read comments contributed by other students. Hsi began all discussions by posing a problem, such as whether a cake would cool faster if it were in a metal pan or a glass pan placed on a metal surface. Students began by making their own prediction and then reading the comments of others. Second, it was beneficial for students to describe the character of their contribution. Thus, students indicated whether they were elaborating on a comment, asking a question, contradicting an idea, or starting a new discussion. By considering how their idea fit into the overall classroom discourse, students were more reflective about the nature of their contribution, and more likely to benefit from interacting with their peers. Third, we improved online discussions with "seed comments" that introduce ideas that students might not have considered or that highlight ideas in ways that contribute to an effective discussion (Hsi & Hoadley, 1997).

Chris Hoadley (1999) studied the value of adding personalized versus textbooklike ideas to the discussion. In the personalized format, a fictional individual periodically made contributions to the discussions, adding new ideas. In the textbook condition, new ideas were contributed by a neutral, authoritative guide. Hoadley found that by personalizing comments and associating a series of comments with the same character, discussions were more effective than when the ideas were introduced using textbooklike comments.

In addition to online discussions, there are many other ways that students could learn from one another in the curriculum. Many WISE projects include peer review activities where students are guided (by Web forms and reflection prompts) to critique the designs or arguments of their classmates. For example, in the WISE "Houses in the Desert" project described in Chapter 2, students critiqued one another's initial house designs, identifying aspects where the designs could be improved. Students benefit not only from the feedback that they receive from their peers in such activities, but from the process of identifying criteria and determining the gaps in someone else's design.

When students learn from one another, they can expand their repertoire of ideas, negotiate criteria for distinguishing among their ideas, and learn new ways to articulate their views. This can happen when pairs work together to make predictions or write notes, in online class discussions of various types, and in critique activities. When students hold distinct ideas, peer interactions provide an opportunity to develop criteria they can apply in future situations. Ultimately, in order to sort out the ideas in their repertoire and build a more coherent understanding, students need criteria, and collaborative learning activities emphasize the formation and selection of such criteria.

Promote Autonomy

The fourth tenet of the knowledge integration framework concerns activities that engage students in the lifelong process of integrating, distinguishing, and sorting out their ideas. Knowledge integration is an ongoing, continuous, and important aspect of scientific reasoning. Students benefit from multiple opportunities to reflect on their ideas and make them more coherent. Often, scientific activities in classrooms guide students to do specific tasks rather than helping them engage in the long-term process of integrating their ideas.

Activities such as comparing ideas, preparing an argument, or planning an experiment require autonomous reasoning. Promoting autonomy involves helping learners evaluate their repertoire of ideas, determine whether new ideas are valid, seek out new ideas when contradictions or uncertainties arise, and develop criteria for distinguishing among ideas. This includes sorting out ideas to develop a more coherent or convincing argument based on evidence.

Typical classroom instruction does not promote autonomous learning, leading students to prefer an economical approach where they respond to specific assignments. In our earlier work, we described students as cognitive economists, always wanting to know when they have done enough. We found that students often asserted that two situations were unrelated in order to avoid the difficult task of establishing similarity or synthesis. Thus, one student argued that heating a casserole is completely different from heating water, so the two situations do not need to follow the same principles. Another asserted that heating and cooling are completely different, so it was not necessary to incorporate information about heating in order to interpret cooling. Indeed, it can be challenging to motivate the intensive, self-directed kinds of learning and reflection that lead to knowledge integration, and certainly the typical atmosphere of the classroom does not promote such a mental frame. Encouraging students to recognize the benefit of autonomously integrating and evaluating ideas is an important goal of the knowledge integration framework.

There is substantial evidence concerning the benefits of autonomously monitoring and integrating ideas, which can be gathered from several research programs. For example, cognitive research on self explanations conduced by Micki Chi and her colleagues (Chi, Bassok, Lewis, Reimann, & Glaser, 1989; Chi, 2005) shows that when students spontaneously explain something to themselves they learn more than students who do not engage in such "self-explanations." In the KIE project, Betsy Davis (1998; 2004) reports that learners who compose coherent letters integrating a variety of evidence are more success-ful in subsequent activities than those who finish all the assignments but neglect the overall argument. In sum, research suggests that when students are encouraged to explain their own thinking or make sense of complex information, they are more successful learners. Activities that promote autonomous learning and reasoning have the potential to help students use techniques such as self-explanation and become more effective at monitoring their own understanding.

The cognitive mechanisms involved in autonomy or lifelong sci-ence learning involve a self-reflective process of comparing ideas, seek-ing evidence to determine which ones are most valid, looking for ways to make connections across seemingly disparate situations, and ulti-mately seeking a coherent understanding or account of the problem. Students often have difficulty making their ideas coherent, and may not pursue a coherent understanding when engaged in traditional forms of science instruction (e.g., lectures, homework, and exams). When students encounter too much information, as occurs in the typ-ical science classroom today, they may legitimately be unable to find a way to engage in any kind of autonomous knowledge integration pro-cess. This tenet of autonomous lifelong learning aims to counteract that tendency, claiming that knowledge integration cannot happen unless students are engaged in sustained, autonomous reflection and reasoning. Clearly, this is a challenge for any science curriculum, and it is one of the tenets that we take most seriously in all of our designs. In order to enact a knowledge integration approach, teachers must be willing to allow some time, space, and incentive for students to en-gage in their own self-driven learning processes.

In order to enhance the opportunities for students to become au-tonomous learners, the CLP project began investigating the best de-signs for reflection prompts. These are simple requests for reflections, such as "What do you think will happen?" or "What are some expe-riences you have had with this topic?" However, the design of such reflection prompts has great consequences for autonomous learning. When students are asked to explain their thinking at various points during the learning process, they have the opportunity to autono-mously question or think through their ideas. They might be asked to compare two alternative views or to generate some evidence to sup-port an assertion.

Reflection prompts have proven successful in a wide range of re-search studies, and there is considerable research to show that the kind of prompts that students encounter has a serious impact on their developing of coherent understanding of science topics. For example,

Betsy Davis (1998; 2004) compared the use of generic prompts, which ask students quite generally to reflect on ideas and determine how valid they are, with specific prompts that ask students to compare certain situations. Somewhat surprisingly, Davis found that the generic prompts led to more autonomous, thoughtful reflections than specific prompts, because students often misinterpreted the specific prompts and because the generic prompts encouraged autonomous interpretations. Thus, students might be asked to compare two specific situations (using a specific prompt), but if those situations didn't make sense to the student, then the student wouldn't have anything very useful to say. If, on the other hand, the prompt asked students what they were thinking at the moment and what information they needed to make sense of the situation, then they could pick something they did not understand and explain their confusion.

Students gain opportunities to practice autonomous reasoning about science when prompted to reflect. But there are many other ways to encourage autonomous reasoning as well. WISE was designed to support autonomy, as students must work on their own interpretations, designs, arguments, and critiques, and not simply listen to lectures or demonstrations from the teacher. WISE has incorporated many different tools and activities to promote autonomous learning, such as graphing, drawing, data collection, online discussions, note-taking, concept-mapping, and peer review. All of these activities, if they are well designed, can foster a general attitude of autonomy, peer exchange, and reflection. The WISE project supports students during such activities by providing scaffolding in the form of technology tools, cognitive guidance, and the inquiry map that helps them navigate through the project. Figure 3.4 shows the WISE "How Far Does Light Go?" project, with the Sensemaker scaffold guiding students in designing an argument and a reflection note popping up to encourage them in this process. By providing such guidance and scaffolding, WISE helps students to emulate the kind of autonomous or lifelong reasoning processes that are the hallmark of science.

ENGAGING STUDENTS IN INQUIRY

The reader may remember from Chapter 1 that our ultimate goal is to promote an atmosphere of inquiry, autonomy, and critical thinking in science class, engaging students and teachers in a more dynamic, collaborative form of learning. The knowledge integration framework is our effort to provide a theoretical foundation for such forms of learning and instruction. It guides our design of technology environments, cur-

Figure 3.4. The WISE Sensemaker tool helps students sort their ideas, placing evidence from the Web into related categories and rating the strength of evidence and counter evidence with respect to different arguments. The image shows Sensemaker being used in the "How Far Does Light Go?" project, where students debate whether light dies out or goes on forever. Students use their Sensemaker file as a scaffold in subsequent classroom debates.

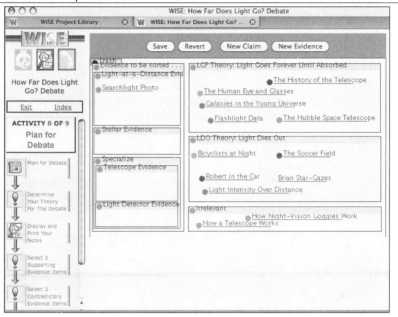

riculum materials, and assessments and guides interpretation of learning processes that occur when classrooms engage with our designs.

The guidance provided by our technology-enhanced learning environments helps students adopt a more autonomous form of learning that reflects the nature of scientific investigation. The scaffolding provided by such curriculum environments also helps to ensure that students complete the full activity and never feel disoriented. The availability of such guidance helps teachers feel confident in allowing students to engage in complex activities that involve a wide spectrum of visualizations, collaborations, and autonomous investigations. Such designs are challenging for teachers, because every student or small group requires individualized attention. WISE was designed to address this need. Because of the scaffolding and curriculum structure that it provides, teachers are freed to work with the students who are having difficulty while others in the class continue to conduct their investigations. The process of teaching with WISE is detailed fully in Chapter 7.

In summary, by providing scaffolding tools and inquiry maps, WISE can support students as they engage in complex inquiry activities that include the full range of an investigative sequence—making predictions, designing experiments, conducting experiments, drawing conclusions, writing reports, critiquing the reports of others, and identifying next steps. By guiding students through such inquiry processes, WISE provides them with valuable experiences in knowledge integration. With repeated experiences, they become adept at identifying the pitfalls and opportunities in scientific investigations, and gradually become more autonomous scientific reasoners.

RECOMMENDED READINGS

Linn, M. C., & Hsi, S. (2000). *Computers, teachers, peers: Science learning partners*. Mahwah, NJ: Lawrence Erlbaum.

> This book offers a comprehensive description of the Computer as Learning Partner (CLP) research project, and a thorough review of the theoretical perspective of scaffolded knowledge integration. It offers rich anecdotes and illustrations from the classroom, with selected commentary from a teacher, "Mr. K."

Linn, M. C., Davis, E. A., & Bell, P. (Eds.). (2004). *Internet environments for science education*. Mahwah, NJ: Lawrence Earlbaum.

> This edited volume includes chapters from several Ph.D. students who completed their doctorates in our research group, working on the Knowledge Integration Environment (KIE) research project. The volume includes several overview and methodological chapters (Linn and colleagues), as well as specific chapters on argumentation (Philip Bell), experimentation (Doug Clark), prompting (Betsy Davis), collaboration (Chris Hoadley), and future directions with WISE (Jim Slotta) and other projects (Philip Bell, Marcia Linn).

CHAPTER 4

Instructional Patterns for Knowledge Integration

Instructional patterns are sequences of activities that help students develop a coherent understanding of science. In the last chapter, we identified features of our materials, such as visualizations or online discussions, that help students learn. To get the full potential of these features, we have identified patterns of activities that strengthen their impact.

For example, in his research on student argumentation, Philip Bell (2004) found that a WISE debate project is much more effective when it culminates in a written report or reflection where students are asked to elaborate their position. Similarly, Doug Clark (2004) found that students benefit from reflecting on their statements of personally held principles after they have engaged in collaborative argumentation activities. A number of studies showed that online discussions are more successful when they are followed by an opportunity for students to summarize the main argument or ideas that appear in the discussion (Linn & Slotta, 2006).

In the previous chapter, we organized the promising features of knowledge integration in the form of four basic tenets. To make science accessible, we chose problem contexts that resonated with students' everyday experiences. To make thinking visible, we developed visualizations to illustrate ideas for students. To help students learn from one another, we identified numerous ways to promote collaboration and exchange among students and their peers. To encourage autonomy, we developed checklists and inquiry maps that helped students manage their own progress as well as reflection prompts that enabled students to organize their ideas.

We began to recognize certain regularities in the use of these features that serve as a basis for instructional patterns. By examining successful and unsuccessful instructional sequences across numerous research studies, we have refined our theoretical account of knowledge integration. Ultimately, a goal of our research group is to create a design that translates the knowledge integration framework into specific guidance. This would ensure that any curriculum project designed according to the structure would adhere to the theoretical basis and promote knowledge integration. In this chapter, we describe the processes of knowledge integration and introduce instructional patterns that capture those processes.

THE NATURE OF KNOWLEDGE INTEGRATION

Every student comes to science class with a repertoire of ideas that has grown as a result of myriad experiences and countless endeavors in reasoning and learning. This repertoire is a primary resource for the student as he or she encounters any new material, and it is an essential feature within the knowledge integration approach to learning. By respecting the varied ideas that students bring to science class and placing them at the center of instruction, we ensure that students develop a coherent understanding of any instructional material. We have identified three characteristics of learners that account for the varied ideas that students bring to class, and are thus important in the design of instruction. We refer to these as the cultural, interpretive, and deliberative nature of the learner.

Students come to science class with their own cultural experiences, and their repertoire of ideas reflects their unique cultural background. For example, if they cook on a stove with a gas flame at home, students might develop ideas about which materials transmit heat, whereas if they live in a home where the microwave is used for most cooking, they may not develop strong ideas about the thermal properties of materials. The cultural norms and expectations that students develop within their families are very important. For example, some students celebrate the excitement and importance of science at home, whereas others might reduce emphasis on the importance of science, or even reinforce the idea that science is boring. The knowledge integration approach to instructional design responds to these views by considering and respecting the role of cultural context in a student's repertoire of ideas.

The second characteristic is that students interpret new information in light of their preexisting ideas and experiences. If students think that heat and temperature are the same thing, they are likely to ignore information that assumes these terms have scientific meaning. Those students who have a broad array of relevant experiences may interpret a scientific situation differently from those with few relevant ideas. To elicit these preexisting ideas and to make sure they are considered, designers can use a number of different contexts in order to make a scientific topic accessible to the full range of students. Thus, some students might have relatives who had cancer and find it easy to connect to the topic of mitosis because of that perspective. Others might have used microscopes to observe cell division, or might have read science-fiction accounts of cells running wild. Science instruction that allows students to build on and reconsider their prior ideas and experiences will ensure that all learners take advantage of their interpretive skills.

A third characteristic of learners is that they are more or less intentional or deliberate in their approach to learning. Students vary in how actively they monitor their own progress and in how autonomously they guide their own learning. Students who monitor their progress, explain their ideas to themselves, and identify conundrums are likely to avoid getting stuck or becoming committed to multiple conflicting ideas. Those who are less deliberate may not realize that there are gaps or inconsistencies in their understanding of a science topic. Ultimately, we would like all students to become effective at guiding their own science investigations, but because students vary so greatly along this dimension, it is important to offer instructional experiences that meet the needs of a broad range of learners. To be effective, science instruction must take advantage of the cultural, interpretive, and deliberative nature of science learners by supporting students in complex, sustained projects where they carry out individualized investigations. In the next section, we identify four fundamental processes of knowledge integration that, if included within a curriculum design, can help students improve in their ability to monitor their own progress.

ELICITING, ADDING, AND REFINING IDEAS: THE PROCESSES OF KNOWLEDGE INTEGRATION

In order to understand when, how, and why inquiry projects can foster knowledge integration, Linn and Eylon (2006) reviewed the research literature to look for successful instructional patterns. They examined all of the work cited in Chapter 1 of this volume, as well as the wider literature in instructional design and science education. They began by articulating four fundamental processes that constitute the cognitive mechanism of knowledge integration: (a) elicit ideas, (b) add new ideas, (c) develop criteria, and (d) sort out ideas. When combined into an instructional pattern, these processes ensure that curriculum activities capture the tenets of knowledge integration. Below, we describe each of the four processes, including a detailed example of how they appear in the WISE "Mitosis" curriculum.

Elicit Ideas

Each instructional pattern includes the process of eliciting ideas. Only when ideas are elicited can they be evaluated and reconsidered. The knowledge integration process involves making sure that students have an opportunity to build connections between any ideas they may possess and the topic of instruction. If only some of a student's ideas about a scientific phenomenon are considered, then the ones that are neglected might emerge in future activities, perhaps even as compelling alternatives to the desired scientific interpretation. For example, in CLP, we investigated students' ideas about heat and temperature, engaging them with simulations of thermal conductivity and insulation. Recall that when we asked them which materials would be best for keeping their canned soft drink cool until lunch, students rejected the choice of wool, even though it was the best insulator listed. When interviewed about their reasoning, they revealed that wool should be considered a poor choice for keeping things cold, since sweaters are made from wool and sweaters are meant to keep a person warm (Songer & Linn, 1991; Linn & Hsi, 2000). Thus, an effective instructional sequence that promotes knowledge integration must include the process of eliciting a broad number of ideas from the participants. When students are prompted to connect their full range of ideas with the topic of instruction, they are in a better position to compare, contrast, and distinguish these ideas.

It is challenging to elicit all the ideas that students have, because the ideas are contextualized. For example, even if prompted to think about other ideas they have that relate to insulation, students might not consider the wool sweater, because their past experience of this idea is not within the context of thermal science. To create successful instruction, the designer has to consider the broad range of contexts where the topic arises. By using a range of contexts, curriculum designers have a better chance of eliciting the full repertoire of students' ideas.

Consider the WISE "Mitosis" project (see Figure 4.1) where students are asked initially to generate their ideas about mitosis in a brainstorming activity concerning cancer and cell division. Then they are presented with an animation of mitosis and asked to make their own decisions about when distinct phases begin and even to assign their own names to the phases. By using two different methods for soliciting ideas about mitosis—one, in the context of cancer and cell division, and another in the context of an animation of mitosis—the WISE "Mitosis" project aims to elicit a range of relevant ideas from students.

Figure 4.1. WISE Reflection Notes help to reveal student ideas by prompting for reflections, as shown in the image. After reading about the role of cell division in cancer, students are prompted for their predictions about what might happen to a human organ if its own cells were to divide uncontrollably. WISE Brainstorm allows a student to see all the comments added by peers after he or she has submitted a reply.

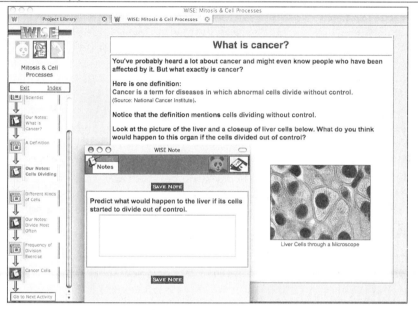

Add New Ideas

A second process that is vital to knowledge integration is that of adding new scientific ideas. Students do not come to science class with all the answers. It is important to add new information. However, like eliciting ideas, this process is not straightforward. For new ideas to be comprehensible and effective, they need careful design. Thus, a lecture with complex ideas embedded in a detailed narrative is not as successful as a visualization that students can readily interpret. In order to make sense of science topics, students must be provided with new, scientifically normative ideas that can then be connected to their preexisting ideas and experiences with the aim of developing a coherent understanding.

Of course, science educators have a strong interest in adding new ideas but they do not always consider how to add ideas that will be connected to students' existing knowledge. Because instructors seek to engage students in the rich content of science knowledge, they likely introduce many ideas and entire conceptual categories that students have not previously encountered. Curriculum designers must address this basic process of adding new ideas carefully in order to help students build connections to their existing repertoire of ideas.

One way that WISE adds new ideas is by using interactive, scientific visualizations where students see concepts such as mitosis or chemical bonding in new ways, and are prompted to reflect and describe their interpretation of these new representations. Another approach to adding new ideas is the use of narrative examples, which allow students to encounter scientific concepts within an interesting context or scenario that includes a coherent treatment of the science topics. A third way that we have added new ideas is through student-driven investigations, where students are guided to conduct experiments that reveal new ideas about a scientific phenomenon. Students also encounter new ideas in textbooks, through Internet searches, and in teacher lectures. Rather than assuming that new ideas will be considered by learners, it is important to determine whether students are taking up the intended idea or whether they are neglecting or contorting the idea in some way.

The WISE "Mitosis" project introduces variation in the rate of cell division using visualizations. The activities within this WISE project engage students in comparing the cell division rates of muscle, liver, nerve, and skin cells. This activity helps students consider the mechanism of cancer, which is the result of cells reproducing too fast. By comparing the cell division rate of muscle, liver, nerve, and skin cells, students begin to think about why cells might reproduce at different rates. Another way that WISE "Mitosis" introduces new ideas is by having students compare their own ideas about the phases of mitosis (as captured in the visualization activity) with those defined by scientists. Students break the mitosis animation up into sections and name their sections. Then they compare their segmentation and naming with the scientifically normative view, reflecting on similarities and differences.

Students benefit from ideas that are offered in a way that allows them to probe, interact, and test those ideas. Students also benefit when ideas are offered in a broad range of formats and contexts. Employing a range of ways to introduce new ideas is important because each student has a unique repertoire of ideas that influences how he or she responds to new ideas. In addition, students need practice gathering ideas from a broad range of media because they will need to continue this process of adding ideas throughout their lives.

Develop Criteria

Students need effective criteria to distinguish among ideas in their repertoire, including new ideas that have been recently added. Students need some standards or criteria to determine which ideas are more effective, valuable, or scientifically sound than others. Often, the norms for scientific decision-making are quite abstract or implicit. Students are told that they should prefer those ideas that are scientifically supported with evidence, or were tested using the scientific method. These criteria are obviously important, but they may seem confusing or inaccessible to students. Thus, we identify an important process within knowledge integration as that of identifying and using criteria to distinguish among ideas.

The most important way that students distinguish among ideas in a science curriculum is by using evidence. However, often students must figure out what constitutes scientific evidence in a given situation. If they are unfamiliar with the methods of a particular domain, they may not know how to gather or evaluate evidence. Many Web sites make connections between the use of cell phones and the incidence of cancer, for example, and some students might assume that if information is available on the Internet, it is valid. These students would need to learn how to distinguish among valid and persuasive messages. Even if they place a high value on evidence that is supported by scientific experiments, students may not be able to recognize the methodologies that are appropriate within a particular scientific discipline. For example, while it is easy to conduct experiments to compare insulation material, in order to understand the extinction of dinosaurs or the causes of earthquakes, students would need dramatically different methods that address the geological or historical record.

WISE "Mitosis" employs a number of activities to help students develop criteria. After they compare rates of cell division at the beginning of the project, they then develop criteria for distinguishing among rates and explaining why one cell type has a more rapid rate of division than another cell type. For example, students might say that skin cells change and divide more rapidly based on their observations of how rapidly wounds heal or how skin cells flake off when they are sunburned. They compare these observations about skin to their ideas about muscle or nerve cells and seek additional information and evidence in order to make decisions about the relative rates of cell division for these different cell types. Another place where "Mitosis" helps students develop criteria for distinguishing among their ideas is in its use of an online electronic discussion about the ways in which they've subdivided the mitosis animation. Students compare their choices for breaking up the mitosis animation with the choices made by other students. They discuss their decisions, citing evidence from the animation to defend their views, and then revise their segmentation if they are convinced by the discussion.

Thus, there are many ways that students can develop criteria for distinguishing among ideas. In fact, instructors can actually help students learn to develop their own criteria, or to distinguish between the criteria that are appropriate in different situations. For example, in CLP, we created an activity that was aimed specifically at helping students develop their own criteria. It began when we noticed that students often have difficulty recognizing what constitutes a good report on an experiment (Songer & Linn, 1991). We realized that it would be hard for them to submit a good report if they did not have the criteria for determining what constitutes a good report. In order to help them develop criteria for such judgments, the classroom teacher (Mr. K) created an example report that included much of the confusion that students had encountered in writing up their experimental findings. Mr. K then conducted a class activity where he divided the class into small groups to examine this composite report and identify what they thought were promising and questionable aspects. He then led a class discussion where the students pooled their ideas and made a list of criteria that they could use to evaluate reports on experimental investigations. Later in the term, after students had conducted their own experiments, they were reminded of these criteria, and used them in creating their own experimental reports, as well as in evaluating reports generated by other class members.

Sort Out Ideas

The fourth and final fundamental process of knowledge integration is to sort out ideas. Students must learn to distinguish among the various ideas that they possess within their repertoire—including new ideas that have been added through instruction or generated autonomously, as well as any of their preexisting ideas—and then apply the suitable scientific criteria to sort out which ideas are the most appropriate for reasoning about scientific topics. Often, science instruction neglects this process of sorting out ideas, simply assuming that students have replaced their idiosyncratic or personal ideas with those presented in science class. A large body of research shows that, although students do entertain the new ideas offered in science class, they do not simply adopt them and dispose of all other understandings (Reiner, Slotta, Chi, & Resnick, 2000). Rather, students tend to retain their previous non-normative ideas, which are not integrated with any new ideas gained in science class because no effort was made to help the students sort out the similarities and differences, and build a coherent understanding.

In order to enable students to sort out their ideas, science instruction must provide suitable activities and time for students to compare, contrast, consider, and reconsider their ideas, helping them come up with a more coherent account of the scientific phenomenon. For example, WISE "Mitosis" (see Figure 4.2) helps students sort out their ideas about the rate of cell division by asking them to hypothesize about the frequency of division in cancer cells compared to other types of human cells. At the end of the activity—after they've gained more insight into the process—they are engaged in sorting out their ideas about what kinds of cells reproduce quickly and the relevance of these ideas for cancer treatment (e.g., to help make the connection to why patients' hair often falls out). "Mitosis" also provided students with an opportunity to sort out ideas by asking them to reflect on any differences between their ideas and those of scientists when comparing the way that the mitosis animation is broken into parts. Other activities that enable students to sort out their ideas include writing reports,

Figure 4.2. WISE Reflection Notes are used for many purposes, depending on the pedagogical context within the inquiry project. Here, the note is prompting students to consider the challenge of how to develop a cancer medicine by targeting cell division. Such reflections help students work with their ideas and develop a coherent understanding of science topics.

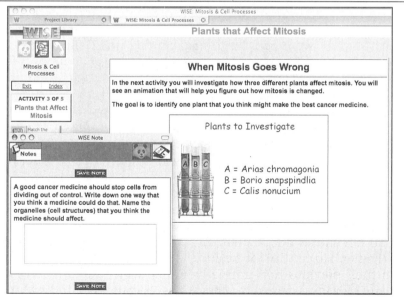

making presentations, engaging in debates, and keeping a journal, which can all be effective depending on the specific instructions and scaffolding provided in those activities.

EFFECTIVE INSTRUCTIONAL PATTERNS

The basic cognitive processes that make up knowledge integration offer a way to evaluate instructional designs. Features such as visualizations or experiments are more successful when they occur in a pattern using all four processes. To illustrate how the processes can improve the effectiveness of features of instruction, Linn and Eylon (2006) reviewed many successful activities and extracted instructional patterns that are effective in supporting knowledge integration. They articulated their top 10 patterns (see Table 4.1).

WISE critique, debate, and design projects that were introduced in Chapter 2 are made up of a series of patterns. Ensuring that activities take advantage of the patterns also means that the activities use the knowledge integration processes over and over again. To illustrate, we describe how WISE "Mitosis" implemented two of the patterns, Experimentation and Collaboration, focusing on how these patterns incorporate the four processes of knowledge integration.

WISE "Mitosis" implements the Experimentation pattern, where students compare three hypothetical candidate plants as possible sources of cancer drugs, as shown in Figure 4.2. The Experimentation pattern uses all four of the knowledge integration processes described above. It starts by eliciting student ideas about the candidate plants, named Arias chromagonia, Borio snapspindlia, and Callus nonucium. Once students have generated their preliminary ideas about how these plants might impact cancer, they add new ideas to their repertoire by conducting simple experiments by treating a cell with each plant using the mitosis simulation. They discover that Arios destroys one set of chromosomes during anaphase, Boreo destroys the spindle fibers during metaphase, and Callus destroys the entire chromosome after anaphase. The investigations provide students with new ideas and help them build connections to their preexisting ideas. The WISE project then helps students develop criteria by asking them to use evidence from their investigations in evaluating the three candidate plants.

By comparing the impact of the three plants on a cell's mitosis, students consider what evidence makes sense for distinguishing among the plants and make connections to their own ideas. To encourage students to sort out their ideas, WISE "Mitosis" asks them to make a recommendation about which plant should be used as a cancer medicine. Students use the evidence from their investigations and their

Table 4.1. Effective Instructional Patterns.

Pattern	Description	Relevant Research
Orient, diagnose, and guide	The *orient, diagnose, and guide* pattern recursively defines the scope of a topic, connects the topic to personally relevant problems, links the new topic to prior instruction, identifies student entering ideas, and adds ideas to stimulate knowledge integration.	Instructors often find student ideas surprising (Linn & Hsi, 2000). Benchmark lessons (diSessa & Minstrell, 1998), bridging analogies (Clement, 1993), didactic objects (Thompson, 2002), and pivotal cases (Linn, 2005) help diagnose understanding. Designing instruction to respond to student ideas can improve learning (Crouch & Mazur, 2001).
Predict, observe, and explain	The *predict, observe, and explain* pattern involves recursively eliciting student ideas about a topic, demonstrating the phenomenon, and asking students to reconcile contradictions (Songer, 1996; White & Gunstone, 1992).	Using this pattern improves student learning compared to demonstration alone (Sokoloff & Thornton, 2004; Linn & Hsi, 2000). Predictions enable students to test their ideas (Linn, Songer, & Eylon, 1996).
Illustrate ideas	The *illustrate ideas* pattern models authentic reasoning about a topic, making visible strategies for grappling with complex questions. Students try out the strategies and reflect on their results.	Case studies and historical notebooks illustrate how scientists framed and explored problems to improve student outcomes (Clancy et al., 2003; Palinscar et al., 2001).
Experiment	The *experiment* pattern involves a recursive process of framing a question, generating methods for investigating the question, carrying out an investigation, evaluating the results, and using the findings to sort out the repertoire of ideas.	This pattern enables students to make decisions about what is a good experiment and what can be learned from an experiment. Teachers need experience to use the pattern successfully and improve outcomes (Linn, et al., 2004; Polman, 2000).
Explore a simulation	The *explore a simulation* pattern involves a recursive process framing a challenge, contest, or question; testing conjectures with a simulation; applying criteria supplied by the simulation; and revising ideas.	This pattern requires well-designed environments to succeed (Pallant & Tinker, 2004). Simulations of the layers of the Earth improve student understanding (Kali, Orion, & Eylon, 2003).
Create an artifact	The *create an artifact* pattern involves a recursive process of framing a question, selecting or creating a draft artifact, evaluating the results and improving the artifact, and connecting the results to views of the topic.	Learners gain deeper understanding of complex systems such as behavior of ants, planetary motion, electricity, genetics, heat flow, or oxygenation of blood using this pattern (diSessa, 2000; Pallant & Tinker, 2004; Redish, 2003).
Construct an argument	The *construct an argument* pattern involves selecting a question, generating ideas, identifying evidence, articulating a viewpoint, and revising the viewpoint based on feedback or new evidence.	Debates where students emulate the techniques used by practicing scientists to defend competing hypotheses about topics like dinosaur extinction improve understanding of science (Linn et al., 2004).
Critique	The *critique* pattern asks learners to recursively evaluate ideas about scientific phenomena, apply criteria, and warrant assertions with evidence.	Critique, although neglected in science courses is often easier than creating a solution and can help students begin to formulate criteria (Slotta & Linn, 2000; Linn & Hsi, 2000; diSessa et al., 2002).
Collaborate	In the *collaborate* pattern, students generate their own ideas, respond to group ideas, support their views, and reach consensus. Negotiating meaning is central to student understanding (Linn & Slotta, in press).	Consistent with Vygotsky's (1978) notion of the zone of proximal development, the collaborate pattern succeeds when groups respect the ideas of each participant (Brown & Campione, 1994; Cohen, 1994).
Reflect	The *reflect* pattern encourages learners to analyze the connections they make between their ideas and monitor their understanding. Varying prompts reveals which approaches succeed (Linn, Davis, & Bell, 2004).	Reflection stimulates metacognition, encouraging learners to identify gaps in their ideas and seek ways to fill the gaps (Bjork, 1994; Chi, 1996; Krajcik et al., 1999; Schoenfeld, 1987).

knowledge of the mitosis phases to recommend a plant that could be effective for treating cancer. They justify their answer using evidence from the project. Thus, the Experimentation pattern includes all four of the knowledge integration processes: eliciting ideas, adding new ideas, developing criteria, and sorting out ideas.

Another pattern identified by Linn and Eylon is the Collaboration pattern. While many researchers have advocated collaboration, and it is even one of the four tenets of knowledge integration, the pattern is meant to provide more detail about how to foster effective collaborations among students that include the processes of knowledge integration. The Collaboration pattern starts by eliciting student ideas, which can be achieved through brainstorming, reflections, or class discussions. WISE "Mitosis" engages students in an online discussion where they reflect on evidence from their experiments and introduce their ideas to peers. The next stage in the Collaboration pattern is for students to explore their ideas through exchange with peers. So, in "Mitosis," each student works closely with one peer to explore information about current cancer medicines and treatments, determine side effects, and discuss the possible impact of the treatment. This activity also allows students to combine their evidence from their experiments with additional information about side effects and challenges to sort out their ideas about cancer treatments. Students take advantage of the ideas they gained from their peers in the online discussion as well as the collaborative phase, and make a final recommendation based on their experiments, discussions, and reflections. This final report gives students an opportunity to compare and contrast their ideas, review the evidence that they have for various plants, apply their criteria, and develop an argument to support their point of view.

The knowledge integration perspective on science learning and instruction represents a consolidation of the experiences of many researchers, classroom teachers, technology designers, and assessment specialists, and has emerged from reflection on a broad range of empirical evidence. By using the knowledge integration processes to incorporate promising curricular features into instruction, designers can strengthen instruction. Although combining features and processes is not sufficient to ensure that instruction achieves knowledge integration, this is an excellent starting point. The processes can also help instructors and designers refine instructional approaches based on evidence from classroom trials. The next section describes some of the issues and opportunities that come with designing such curriculum.

DESIGNING KNOWLEDGE INTEGRATION
CURRICULUM AND ASSESSMENTS

The knowledge integration approach to curriculum design focuses on the processes that students use to make sense of science, and harnesses these processes to engage students in developing a more sound, coherent, and articulated understanding of complex scientific phenomena. As illustrated for the topic of mitosis in this chapter, WISE curriculum designers combine a range of activities to form knowledge integration patterns, so that students have the opportunity to follow a sequence of activities that ultimately enable them to consolidate their ideas and develop a coherent conceptual understanding.

Knowledge integration patterns are crucial to the effective design of activities. If activities only elicit ideas but don't add new ideas, develop criteria, or have students sort them out, then they have little chance of fostering knowledge integration. The patterns emphasize aspects of science instruction that have proven successful in research but are rarely implemented in typical lecture- and textbook-based courses. Typical courses may or may not elicit student ideas, but even if student ideas are elicited, frequently they are elicited only in order to be critiqued or revised rather than as a source of information to be built upon. Instead of encouraging students to generate their ideas and distinguish them from normative ideas—to "sort them out"—a more common approach in science classes is to identify ideas that aren't fruitful and encourage students to replace them with the normative ideas. This approach may succeed in the short run, but leaves open the possibility that students will return to their personal views once they put the class behind them. Students have spent much more time developing their own ideas than they have considering the new ideas presented in science class.

Typical instruction also frequently neglects the process of developing criteria. Science teachers often present criteria as being well established, such as the scientific method, and try to help students understand how such criteria apply in different situations. This is unlikely to be an effective approach because students lack insight into the complexities and nuances of scientific investigations. For example, students often have difficulty determining whether a scientific argument includes sufficient evidence to support a conjecture, or whether it has sufficiently entertained all counterarguments. This situation is well illustrated by the pervasive, persuasive messages that are offered to citizens by pharmaceutical companies in magazines, on television, and on the Internet concerning various new drugs. Given the advertising budget for these drugs, it appears that these messages are successful, yet they often neglect crucial information such as whether the new dug is actually any more effective than an older drug designed to perform the same task.

Another interesting comparison between the knowledge integration approach and that of typical instruction concerns the use of hands-on experimentation by students. Many research studies and some science teachers complain that hands-on experimentation is an inefficient and unsuccessful approach. Viewed through a knowledge integration lens, this is not surprising if hands-on experimentation is intended to add new ideas in the same manner as textbooks and lectures. Without the additional processes of eliciting ideas, developing criteria, and sorting out ideas, the hands-on experiment becomes a fun but not particularly effective instructional activity. Students learn a new idea about science but have no opportunity to connect it to their existing ideas or to distinguish it from other perspectives. Without the opportunity to make predictions before they experiment, then conduct the experiment, then reflect on the criteria for distinguishing the findings from the experiment from other ideas that they might have, and then engage in a reflective process to sort out the ideas from the experiment, students are unlikely to gain the full advantage of hands-on experimentation.

Instruction that is designed to incorporate the knowledge integration patterns will engage students in the full range of processes necessary to develop a more coherent understanding of science. Students benefit from the opportunity to connect new ideas and reorganize their repertoire of ideas. The approach of implementing the knowledge integration patterns to create activities that capture the four tenets of knowledge integration will result in curriculum where students gain a more robust understanding of scientific phenomena. By using the knowledge integration patterns to design curriculum, teachers and researchers have the opportunity to create instructional materials that students can use to build on their own ideas, sustain their understanding of scientific phenomena, and become lifelong autonomous learners.

DESIGNING KNOWLEDGE INTEGRATION ASSESSMENTS

In order to effectively measure the learning outcomes achieved by students using WISE projects, we have developed an approach to designing "knowledge integration assessments." When assessments align with instruction, they measure the goal of the curriculum and can determine the effectiveness of the instruction.

To assess the impact of "Mitosis," we used a pre-test–post-test design. To specifically assess the knowledge integration impact of the module, we designed knowledge integration items, shown in Figure 4.3. In addi-

Figure 4.3. This figure shows an example of a pre-post test question that students would answer to determine their understanding of mitosis and the process of cell division. The Figure shows the assessment as it appears in the WISE authoring mode.

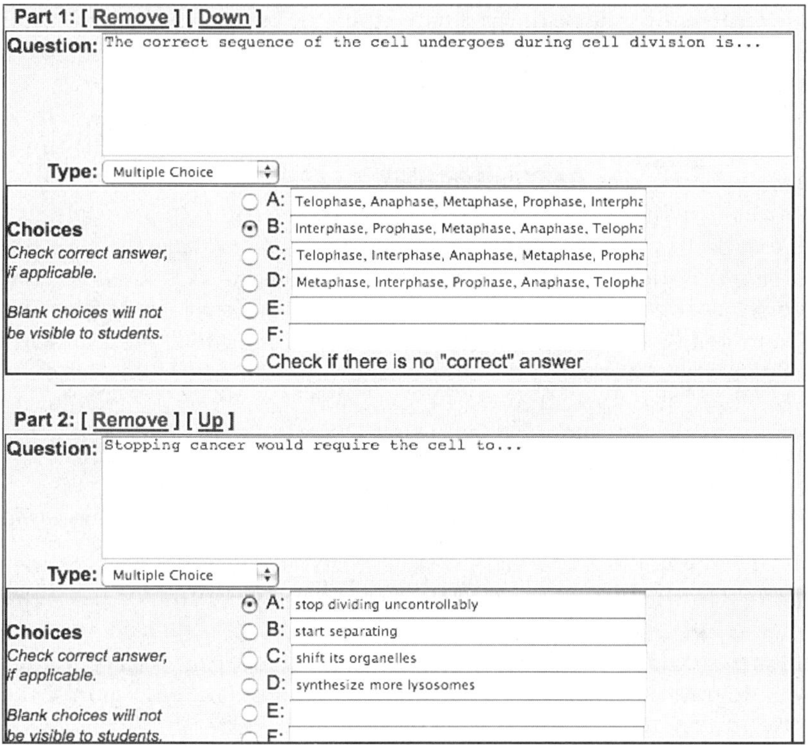

tion, we used standardized items and scored them using a knowledge integration rubric. We found that, across all the classes using the module, there was a substantial improvement in understanding of mitosis and the process of cell division (Figure 4.3). Using the end-of-year assessment from the cohort comparison study, we also found that the mitosis module was very effective in improving students' understanding, compared to students who studied the typical textbook account of mitosis.

In conclusion, the knowledge integration instructional patterns combine promising curricular features with powerful processes. This combination has emerged from careful analysis of successful instruction. This empirical process has produced the knowledge integration framework for the design of instruction that reflects extensive research in the learning sciences and resonates with the findings of numerous other teams studying science learners. The key to the success of knowledge integration instruction is to build on the ideas that students have. Students have worked hard to come up with these ideas; these ideas represent intellectual undertakings and learning processes that are valid and useful. By capitalizing on these processes, which include sorting out ideas, distinguishing ideas, making sense of complex situations, and generating new conjectures, science education has the potential to help students become lifelong science learners.

RECOMMENDED READINGS

Edelson, D. C. (2001). Learning-for-use: A framework for the design of technology-supported inquiry activities. *Journal of Research in Science Teaching, 38* (3), 355–385.

> This research article describes Edelson's design framework, called "Learning for Use," which was designed according to principles of cognitive and educational research, and seeks to guide designers to create curriculum that fosters engagement and understanding. The goal is for students to develop useful knowledge.

Linn, M. C. (2006). The knowledge integration perspective on learning and instruction. In R. K. Sawyer (Ed.), *The Cambridge Handbook of the Learning Sciences* (pp. 243–264). New York: Cambridge University Press.

> This chapter in the recent *Cambridge Handbook of the Learning Sciences* summarizes Linn's notion of instructional patterns.

Linn, M. C., & Eylon, B.-S. (2006). Science education: Integrating views of learning and instruction. In P. A. Alexander & P. H. Winne (Eds.), *Handbook of Educational Psychology* (2nd ed., pp. 511–544). Mahwah, NJ: Lawrence Erlbaum.

> This chapter in the *Handbook of Educational Psychology* details the efforts of Linn and Eylon to synthesize a wide literature form the learning sciences into a set of instructional patterns.

CHAPTER 5

Designing WISE Curriculum: A Partnership Approach

Today more than ever before, we need efficient and effective curriculum materials in science. The corpus of science knowledge is expanding, standards-setting groups are only adding new topics, and students are more likely to require an understanding of complex science for a career. As described in earlier chapters, the theoretical perspective of knowledge integration offers insights and methods that can guide the development of instructional materials. We have built upon this research to develop a process for designing technology-enhanced inquiry projects that promote integrated understanding of complex science topics.

The tenets, processes, and instructional patterns described in previous chapters can help designers evaluate whether curriculum activities and materials will be likely to foster knowledge integration. But the actual development of those materials, from selecting suitable Web sites to writing effective reflection prompts and discussion topics, is a matter of careful design and composition, classroom trials, and iterative refinement. This chapter presents a detailed discussion of how we develop effective curriculum and assessments for WISE. We present a collaborative model where teachers, researchers, technology specialists, and scientists work together to ensure that all materials are scientifically accurate, age-appropriate, and sensitive to student ideas and knowledge integration processes.

CHALLENGES AND OPPORTUNITIES FOR DESIGN PARTNERSHIPS

Creating engaging science inquiry activities that meet curriculum standards, take full advantage of the technology environment, and adhere to a theoretical framework requires many talents and considerable effort. From the very beginning, the design and development of WISE curriculum has been conducted by teams that include science teachers, science disciplinary experts, technology specialists, and educational researchers. Usually, a team is convened to create a new WISE project for a specific science course or research project.

The first thing the team must do is to find a suitable inquiry topic for the new WISE project, a process described in more detail below. The ideal topic for a WISE project is one that is central to the curriculum yet traditionally difficult to teach, so that the WISE technology tools and pedagogical approaches provide a unique advantage. For example, the topic of mitosis described in Chapter 4 was chosen because biology teachers in our research project felt that their students were not gaining a deep understanding of this fundamental topic. It is then quite a challenge for the team to develop a technology-enhanced inquiry curriculum that captures the knowledge integration processes, promotes lifelong science learning, and includes embedded assessments so that teachers can monitor students' progress.

One of our earliest WISE projects, called "Sprouting Space Plants," engaged upper elementary and middle school students in designing a terrarium for use on the international space station *Freedom*. Members of the WISE research group had been invited by NASA life scientists to create an engaging inquiry science activity, and we realized that this could only be achieved if the NASA scientists were deeply involved in the design process. We also realized that we would need to include the science teachers who would be the first to try out the new WISE project. A third perspective was added by the WISE researchers, who came to the table with specific research questions they wanted to address using this project as their experimental materials. In the case of "Space Plants," the researchers also wanted to investigate the use of visual representations by taking advantage of a new "WISE Draw" tool that would allow elementary-age students to depict their ideas graphically.

At the heart of the WISE design process is a healthy and ongoing debate between the scientists, who often seek to "translate and deliver the science content" (similar to a textbook), and the educational researcher, who is eager to "engage students with inquiry." Teachers generally seek a balance between inquiry and knowledge transmission. They advocate for important matters such as age-appropriateness and coverage of curriculum standards.

One persistent challenge is the temptation to use WISE as a kind of electronic textbook, delivering well-written science content that engages students in reading multimedia materials, from which they are meant to "learn" new content. Such materials are easy to write because they convey the content in a straightforward fashion, much as a lecture or textbook would do. But they do not generally support a knowledge integration approach to instruction. Certainly, there is a place for such materials within WISE projects, in the form of background or introductory content that helps prepare students for subsequent inquiry activities. Problems arise, however, when partnerships neglect inquiry or add inquiry activities that do not engage students in the processes of knowledge integration. To succeed in promoting knowledge integration, inquiry activities not only need to encourage investigation, but also to elicit student ideas and help students develop criteria for distinguishing and sorting out their ideas.

One of the most difficult design challenges is finding an engaging "inquiry theme" that will serve as the pedagogical basis of the project. In the case of the "Space Plants" project, the partners selected a theme that captured the Experimentation pattern described in Chapter 4. It was proposed that students could conduct hands-on experiments concerning the best plants for astronauts to use as a food source during long-range space flights, such as a human mission to Mars. Specifically, the project guides students as they investigate the characteristics of "NASA Space Plants" that have been specially bred so that they grow more quickly than ordinary plants and can sustain more hours of direct sunlight. Determining a suitable inquiry theme for a WISE project is crucial to its success because it must offer students engaging activities in which they can make rich connections to the relevant science topics.

After finding a suitable inquiry theme and outlining some possible activities for the new WISE project, the authors must plan the more detailed activities and materials that will make up the project. Thus, each project consists of a sequence of distinct activities that are designed so as to require approximately one class period (approximately 45 minutes). Each of these activities in turn consists of a sequence of steps, each of which can be any one of the existing WISE step types—such as reflection notes, journals, online discussions, drawings, and so forth (see Table 2.1 and Figure 5.1, which shows the steps within the third activity of the "Space Plants" project).

In order to promote knowledge integration, the authors must create a sequence of steps that implement one or more of the design patterns described in the previous chapter. These patterns, such as the Experimentation pattern, have been determined by prior research to promote student reflection and synthesis of ideas. But the patterns are not highly specific in terms of suggesting an implementation. For example, the Experimentation pattern calls for framing an experimental question and embedding the investigation in the knowledge integration processes described earlier. First, students need to generate their own ideas so they can connect them to the new ideas. Second, students need to generate methods of investigating the open questions and criteria for evaluating the results. Third, students need to add new ideas by carrying out the investigations. Finally, students have to use the criteria to evaluate their results and sort out all their ideas. Thus, curriculum designers must take this powerful but fairly general recipe and formulate specific materials and assessments.

Figure 5.1. WISE inquiry projects are structured as a series of activities, each of which consists of a sequence of steps. Each step can have a particular "type," such as viewing a Web page, taking a reflection note, or joining an online discussion. The process of authoring a WISE project is essentially one of determining the best sequence and content of such steps. Shown in the image is step 2 ("View Evidence") in the third activity ("Conditions in Space") of the WISE "Space Plants" project.

In "Space Plants," for example, the designers implemented the Experiment pattern by developing a sequence of WISE steps that support students as they plan, conduct, and interpret their experiments using the NASA Fast Plants. The project uses the Experimentation pattern for several distinct investigations. Students compare the growth patterns of a NASA Space Plant and an ordinary radish plant. They conduct a series of experiments in which they compare the growth of the two "mystery" plants under different lighting conditions. The project takes advantage of the WISE Draw technology to enable students to analyze the growth process for each plant by graphing the height and the state in the life cycle of each plant. They represent their observations in WISE Draw using what we call "WISE rubber stamps" to indicate the state of the life cycle of each plant in their experiment. The stamps show no growth, growth, more growth, flowers, and seed pods. The graphs thus show the height of the plant as well as its developmental stage (see Figure 5.2).

In this chapter, we illustrate how a WISE project moves from the initial status of an inquiry theme to a more specific instructional pattern (e.g., Experiment), and finally to a well-defined series of activities and steps.

Scientists and teachers often hold strong ideas about science curriculum, and yet neither may have much experience in writing curriculum materials or designing inquiry-oriented activities. Educational researchers bring experience with the knowledge integration framework, which offers a source of direction for design discussions. Even with such a helpful framework, however, there remain many concrete challenges associated with authoring. For example, the partnership has to select Web resources, create inquiry activities (e.g., concept maps, drawings, online discussions), and identify assessments. Once a full version of the project is created, it requires review from several different perspectives, feedback, and revisions before it can be taken into the classroom. Only then will the new WISE project deliver on its promise as a technology-enhanced curriculum lesson (for the teacher), a method of dissemination or outreach (for the scientist), and a well-designed research resource that will allow specific questions to be addressed (by the educational researcher).

Figure 5.2. This image shows the WISE Draw tool being used within the "Space Plants" project to implement curriculum patterns. Here, students use the rubber stamp feature of WISE Draw in order to create a graph that compares the growth of their two kinds of plants. Note that the taller plants, (which are actually Wisconsin Fast Plants) have grown much more quickly and have flowered, whereas the other plants (a normal radish) have not grown nearly as tall and have not flowered yet.

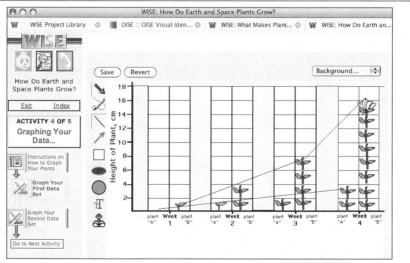

THE WISE PARTNERSHIP MODEL

As WISE matured through the years, the authoring partnership approach also matured as a general model that includes several distinct phases and components. If this process is followed with careful attention, it can result in more than just an effective new WISE inquiry project that adheres to the knowledge integration framework. It can also serve as a meaningful professional experience for all participants, connecting each member with peers from other disciplines and enabling productive discourse about student learning and teacher practices. A key feature of the process is a design review from several different perspectives. This design review ensures that the project includes the diverse perspectives of the team and incorporates the proven design patterns.

We began to formalize our "WISE partnership model" as a design process that could be reliably established in future efforts. We recognized that our own investigations required us to develop many new WISE projects for our research program, and we wanted to capture the successful atmosphere of inquiry and iterative improvement that we experienced in the early partnerships. All participants are stakeholders in the success of the curriculum, and their curriculum development efforts can be interpreted as a knowledge integration process where the designers are engaged in collaborative inquiry activities. Each member of the partnership enters the process with some initial ideas about learning and instruction that will invariably influence their experiences as well as the products of their work.

Indeed, it is useful to interpret the interactions among the partners as a knowledge integration activity, drawing upon the four tenets of knowledge integration that were outlined in previous chapters. First, we support the addition of ideas in such a way that they are accessible to each individual in the partnership and are easy for other members to elaborate. Second, we seek ways to make the ideas of each partner visible through representations, examples, and discussions. Third, we help the partners learn from one another by conducting reviews from each participant's perspective (e.g., assessment, discipline, visualization, grade-level appropriateness, communication potential). Fourth, we help the partners become lifelong learners, gaining important skills and perspectives that lead to a continuous improvement not only of their designs but also of their own design process.

WISE researchers have now participated in many successful partnerships that have included scientists from various governmental and nongovernmental agencies, as well as dozens of classroom teachers and educational researchers. These efforts have yielded a small library of WISE inquiry projects and secured the continued participation and interest of many scientist and teacher partners. Along the way, we have researched both the methods and the technology that can help support such partnerships, which now serves as the basis for all of our own curriculum design. For instance, the NSF-funded center called Technology-Enhanced Learning in Science (TELS—see Chapter 9) employs this model for its development of many new curriculum projects. The next section reviews the model in greater detail, drawing on examples from various WISE partnerships, particularly "Space Plants."

PHASES OF DESIGN

Over the course of several WISE partnerships, we identified three phases of the partnership model: (1) planning, (2) design, and (3) enactment and revision. In the planning phase, the partnership is formed, typically with at least one educational researcher who represents WISE and the knowledge integration perspective, one science partner who contributes disciplinary knowledge, and one teacher who brings classroom experience and who helps tailor the project to fit well within his or her science course. In the design phase, partners collaborate to create the first versions of the projects, with teachers outlining the content standards and advising about students, educational researchers guiding the development of the curriculum, and science experts shaping the communication of the scientific information. In the enactment and revision phase, teachers test out the projects in their classrooms, members of the design team analyze the evidence from the classroom trials, and the scientist continues to advise in content areas, adding any new or emerging findings that are relevant to the project. The cycle of iterative refinement continues until the partnership feels that the project is in a stable form that achieves the desired learning outcomes.

Planning

In this early phase of the curriculum design, the partners meet to establish their goals and talk over some possible approaches. The partners spend considerable time in this phase of work identifying topics that are well suited for the teacher's science course, that capitalize on technology, and that might engage students in knowledge integration. If there is an important perspective missing from the partnership, such as that of a scientist or teacher, then a representative from this group must be located. Often, new members are added to the partnership as it matures through this and the next phase.

In the case of the "Space Plants" project, the partnership began with just two partners: an educational outreach specialist from NASA's Ames Research Center who had worked with our group previously, and Michelle Williams, a graduate student researcher in our group who wanted to investigate the extension of WISE to upper elementary students and teachers. The two began meeting to discuss ideas, and soon added an elementary teacher, Mr. W. The team also recognized that their efforts would benefit from more specific expertise in the area of plant growth, and soon they added two additional science experts from the University of Texas. In addition, there was a new graphical drawing tool being added into WISE at that time, and another researcher from the WISE group as well as a computer programmer joined in order to help integrate a graphical activity into the project.

The earliest discussions within the partnership typically focus on identifying the most suitable science topics for the project, given the grade level and course topic. The best topics are the ones that are central to the science discipline, yet challenging for teachers to address through lecture, lab, or other conventional methods. WISE researchers often begin by asking teachers, "What topics are the ones that always seem to give you and students the most trouble? Where do students always seem to have misconceptions, despite your best efforts to target those misconceptions?" Invariably, teachers can identify the topics that fit this description.

In the case of middle school physical science, for example, we have often heard teachers identify the topics of force and motion as being particularly challenging ones. In high school biology, teachers readily volunteer topics such as natural selection, adaptation, or meiosis and mitosis. In the "Space Plants" partnership, the 5th-grade science teacher, Mr. W, identified plant growth as an area where urban students often have few experiences. He recounted that many students assert that "plants eat dirt," which interferes with their consideration of chemical nutrients and sunlight. He felt the current materials in the curriculum were limited. He had conducted plant growth labs in class, where students grew plants in small containers, but he had not been able to successfully connect the lab activity with the relevant science content, including the topic of photosynthesis. He also felt that students were not actively engaged with the ideas, and that they did not readily make connections to any aspect of plant growth in their everyday lives.

Early in the design process, WISE authoring partnerships seek to identify a suitable inquiry theme or pattern for the new project. It is impossible for the team to begin designing a WISE project without a consensus about what its basic approach will be and what instructional patterns (see Table 4.3 in the previous chapter) it will employ. In designing the "Sunlight, SunHEAT" project, the team chose the Critiquing pattern, and sought to engage students in critiquing the energy design of passive solar homes. In the "Deformed Frogs" project, the inquiry theme was to compare two different theoretical perspectives about the cause of frog deformities, drawing on the Argumentation pattern. Identifying this fundamental aspect of the project can be a difficult and elusive process. Often, creativity is required to envision a promising inquiry approach for a particular science topic.

In negotiating an effective, engaging inquiry theme for their project, authors may find themselves captivated by an exciting idea, only to realize that the inquiry theme would not directly engage students' ideas about the topic. Often, the team's initial ideas prove to be akin to a technology-enhanced textbook or online adventure game, passively leading students through carefully prepared science content. The key to developing an effective inquiry theme is to find a central activity that engages students in some form of active conceptual process relating to the ideas within the project. For example, in "Sunlight, SunHEAT," students do more than read about the energy designs of passive solar homes; they critique the quality of the designs using scientific criteria. This requires that they ask several questions about the details. In WISE, the inquiry theme has often taken the form of critiquing, comparing, debating, or designing.

In designing the "Space Plants" project, the team met several times to discuss issues such as the teacher's prior experiences with the topic of plant growth, the research literature that is concerned with the nature of student reasoning in this topic area, and the various possible inquiry themes. They identified one interesting pivotal case that had to do with the mass of plants: Where does all the matter within a large plant come from? In the 17th century, a Belgian scientist named Jan Babtist van Helmont had conducted an experiment in which he grew a willow tree from a sapling over a period of 5 years, at which point he weighed the overall plant material. He also weighed the soil in the container in which the plant had grown, and found that, although virtually no soil had disappeared, the tree had gained approximately 150 pounds (70 kg) in weight. Van Helmont reasoned that the plant had drawn all of its mass from the water. Although this interpretation was not correct, because plants also draw some of their new mass from the air itself through the process of photosynthesis, it illustrates an important pivotal case that can be used to engage students in conceptual reasoning (see Figure 5.3).

Figure 5.3. The WISE curriculum is most effective when it can engage students with pivotal cases that prompt them to reconsider their understandings. In this case, the curriculum authors found an historical case where van Helmont, a scientist, tried to identify where the mass of a large plant came from and through experimentation confirmed that the plant's mass does not come from the soil, motivating a curious question about the origin of the plant matter.

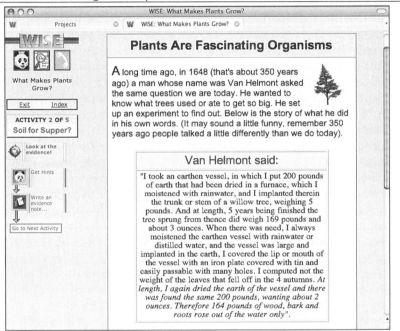

Building on these early discussions, the teachers, scientists, and researchers in the "Space Plants" partnership settled on a topic of "factors affecting plant growth" (including air, water, and soil nutrients). They further selected light and photosynthesis as a specific topic area that would be investigated by students. When it came to selecting an inquiry theme, there was considerable discussion about how 5th-grade students could be engaged in a hands-on activity that connected to the desired topics. Eventually, everyone agreed on an activity where students grew plants in the classroom under different light conditions. This inquiry theme allows students to engage deeply with all of the ideas within the project as well as with the ideas they bring with them to the classroom. So it was decided that students would experiment with real plants growing under different conditions, and the WISE project would be developed to support their experimentation and re-flections, as well as the logistical process of setting up the plant terrariums and the different lighting conditions.

Project Design. Although there is not really a clear boundary between the end of the planning phase and the beginning of the design phase, at a certain point the partners find themselves much more focused on the process of creating the detailed design of their WISE project. They continue their earlier discussions of the most effective kinds of activities, making frequent reference to the knowledge integration framework as well as to prior successful patterns. These discussions help them to outline the basic sequence of activities that will produce the intended inquiry theme while also addressing the science content learning goals.

Different viewpoints within the team are held in productive tension. Teachers are on guard for materials that are beyond their students' capabilities, and for any designs that may be too unwieldy or take too much class time. Scientists monitor the treatment of the conceptual material, making sure that nothing is lost in translation (in the case of "Space Plants," scientists monitored the translation from sophisticated materials about photosynthesis to materials that are age-appropriate for 10-year-olds). Educational researchers seek a final product that holds true to the theoretical framework and engages students in the kinds of inquiry and collaboration for which WISE was intended. If the project is part of an experimental study, the educational researcher can contribute ideas about innovative instruction and design a test of these ideas. Technology specialists on the team listen to all design ideas and help respond with recommended uses of the software systems, or even by developing new tools or features for WISE.

Technology Supports for Authors. WISE provides a technology infrastructure to help the authors convert their ideas about the sequence of activities into actual WISE steps, and to enable them to work as a team. First, the WISE portal allows partners to share authoring permissions with one another, so that anyone can login to the WISE authoring tool and work on editing the project. Second, in order to help authors get started in their design, the WISE authoring tool provides a "New Project Design Wizard" (see Figure 5.4). This is a special-purpose Web form, launched whenever a new WISE project is created, that prompts the author for descriptions of the learning goals, as well as any high-level design of activities.

Working through the New Project Design Wizard can help authors develop an overview of the broad activity structure of the project. For example, the "Space Plants" authors initially identified four main activities, each of which would eventually include a number of WISE steps. The first activity would provide students with some high-level information about plants and the factors that affect their growth. The second activity would provide instructions for students to build their terrariums

Figure 5.4. The WISE Project Design Wizard. We created a simple Web page to guide project authors' basic design discussions. This page is completed before any detailed authoring of WISE steps, and it helps the authors consider the learning goals of the project, the ideas that students will bring with them to the activity, and its overall activity structure.

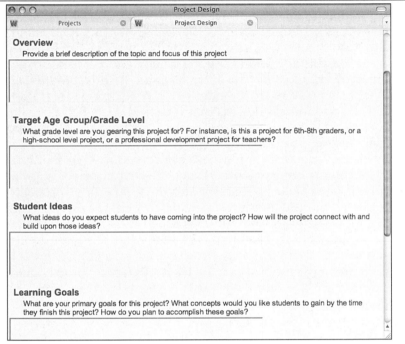

and get their plants started in various growing conditions. A third activity would engage students in reflecting about the challenges of gardening in space, and a fourth and final activity would support students as they applied their observations about plant growth to the challenge of designing a space garden. By helping the design team consider the basic flow of activities within the project in advance of authoring any specific steps, the New Project Design Wizard helped them articulate and critique their basic design before diving into any specific details.

The authoring tool (see Figure 5.5) is quite simple to use, allowing authors to set up new WISE steps or activities, change the sequence of existing steps, and create the content for any specific step. For example, an author might choose to add a step of the type "Online discussion." Once this step type is selected using the "New step" menu, WISE automatically presents the authoring module for online discussions, which asks for the discussion topic as well as several settings that apply to WISE online discussions. In this way, authors create the many steps

Figure 5.5. The WISE Authoring Tool allows new curriculum steps to be created by selecting from a list of available types and then adding content. This image shows an author creating a new step to the "Sunlight, SunHEAT" project by clicking on the "Add Step" link in the second activity ("Web Evidence"). The author selects the "Display Page" step type and will then be prompted to provide the contents of the new page to be displayed.

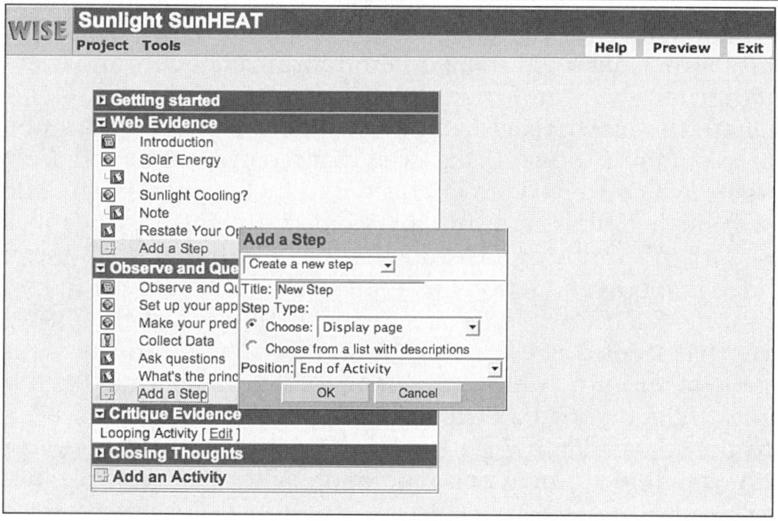

within a project, with a variety of different step types, such as Display Page (which displays an html page, so the authoring module asks for html input), WISE Draw (a drawing tool, where the author specifies the non-editable background of the drawing, as well as a set of rubber stamps that can be employed by students when they make their drawings), or Notes and Journals (student reflection tools, where the author specifies the reflection prompts that help guide students). The full list of step types was provided in Table 2.1. The WISE authors create steps one at a time, resequence them as necessary, and specify the content of each step. At any point, they can launch the "student preview" of the project, which shows them what their project will look like to students.

Authoring Team Dynamics. Along the way, the authors encounter many interesting points in the design process where they engage in dialogue about design decisions. Most partnerships meet regularly, with different individual team members working within the WISE authoring tool in between the meetings. Authors can share the burden of creating specific materials within the authoring tool because of the shared editing permissions managed by the portal. One person can volunteer to create some parts of the content while another creates other parts. Still others review the work and give comments. In the case of the "Space Plants" project, the educational researchers created new webpages that helped translate the van Helmont story into a narrative form that would be accessible to fifth graders. The NASA scientists created some new materials to describe the Wisconsin Fast Plants, and the teachers worked on a good set of instructions for students to create growing conditions. Over the duration of the design phase, most members of the "Space Plants" partnership spent some time authoring materials, and everyone spent time reviewing and making comments.

Often, the materials grow more sophisticated and voluminous as the process moves forward. Activities that seemed quite short and simple when first conceived are discovered to include more than a dozen steps. Other activities that initially seemed straightforward appear to be potentially confusing for students. Webpages that were meant to provide simple introductions to topics are found to be hundreds of words long. Such discoveries are an inevitable part of the process. A project that seemed like it would be short and sweet in the planning phases is often found during the design phase to be longer and more complex than anyone had expected.

In the "Space Plants" partnership, the design process revealed a wealth of rich ideas, materials, and approaches that were deemed essential for the project's treatment of the topic of plant growth. For example, in the introductory activity of the project, WISE steps were created to introduce topics of photosynthesis, as well as soil and nutrients. This, in turn gave rise to a step about a plant's roots and various ways of growing plants (e.g., hydroponically, without soil), which led to another step concerned with photosynthesis. For each of these steps, a WISE reflection note was needed to help students integrate their understanding. Unfortunately, the number of steps within the introductory activity soon became so numerous that some of the partners felt it was too long, with too much reading for students.

An ongoing challenge for the design team is to ensure that the overall inquiry theme and patterns are connected to student activities and materials within the project. Two of the scientists were experienced with "Wisconsin Fast Plants," a special type of radish plant that was developed by professor Paul Williams at the University of Wisconsin. These special plants are well suited for classroom-based activities as well as space missions because they grow very quickly (10 times the speed of normal radishes), they grow well in crowded conditions, and they are unharmed by continuous lighting conditions. They are also sometimes referred to as "NASA Space Plants," because the U.S. Air and Space Agency has made use of these plants in research aboard the *Mir* space station, the space shuttle, and the space station *Freedom*. It occurred to the designers that students could compare the growth of the NASA Space Plants with that of regular Earth plants under different lighting conditions. In order to engage students productively in such comparisons, the project would require them to set up various experimental conditions where two different kinds of plants grew under a variety of lighting conditions. Over the course of several design discussions, the authors of "Space Plants" created a sequence of WISE steps designed to help students implement this pattern of experimentation and reflect about their observations.

The teacher, Mr. W, was deeply engaged in these discussions, and was concerned about the amount of material that was being added to the project. He communicated his concerns to Michelle Williams, the educational researcher who was investigating how WISE could engage students at the upper elementary level. Mr. W expressed a concern that there would be too much focused time reading and writing on the computer, which didn't fit within his normal mode of teaching. He suggested an interesting compromise, that students would not need to complete the WISE project within a single week or even two weeks of instruction, as they do in the middle and high school contexts. Rather, students could be supported to have periodic time on the WISE project throughout the school term, spending a bit of time on the computer each week but extending the project over a much longer period of several months.

Mr. W also suggested that the project include substantial offline discussions led by the teacher that would be interwoven with online components of the project. He wanted to blend this project into his broader curriculum, engaging students in regular and ongoing observations of their plants, encouraging whole-class discussions, and making good use of WISE online elements as well.

Another interesting addition that came about as a result of this design process was the application of the WISE Draw tool in a unique approach to supporting young children in a basic graphing activity. This was not one of the initial learning objectives of the project, but due to the interdisciplinary nature of the elementary curriculum, Mr. W saw value in connecting this project to the important mathematics and science goal of graphing. The team thus added a graphing component to the project where students graphed the height of the two kinds of plants over time. It occurred to the technology specialists on the team that the WISE Draw tool could be used toward this purpose, if, instead of entering a measurement of the height, students simply drew their plants using the rubber stamp tool as described in Figure 5.2. In this way, they were engaged actively in measuring the height of plants and then drawing the heights at different times.

After weeks of meetings, emails, and online authoring activity, the authoring partnership presented its results within the wider community of WISE educational researchers, teachers, and scientists. As with any-thing that we create (including this book!), it is usually of great value to allow our colleagues to review the first draft and provide feedback. Of course, reviews can be conducted from a variety of perspectives: editing and typographical errors, validity of science content, age-appropriate-ness and equitability of curriculum materials, effectiveness of assess-ments, and theoretical integrity in terms of the knowledge integration framework. Different reviewers might be best suited to comment on different aspects of a new WISE project, and for this reason, several members of the community are typically recruited to conduct such re-views. To facilitate the review process, we even developed another Web form that would support the reviewer, collect their reflections, and send them off automatically to the appropriate authors.

Once they have received feedback from the various reviewers, the authoring team meets to evaluate possible revisions that will address any concerns. After such final revisions, the project is ready for presen-tation and discussion at a research group meeting. This group serves as an important sounding board for any new ideas, as well as a final testing ground for curriculum that is about to go into classrooms. In-variably, this final review serves to catch a few typos or even some larger problems that may have escaped the individual reviewers. After this final community review, the project is ready to be taken to the classroom, which marks the beginning of the final phase of the WISE partnership model.

Enactment and Revision

No matter how careful the design, nor how many reviews and re-visions it has undergone, no curriculum material can ever be fully pre-pared for the rigors and unexpected findings that arise in classroom trials. WISE projects are no exception, as invariably the authors dis-cover things about their project design that must be improved in or-der to better support inquiry and respond to student ideas. Of course, the teacher is the first in line to detect any possible problems, such as materials that are confusing to students, opportunities for instruction that may have been underdeveloped, or alternative interpretations of ideas that had not been anticipated. The educational researcher will also typically be present in the classroom for the initial trials, paying close attention to see whether the project supports the processes of knowledge integration. The teacher and researcher will also regularly ask students what they think of the project, whether they are con-fused, whether they are enjoying the project; and what questions they may have about the science.

Another important source of information for the evaluation of projects comes from looking carefully at the student assessments that are embedded within the project. Assessments in WISE are designed to provide opportunities for students to reflect and build their understanding and offer teachers a source of information about how students are thinking. One form of assessment that is used commonly in WISE projects is the reflection notebook. WISE prompts students for reflections throughout the project, and teachers can easily read their ideas by going to the WISE portal. During the first enactment of a WISE project, student reflections often reveal unexpected ideas, misconceptions, and confusions.

For example, in the "Space Plants" project, one of the webpages that was provided to students was concerned with the nutrients that plants need to survive. In designing the reflection note that would help students make the most of this curriculum content element, the authors considered what ideas they wanted to make sure students gained and how they could engage students in sorting out their ideas. Initially, the reflection note was quite simple, asking, "Why do plants need nutrients?" However, when the project was first tested in a classroom, it was noted that students provided short, simplistic replies, such as "Plants need nutrients to live." When the authors noticed such responses, they revised the reflection note to include a more directed question: "How will the plants change if they do not receive the correct amount of nutrients?" By encouraging students to consider the physical changes that will occur in plants that are deprived of nutrients, this reflection note added a greater focus on the specific roles and mechanism of nutrients, which in turn helped students provide richer answers to a second portion of the note that inquired about why nutrients are important.

By closely examining student responses to reflection notes, online discussions, journals, and other embedded assessments, the authoring partners can evaluate whether their project is achieving the desired kinds of reflection and inquiry. In particular, the educational researcher, often a Ph.D. student, can evaluate whether the project is serving its intended purposes for research. In the case of the "Space Plants" curriculum, the Ph.D. student was Michelle Williams, who was quite avidly involved in the first enactment of the curriculum within Mr. W's class. Michelle's research questions were concerned with the adaptations that would be required for WISE to fit well within an upper elementary school science context and support teachers who wished to implement inquiry instruction. She monitored aspects of the curriculum where students were disengaged or confused, or where the teacher felt that things were not age-appropriate. She sought ways to ensure that students were engaged in answering compelling questions and able to revise or integrate their ideas. Based on the first trials, many revisions were made to the "Space Plants" curriculum, in preparation for a formal study of the trajectories teachers follow as they learn to teach science with inquiry. These questions became the basis of Michelle's Ph.D. research (Williams & Linn, 2003).

In every case of authoring, the iterative process of classroom trials, observations, analysis, and refinement is required to make sure that WISE projects are engaging and effective for students and teachers alike. It begins with close observations and analyses of the preliminary trials, which are conducted in the classroom of the partner teacher. The WISE technology serves to capture student ideas and help the design team learn about how students learn and reason within that particular domain. Finally, the iterative design process has contributed to our continued improvement of the WISE theoretical framework, which seeks to capture the effective pedagogical patterns that emerge from all authoring partnerships

SUSTAINING OUR PARTNERSHIPS:
RESEARCH AND CURRICULUM COLLABORATIONS

WISE has served our research group quite well as a platform for the design, development, and delivery of technology-enhanced curriculum materials. It can also offer the same functionality to the wider research community: the capability to author interactive learning materials that can be delivered immediately to classrooms via the Internet, scaffolding student activities and storing all data automatically in a Web-accessible database that can be accessed at any time. Changes to the curriculum materials can be made overnight or even during a school day, allowing an unprecedented level of control over the design and delivery of materials, the collection of data, and the coordination of various research conditions.

In some cases, our colleagues inquired whether they could use WISE as a platform for their own research. Some asked whether they could submit grant proposals that cited the availability of WISE for the creation and delivery of materials. For example, researchers at the Concord Consortium in Boston, Massachusetts, developed a new WISE project to research student collaboration using scientific visualizations. Other researchers chose to adapt existing WISE curriculum projects for new purposes. Investigators at the University of Tubingen in Germany have adapted the WISE "Deformed Frog" curriculum, translating it into German and adding new "collaboration scripts" to

help students succeed in constructing formal arguments. Such extensions of WISE have helped us understand its potential applications as
a flexible multipurpose research platform for the learning sciences.

We have also established partnerships with scientists and educational
specialists from governmental organizations such as NASA or NOAA,
local departments of forestry or natural resources, nonprofit organizations such as the National Geographic Society or the International Wolf
Center, or science disciplinary groups such as the American Physiology
Society or the Thousand Friends of Frogs. Representatives from organizations are motivated for various reasons to create educational resources
for K–12 science instruction. In some cases, as with NASA, the goal is to
help students and teachers connect to scientific expeditions or research
projects; other organizations, such as the American Physiology Society,
wish to promote education within their domain. These science partners
have been enthusiastic about WISE because it can offer: (1) pedagogical
designs for their materials, (2) a technology-rich learning environment
that serves the curriculum to a wide audience of students and teachers,
and (3) a stable, well-supported community of teachers who will return
from one year to the next and will try out new activities as they become
available.

WISE built on such opportunities to help create sustainable, dynamic partnerships. There is a great difference between simply offering a project like "Wolves in Your Backyard" in the WISE curriculum
library with little sustained presence from project authors, and providing it in a context where its authors remain in contact with the
curriculum and improve it based on current science, feedback from
teachers, or new ideas that emerge within the partnership.

Using the partnership model, WISE curriculum authors can improve
their designs as well as their own understanding of inquiry learning, assessment, and teacher practices. Strong personal relationships among
the members of the team are obviously an important key to achieving this goal. The partnership must be professionally rewarding for all
members as well, and must be supported by a technology environment
within the WISE portal. By enabling the process of design and revision
to run smoothly, the WISE portal can help participants remain involved
even after the initial version of the project has been completed.

To support authoring partnerships, WISE created a new area within
the portal called "Communities," where individuals or groups who are
interested in a specific curriculum topic can aggregate their materials, lesson plans, and assessments. For example, consider the interdisciplinary group called the Thousand Friends of Frogs, whose director
contacted us quite early in our project after seeing the "Deformed
Frogs" project online. This group is concerned with the environmental

plight of amphibians worldwide and wished to develop Internet-based curriculum to promote its cause. Biologists and educators from the group helped to establish a WISE Frogs community, resulting in the creation of new versions of the "Deformed Frogs" curriculum as well as the outreach to hundreds of frog-friendly teachers around the world.

WISE Communities offer a private space for their members to keep versions of curriculum projects, maintain annotated Web links, hold online discussions, and many other functions. Figure 5.6 shows the WISE Frogs Community, for which the administrator created five fea-

Figure 5.6. WISE Communities are private spaces within the WISE portal where curriculum authors can maintain relevant resources, drafts of ideas, collaborative whiteboards, and even calendars of authoring activities. Many WISE communities have been created by authoring teams, school district partnerships, or special interest groups. This image illustrates the WISE Frogs community, made up of teachers who are interested in using the topic of deformed frogs for purposes of inquiry science curriculum.

tures that are accessed through the buttons on the right-hand side of the screen: "Members," which simply brings up a list of the members of the community with their personal profiles; "About WISE and Frogs," which is an information page; "Project Descriptions," where community members read descriptions of the various frogs curriculum projects; "Visit the Projects," which presents links to the actual WISE frogs projects; and "Discussions," which brings up a series of threaded online discussions.

Dozens of such communities have now been created in order to support groups of WISE users who share a specific common interest— either a general curriculum topic such as frogs, wolves, or earthquakes; the authoring of a specific project (e.g., the Monterey Bay Aquarium project); the support of teachers from a specific school district (e.g., Denver Public Schools); or the support of a teacher professional development program.

WISE has demonstrated the potential of Web-based communities as a source of development and exchange of educational content. Hundreds of WISE inquiry projects have now been authored by a wide range of participants, including educational researchers with specific questions and content foci, teachers who wish to customize existing projects from the WISE public library, pre-service teachers who participate in a curriculum and technology course, and informal science educators from museums, government agencies, or nonprofit groups who wish to create curriculum materials for their own endeavors. This huge content development effort was not sponsored specifically by any research grant. Rather, the content emerged because WISE was available as an open resource to a diverse community of developers. These professionals have responded to the accessibility of a flexible system that provided the powerful functionality necessary for the design, development, and delivery of interactive Web-based curriculum content. Future extensions of this work will focus on promoting dynamic science curriculum communities that engage a rich array of partnerships and include ongoing contributions from many different teachers, scientists, and researchers.

RECOMMENDED READINGS

Shear, L., Bell, P., & Linn, M. C. (2004). Partnership models: The case of the deformed frogs. In M. C. Linn, E. A. Davis, & P. Bell (Eds.), *Internet Environments for Science Education*. Mahwah, NJ: Lawrence Erlbaum.

This article describes the emergence of the WISE partnership model over the course of the KIE and WISE research projects. It begins by referencing earlier partnerships in KIE, then details the experience of the WISE "Deformed Frogs" partnership.

Williams, M., Linn, M., Ammon, P., & Gearhart, M. (2004). Learning to teach inquiry science in a technology-based environment: A case study. *Journal of Science Education and Technology, 13*(2), 189–206.

> This research article describes the Ph.D. project of Michelle Williams, with details of her experiences in developing the WISE "Plants in Space" curriculum. The paper describes how WISE itself was adapted for use in an elementary level classroom.

Williams, M., & Linn, M. C. (2003). Collaborating with WISE scientists. *Science & Children, 41*(1), 31–35.

> This is a second article about Michelle Williams's efforts with "Space Plants," written in a format that may be accessible to a wide audience of readers.

CHAPTER 6

What Do Students Learn from WISE?

From the beginning, teachers have commented that WISE projects help students learn science. Many of their comments focus on the motivational characteristics of WISE projects, as the teachers remark that students are more attentive, more collaborative, and more intellectually engaged in science when they are using WISE projects.

Frequently, teachers indicate that students whose interest in science had been minimal in the past made impressive contributions using WISE and took science more seriously. For example, one teacher reported that when she used the "Deformed Frogs" debate project, one student who had previously slept during science class not only became involved, but emerged as a leader in the final debate activity. The teacher also reported that, once the WISE project was completed and students were handed a written post-test to complete, this student once again put her head down on her desk and refused to participate. This student complained that the test was for the teacher, whereas the activities were for the students.

This anecdote illustrates how the embedded assessments in a WISE project impact its effectiveness. When assessments have the format of paper-and-pencil tests, they will likely be interpreted by students as being separate from the curriculum, as in the anecdote above. Ideally, assessments for a new WISE project will have a similar look and feel to the learning activities. Assessments should be designed as learning events rather than as supplemental aspects of the curriculum that are solely for the advantage of the teachers or researchers.

Many teachers also comment on the collaborative practices in which students are engaged, noting that students appear to make more productive and thoughtful comments when defending their ideas for their peers. Some teachers also observe that students ask for more feedback on their ideas when using WISE projects than they had done in their previous science instruction. And, as illustrated in the "Deformed Frogs" example, many teachers commented that students who had been previously disengaged in science class displayed surprising energy, made scientifically valid comments during discussions, and contributed interesting ideas on WISE assessments.

But perhaps the most important observations that teachers make are concerned with the written explanations that students provide to WISE reflection prompts. Most teachers report that their students generally have considerable difficulty writing about science, and written reflections have not traditionally been emphasized in standardized tests or even in most classroom science tests. At first, students are not sure how to express their ideas in response to knowledge integration questions and they frequently fail to use scientific evidence to warrant their claims. Most teachers report that over time, however, students become more adept at such reasoning and begin to write sophisticated responses to these kinds of assessments. Teachers who are experienced in the use of WISE draw attention to this expectation when they are addressing the whole class. They also take the opportunity to provide feedback to students concerning their responses to the WISE reflection prompts (which are a form of embedded assessment), emphasizing that they should make connections between ideas and include evidence to support assertions.

As students begin writing more coherent and sophisticated reflections in response to the questions and prompts in WISE projects, they also become more sophisticated in discussing science ideas. Teachers are pleased with the noticeable change in the style and content of discussions, and find it easy to connect discussions to the ideas that students encountered during WISE activities.

Recently, a group of science teachers who were involved in a whole school partnership commented that they were so pleased with the kinds of explanations that students were generating in WISE reflection notes that they wanted to include such questions in their other classroom activities. The teachers even engaged in discussions with their colleagues from mathematics and other disciplines about how to apply a knowledge integration approach to the design of student assignments. This illustrates how the WISE curriculum has an impact that extends beyond science and technology since such extensions have little to do with technology. Although the WISE technology environment was designed to scaffold a certain kind of instruction, there is certainly no reason that such instructional approaches can't be implemented in a wide range of different disciplines and formats, including paper-and-pencil, if designed appropriately.

HOW DO WE MEASURE THE BENEFITS OF WISE?

As discussed in the previous chapter, considerable attention is paid to the design of embedded assessments for every WISE project. Indeed, most student activities within WISE can be interpreted as some form of assessment, in the sense that they can provide insight into students' ideas. In addition to the prompts for reflection, there are many other ways to capture student ideas. To name a few: WISE drawings ask students to perform drawings or place rubber stamps on a histogram or other display; WISE discussions engage students in written exchanges with peers; WISE problem sets present multiple-choice or short-answer problems; simulations and models capture student ideas through their manipulation of variables and controls. While students interpret these activities as being part of the curriculum (which indeed they are), teachers and researchers can make use of all of these data in evaluating the impact of WISE.

Knowledge Integration Assessments

We introduced the idea of knowledge integration assessments in Chapter 3, highlighting items used in the Computer as Learning Partner (CLP) curriculum. One item that we described asked students to explain the difference between heat and temperature and to provide several examples that illustrate their ideas. In order to assess student ideas in such an item, we developed a rubric that rewards both accurate and connected ideas. This rubric results in a scoring of student responses not in terms of whether they are "right or wrong," but rather in terms of their coherence and the connections they make between normative science and the students' own ideas or experiences.

In addition to embedded assessments, all WISE projects have pretests and post-tests that include between 4 and 8 knowledge integration items and require approximately 20–30 minutes of class time. In our research partnerships, teachers are required to administer both the pre-test and the post-test (which include identical items) because they provide an important indicator of student learning. These pre- and post-tests are designed to assess a deep understanding of science concepts, with items that challenge students to apply their understanding to interesting situations. For example, in the WISE "Cycles of Malaria" project, one test item asks students whether they agree with the idea of a law that bans all standing water (in ponds, water troughs, or even filled buckets) in the vicinity of villages where malaria is present (see Figure 6.1). To address this item, students must reason about the life cycle of the mosquito, which carries the parasite that causes malaria. The malaria test item is a knowledge integration assessment because it asks students to extend the learning they went through during the WISE project to a new problem and justify their answer in terms of the science.

In order to capture the accomplishments observed anecdotally by teachers and researchers, we have used knowledge integration items

Figure 6.1. WISE Pre–Post Assessments for Knowledge Integration. This figure shows a pre–post test that was designed to assess students' understanding of how Malaria could be spread or controlled. While these items are not comprehensive, in terms of the medical science regarding Malaria, they are aimed at engaging students' ideas about the spread of the disease.

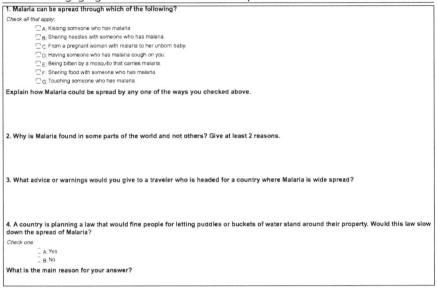

that were co-designed with the instruction and administered in the form of pre-tests and post-tests. Pre–post comparisons on these items show that students make notable gains in their ability to reason with science topics and form coherent and connected explanations of their answers. Since the WISE projects are typically only 1 week in duration, this finding is particularly noteworthy.

Recently, we have used pre-test/post-test designs to probe students' progress in understanding complex science when using WISE projects. Students generally make progress in knowledge integration about complex science topics between pre-test and post-test (see Figure 6.2). When students are grouped based on their pre-test scores, the progress of high and low pre-test groups is comparable (Figure 6.2). Thus, WISE projects have the impact of improving performance for students across the spectrum of pre-test ability. This finding is consistent with the observations of teachers that all students seem to benefit from WISE projects and that a knowledge integration approach offers particular advantages for students who are not typically successful in science.

In order to make progress on knowledge integration assessments, students must display a deep and connected understanding of science. In most of our studies, students start at Level 1 of the knowledge integra-

Figure 6.2. Many research studies have found that students make progress in knowledge integration assessments between pre-tests and post-tests related to a WISE project they conducted in class. This recent study within the TELS project divided the students who scored below and above the median value on the pre-test, and found that they achieved comparable gains at post-test. This findings provides evidence that WISE benefits all students in the classroom.

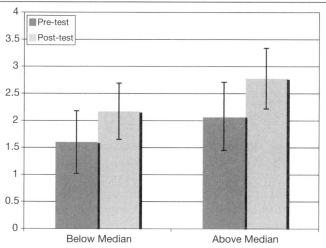

tion rubric, meaning that they display a single isolated idea about a topic and make few, if any, connections to other ideas or experiences. Post-test responses show an average gain of approximately one level on the knowledge integration rubric. That is, students are beginning to link their ideas after they participate in WISE projects. This is a remarkable improvement, given that the projects require only 4 or 5 hours of class time.

Of course, students start out from different places. Some enter the WISE experience with established, linked ideas and thus progress in the direction of linking more ideas and sorting out their repertoire of ideas. Others start with few preexisting ideas and make progress by adding one new idea and linking it with some prior experiences. Averaging across all students, however, we observe the pre–post gains reflected in Figure 6.2.

The pre–post gains that we observe across all of our research studies are compatible with teachers' observations that, when students first use WISE projects, they are unable to link ideas, but then they become more adept at making connections over the course of instruction. Thus, WISE is helping students develop better reasoning and argumentation skills, at least within the specific topic area of the curriculum.

There remains an open question about whether the gains that students make in a specific WISE project are general to other domains of science. Anecdotally, teachers feel that a "small dose of WISE" is able to help the class generally become more reflective and communicative about science. Such a change could stem from both teacher and student experience with WISE. The teacher is also learning as a result of enacting a WISE project, and this learning will propagate to other aspects of the curriculum. Thus, if the students in the class seem to have gained some general degree of reflection and knowledge integration, this might be a consequence of transfer from the WISE project, or it might be that the teacher has gained in skill and understanding about how to instill that atmosphere in the classroom. Even if the pre–post gains we measure are limited to the specific topic domain of the WISE project in which students were engaged, it is encouraging that students begin to link their ideas as a result of participation in the WISE projects.

Does Knowledge Integration Help Performance on Standardized Tests?

How do student gains in knowledge integration affect their performance on standardized assessments of science knowledge that are common to secondary education worldwide? Comparing performance on knowledge integration assessments to performance on standardized tests is important because policy decisions and funding decisions are often linked with student performance on standardized tests. Governments are even introducing legislation, such as the No Child Left Behind act in the United States, that rewards teachers and schools that make progress from year to year in standardized test performance.

A number of studies have analyzed the characteristics of standardized tests. Although they vary considerably from one to another, a surprising and discouraging characteristic of most standardized tests is that they do not require students to link their ideas and apply their understanding to new situations, such as occurs in knowledge integration assessments. Even when test items do ask students to generate rich responses and explanations, such as some of the items from the Third International Mathematics and Science Study (TIMSS), those items are often scored in such a way that they actually give credit to students who generate a single idea (Liu, Lee, Hofstetter, & Linn, 2008).

Analysis of assessments in mathematics across all states shows that, on average, these tests include no items that require knowledge integration (Hyde, Lindberg, Linn, Ellis, & Williams, 2008). This situation means that standardized tests in mathematics have no value as learning events in their own right, do not capture students' ability to make connections to topics, and do not convey the value of linking ideas using evidence to students or teachers.

In the increasingly high-stakes atmosphere of standardized testing, teachers often feel compelled to "teach to the test." Thus, if tests are not measuring knowledge integration, it is unlikely that teachers will feel a strong motivation to help students make gains in that direction. If the most important tests require students to perform only straightforward problems (such as balancing a chemical equation) and memorization of content rather than demonstrate a deep understanding, then teachers will focus on their students' achievement on such tests. When teachers reinforce these goals in the classroom, students become convinced that memorizing information and problem-solving techniques are sufficient strategies for learning science. Students and teachers alike may fail to recognize the value of learning science for lifelong interpretation of complex, real-world dilemmas.

When students learn to read, they practice reading regularly, and when they learn mathematics, they encounter opportunities to use their mathematical accomplishments. However, most individuals feel that they rarely find opportunities to apply the ideas they learn in science class. Standardized tests that prioritize the recall of isolated bits of information reinforce the belief that science is not relevant to everyday life. In contrast, WISE projects situate science concepts in the context of a problem that students might well encounter again in their lives, such as the choice of insulation for home heating, the use of genetically modified foods, or how to interpret different treatments for cancer. Students are likely to revisit such questions throughout their lives and will thus have ample opportunities to utilize their science knowledge. With a knowledge integration approach to science instruction, they will be able to draw on well-connected ideas that support a scientific analysis of the dilemma. As a result, they will strengthen their understanding of science as they encounter each new problem.

Teachers and policymakers often recognize the limitations of standardized tests but argue that they still provide good, basic measures of science learning. However, our research studies have shown that tests of simple recall of information do not offer any measure of knowledge integration (Clark & Linn, 2003). One reason standardized tests fail to measure knowledge integration is that such tests are typically designed to address an entire year's curriculum content and to align questions with specific topics. To encompass the numerous topics mandated by state standards, tests are likely to have very few questions that target any give topic. These items typically address only the most straightforward aspects of the topic, and may not distinguish among the more complex levels of knowledge integration. In addition, items that require knowledge integration are difficult to write in a multiple-choice format, which is the common format for standardized tests.

As Hee Sun Lee found when she analyzed performance on standardized and WISE items, the multiple-choice items failed to distinguish among students because they were too easy. She found that students who succeeded on the standardized multiple-choice items had difficulty with the more challenging knowledge integration items (Lee, Tinker, Husic, & Chin, 2006). Thus, if questions map to a single topic, they may neglect both complex ideas and links across topics. As a result, standardized tests are insensitive to knowledge integration instruction because they lack questions relevant to the topic, lack questions that require links from one topic to another, and lack emphasis on the goal of making connections among ideas.

In summary, WISE pre-tests and post-tests are effective in measuring the progress of students in knowledge integration related to the specific topics being addressed within the curriculum. As observed by teachers, these tests document that students learn more information about the topics that they study, and learn how to link the information into arguments. In contrast, standardized tests often use multiple-choice items that do not have a very deep coverage of the topics used for WISE instruction and therefore are not particularly sensitive to knowledge integration accomplishments. Innovations like WISE that promote knowledge integration should not expect to make a substantive impact on students' performance on standardized tests, because those tests simply do not measure deep understanding. This will be a persistent problem for educators, to the extent that standardized tests remain the focus of attention among politicians and policymakers.

WHAT DO TEACHERS LEARN FROM USING WISE?

Many conversations with WISE teachers reveal their belief that not only do their students make progress in learning science, but they also make progress in their abilities to teach science as a result of using WISE. Teachers point out that they learn some real advantages for technology, particularly in relation to the use of animations and simulations, which communicate information that is simply not available in textbooks but can be confusing for students. Teachers also report enthusiasm for the WISE inquiry map that guides students' activities. They feel that following the map helps students carry out complex scientific investigations without asking the teacher for direction as frequently. As a result, the teacher has time to spend working with individuals who are having difficulty understanding the material.

Teachers feel that WISE helps them learn how to assess student progress in science. They learn to use the knowledge integration rubric to reward students for building arguments, and they learn to use the embedded assessments to gain insight into the trajectories of their students' ideas. WISE assessments help teachers recognize when students are making progress. The embedded assessments allow them to identify problems that are encountered by all students, and then interrupt class to discuss those difficulties. We discuss this process more deeply in Chapters 7 and 8, which are concerned with professional development and teacher learning.

In addition, teachers report that using WISE gives them some new ideas about teaching. They learn how to encourage inquiry on the part of their students, as well as to emphasize coherence of understanding. Some teachers report that they extend this approach to instruction in other courses that they teach and find the strategies valuable in those contexts. Many teachers have tried to create classroom tests that require similar forms of reasoning. Teachers also generally report that the WISE pre-test and post-test items provided with the project can be used as part of their general classroom tests, such as the end-of-year exam.

Teachers acknowledge that it is much more difficult to write items that require students to generate thoughtful scientific explanations than they had anticipated. Those teachers who were part of the authoring partnership for a project understand why these test items are so effective. The items are designed to measure students' understanding, they have been intensively reviewed, and they have been evaluated and revised several times based on classroom trials. Thus, the assessments within WISE projects are typically more effective as knowledge integration items than those created by teachers on their first attempt. This does not mean that teachers cannot design such items, but it does underscore the challenge of designing effective items for classroom tests. Although some teachers are able to find the time and effort required to do this, many others are still developing the understanding of knowledge integration, or cannot make a sufficient time commitment. In order to support teachers as they develop knowledge integration assessments, WISE provides sample questions on our Web site that teachers can use to help develop assessments of student understanding.

HELPING SCHOOL PRINCIPALS SUPPORT
INQUIRY AND TECHNOLOGY APPROACHES

In a recent research project, we have convened a community of school principals to help us understand their schools' assessment needs and to make sure that WISE is providing them with appropriate information. Initially, principals were quite happy with the reactions of their teachers and students as well as with the knowledge integration assessments, be-cause teachers were enthusiastic about WISE and students were demon-strating the insights they gained from WISE. In the early stages of this study, principals reported that the most important factors for their prac-tice were that teachers and students were enthusiastic about science, that students indicated a desire to take more science courses in high school, and that students were considering careers in science. This was reassuring for us to hear, and allowed us to focus our outcome measures on those elements of science learning for which WISE was designed.

However, as California began to implement standardized testing in science in response to the No Child Left Behind legislation, the reactions of principals changed. Principals became more anxious about ensuring that students were learning as many science concepts as possible from their experiences with WISE. In response, we changed our assessments to more completely document the benefits of WISE. Overall, principals have been satisfied with our pre-test/post-test findings, such as those reported above, and have continued to be enthusiastic supporters. In-deed, principals whose teachers were using WISE expressed confidence about the impact of science instruction on their students and increased their support of technology in science classrooms.

Based on this experience and others, we have also provided the opportunity for school principals to form a community that meets periodically and stays in touch online (Gerard, Bowyer, & Linn, 2008). Forming such a community has helped us understand the kinds of evidence to which principals pay attention, and what values are im-portant to their vision for their schools. The principals within this small community encouraged one another, identified ways in which WISE could help within their science departments, and supported the continuing use of WISE. We have documented that schools whose principals are members of this community have more teachers using WISE than those whose principals are not in the community. Some of the principals within the community began requesting that teach-ers use a least one WISE project per year and working to secure ad-ditional computer laboratories or mobile carts of laptop computers for their schools. We also found that the teachers from those schools whose principals are in the community had more resources for teach-ing WISE and more support from their science departments.

WHAT ROLE DOES RESEARCH PLAY IN POLICY AND PRACTICE?

Researchers have the mission of understanding the impact of educa-tional innovations and communicating that impact to a number of different audiences. The research community maintains a literature of publications, and most scholars are aware of all the work that happens within their field. It is important for researchers to publish and present their work, as well as to discuss the broader themes and implications at conferences and workshops. In addition, researchers can help teachers refine their instruction by gathering evidence about the effectiveness of each version of the curriculum. They can also inform the design of effective professional development based on models of a teacher's growth in instructional practices. And they can even help principals lobby for funding by gathering evidence of the impact of WISE.

Another audience that is important to researchers consists of those individuals who are interested in improving science curriculum materials. This audience includes educators from universities, school districts, nongovernmental and even governmental agencies, as well as private companies. To meet the needs of this diverse audience, researchers conduct comparison studies that help clarify the most effective approaches to teaching and learning science concepts. We discussed this process in Chapters 3 and 4, with some examples from the development of WISE curriculum materials. For example, we discussed comparison studies that contrasted students making predictions before exploring a simulation with situations where students did not make predictions.

A final audience for researchers is that of decisionmakers of all sorts: individuals who make decisions concerning what curriculum materials to use, how funds are allocated, topics for curriculum design projects, topics for professional development, and so on. This audience includes state, local, and national policymakers in science education, as well as funding agencies and individual teachers selecting from among instructional options. To help this audience make decisions, researchers can offer clear, concise statements about the implications of their work, such as the policy statements we offer in the conclusion of this book.

WISE Instructional Comparison Studies

In order to meet the needs of these various audiences, WISE researchers have conducted a variety of comparison studies. Some comparison studies contrast alternative forms of WISE projects in order to clarify the best designs for WISE curriculum, and the best ways of teaching with WISE. Other studies compare WISE to typical or alternative forms of instruction. WISE comparison studies tend to contrast two different versions of WISE and employ a variety of students' ideas and artifacts and teaching practices as measures. In Chapter 3, for example, we described studies that compared different formats for

WISE reflection prompts and found that more generic prompts elicited more sophisticated explanations. This study revealed that the specific prompts interrupted students' flow of reasoning because they asked questions that were not personally relevant.

Recent comparison studies by researchers using the WISE learning environment have contrasted various ways to use visualizations within WISE projects, such as simulations of chemical reactions, global warming, or heat flow. These studies are conducted in classrooms with input from teachers, students, and administrators.

Hsin-Yi Chang (2008) investigated the kinds of questions that students respond to when they conduct experiments using visualizations. She noted that students could be asked to conduct experiments, to critique experiments that have been conducted by others, or to critique their own experiments. She designed two conditions, one where students conducted many experiments and another where students engaged in a mix of activities, sometimes conducting experiments and sometimes critiquing experiments. She ran these two conditions in the classrooms of several middle school teachers, ultimately studying about 10 different classes. She found that when students were asked to critique as well as experiment, they were more successful in answering critique and experiment questions than if they were only asked to perform experiments.

This suggests that critique activities are generally valuable in helping students understand complex scientific phenomena. This is not a surprising result, since students often make conjectures about a scientific phenomenon without much evidence to support their ideas. If students have the opportunity to critique experiments as well as make conjectures, they will be more likely to develop effective criteria for distinguishing among experiments.

A second comparison study recently conducted by a WISE researcher investigated the best way to help students interpret a visualization of chemical reactions. Helen Zhang (2008) noted that students typically explored such visualizations for a while, but made no progress in responding to knowledge integration assessments concerning the visualization. She decided that it would be useful to encourage students first to sketch their ideas about the chemical reaction that was happening within the visualization, then to conduct further experiments. In the "sketch" condition, students alternated between exploring a chemical reaction and sketching what they thought was happening in the chemical reaction (see Figure 6.3). In the "explore" condition, students simply conducted as many explorations of the visualization as they desired.

Zhang found that students who had the opportunity to sketch their ideas were more successful at interpreting chemical reactions than students who did not have the opportunity to draw their ideas.

Figure 6.3. Students Sketching Their Ideas. A screenshot of a dynamic visualization demonstrating hydrogen combustion at the molecular level. Lower: Drawings created by a student in the "sketch" condition, exploring the dynamic visualization and explaining what he thought was happening in the chemical reaction.

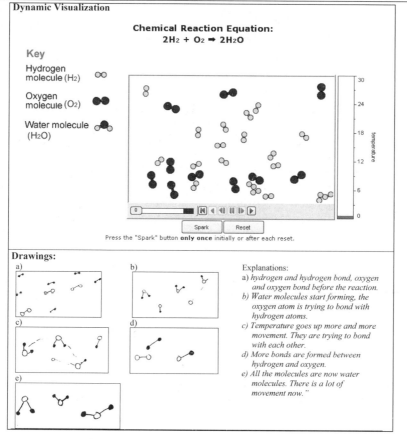

In analyzing this result, Zhang concluded that, in many cases, students rush through science activities and fail to monitor or check their understanding. By sketching their ideas, students are required to construct their own understanding and interpretation of the concepts, and are able to check their understanding.

Kevin McElhaney (McElhaney & Linn, 2008) was also interested in how students interpret simulations, particularly those designed to help them make connections between everyday events and basic science principles. He developed a new simulation of automotive airbags in order to connect to the basic principles of relative velocity. Airbags can be dangerous for small children and short persons because they tend to be seated closer to the front of the car. In a collision, the short driver will lurch forward toward the onrushing airbag from a closer starting point than the tall driver, with the possibility of injury if the expanding airbag is encountered before it has fully deployed.

For physical science students, the airbag scenario can be described as a problem of relative velocities, where two objects are moving toward one another from some initial separation. McElhaney developed a simulation where students explore this problem by varying the distance between a driver and the airbag, as well as several other variables. The WISE "Airbags" project guides students through explorations and discussions of airbag safety, including experimentation with the simulation to determine the conditions under which airbags are safe (see Figure 6.4). Students experiment with the simulation by setting the distance between the airbag and the passenger, the speed of the vehicle, and the amount of time it takes for the bag to begin deploying (which is related to the car's "crumple zone").

In his initial studies, McElhaney observed that there was a negative correlation between the number of experiments performed by students and the quality of the experiments. In order to get students to plan and interpret their experiments more carefully, McElhaney introduced some pre-experiment activities. He asked students to in-

Figure 6.4. This image illustrates how students experimented with the WISE "Airbag Simulation" in order to determine airbag safety. The students were able to vary the distance between the airbag and the passenger, the speed of the vehicle, and the amount of time it takes for the bag to begin to deploy.

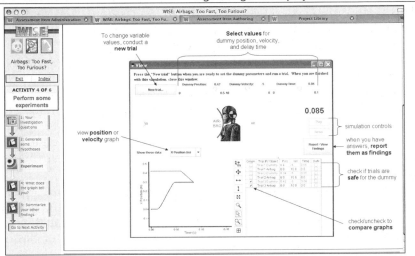

dicate which variable they were investigating and then to specify the purpose of their experiment. In this comparison study, McElhaney found that students who were supported in the planning process—that is, students who were asked to indicate which variable they were investigating and what their research question was—conducted fewer experiments but were more successful. This condition was compared with the open-ended situation where students who conducted large numbers of experiments were quite unsuccessful. Thus, requesting students to articulate their goals before conducting experiments meant that students conducted better experiments and learned more.

These three examples of comparison studies illustrate the importance of helping students become more reflective in using simulations and experiments, resulting in greater insights into the science topics they are studying, as well as the experimentation process. The comparison studies are valuable to several of the audiences named above, including curriculum designers who can benefit from the instructional patterns revealed by all three studies, researchers who can critique the findings and inform their own subsequent studies, and even policymakers who can see that not all simulation activities are of equal value.

Research Comparing WISE with Typical Instruction

School principals and policymakers often ask researchers about the relative value of technology-enhanced and typical instruction. This is an interesting question, in part because it is quite difficult even to define typical instruction, and just as difficult to measure its effectiveness. WISE comparison studies do not tell us whether teaching with WISE is more effective for a certain topic than teaching without WISE. This would involve a level of controlled experimentation that is difficult, if not impossible, in education. For example, if one teacher uses WISE and another uses a second alternative method, any differences we measured between their students could be a result of the fact that there are differences between the teachers themselves. Alternatively, if we use the same teacher for both methods (in order to control for such teacher differences), how can we decide which method should come first? How could we keep one method from affecting the teacher's understanding and application of the other? In general, educational studies that compare one method with another have great difficulty controlling for all possible confounding variables.

WISE has attempted to compare typical instruction with WISE instruction to ascertain the benefit of WISE for student learning. One way that we have approached this challenging question is through cohort comparison studies, which involve testing students in a set of classes at the end of their academic year and recruiting teachers who taught those students to implement a different curriculum the following year.

By having the same teachers teach their typical curriculum followed by the WISE curriculum, this experimental design controls for the possible confounding effect of the teacher, mentioned above. In addition, by having the teacher teach a new cohort of students in the same school, the characteristics of students are held relatively constant. There could be some variations from year to year, but overall, students within a given school are likely to be similar from one year to the next. Finally, teachers in a cohort comparison study can be compared in terms of their instruction before they began using WISE and their instruction that includes WISE.

We conducted a cohort comparison study to evaluate the impact of WISE modules that were designed for topics in 6th- through 12th-grade (ages 10–17) science courses. We recruited teachers from schools across the United States. In the first year, students in all the schools took an annual assessment at the end of the year, after having participated in the typical version of their school's curriculum. The next year, a new group of students engaged in the innovative curriculum using WISE, and received the same end-of-year assessment as the previous cohort.

We compared the performance of the two student cohorts on the end-of-year test and found that students in the WISE cohort performed about one-third of a standard deviation higher than students in the typical cohort, across all six science topics (see Figure 6.5). In middle school,

Figure 6.5. Gains on End of the Year Test in Cohort Comparison Study. We compared student performance on a set of Knowledge Integration assessments that tested students' ability to make connections between topics.

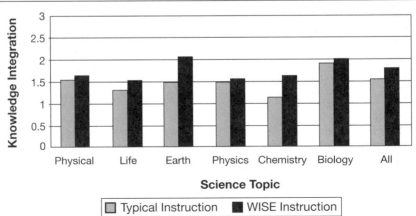

WISE projects addressed topics in Earth science, life science, and physical science. In high school, WISE projects addressed topics in biology, chemistry, and physics. This result shows that technology-enhanced inquiry projects in key science topics can be successful and can enable students to outperform their peers who experience typical instruction.

WISE STUDENT SUCCESS

In conclusion, WISE comparisons studies—those comparing different versions of a WISE project and those comparing typical instruction to WISE instruction—provide evidence that WISE projects are effective instructional materials. They demonstrate that revisions to the design of WISE projects result in more effective curriculum, and that students who participate in those projects outperform their peers who receive typical instruction. Thus, whether you are studying life science, Earth science, chemistry, or physics, WISE projects improve your understanding of science.

RECOMMENDED READINGS

Chang, H-Y. (2008). *Review of research on dynamic visualizations in science learning.* Proceedings of the 8th International Conference of the Learning Sciences. International Society of the Learning Sciences, Inc., Utrecht, The Netherlands, pp. 3-226–3-227.

> This paper synthesizes the findings from research exploring the value of dynamic, interactive scientific visualizations. Visualizations improve learning outcomes. In addition, when visualizations are embedded in instructional patterns, students benefit more from using them.

Linn, M., Lee, H-S., Tinker, R., Husic, F., & Chiu, J. (2006). Teaching and assessing knowledge integration in science. *Science, 313*, pp. 1049–1050.

> This paper compares two cohorts of students taught by the same teachers. The typical cohort followed the usual curriculum and the inquiry cohort used the WISE materials. The inquiry cohort was more successful than the typical cohort.

McElhaney, K. W., & Linn, M. C. (2008). *Impacts of students' experimentation using a dynamic visualization on their understanding of motion. International perspectives in the learning sciences: Creating a learning world.* Proceedings of the 8th International Conference of the Learning Sciences. Utrecht, The Netherlands: International Society of the Learning Sciences, Inc.

> This paper shows that the quality of student experimentation varies depending on the instructional conditions. Students who do more comprehensive experiments learn more.

CHAPTER 7

Teaching with WISE

After the intensive process of curriculum design, classroom trials, and iterative refinements described in Chapter 5, a new WISE curriculum project is finally ready for use in the classroom. This chapter is concerned with the role of the teacher: What kinds of things must teachers do in order to help WISE succeed, and how can WISE help transform the classroom? We discuss how WISE can help teachers add new forms of interaction among students, peers, and instructors, and thereby add new opportunities for teachers to learn about their students. We also discuss the role of the WISE technology in supporting teachers before, during, and after their enactment of a curriculum project.

We begin by describing the experiences of Mr. K, who was the very first teacher to use WISE in his own classroom. By observing and participating as he honed his practice, we developed an understanding of how WISE really worked within a science classroom. These experiences informed our design of several technology tools for teachers, and also helped us understand the professional development trajectory that science teachers could follow in adopting new methods of inquiry and technology.

TRANSFORMING A SCIENCE CLASSROOM WITH INQUIRY AND TECHNOLOGY

When we first introduced Mr. K to WISE in 1997, he was already a veteran of several previous research partnerships with our group, including KIE and CLP (discussed in Chapters 3 and 4). At the time, he was in his third decade of teaching and had a very high comfort level with of the use of inquiry and technology approaches. Still, WISE was offering something new: complete, well-designed curriculum projects delivered through a Web interface, providing all materials to students, prompting them for reflections, and guiding them to use the appropriate tools for various tasks. Mr. K had been a member of the design partnerships that created the first WISE curriculum projects, so he was quite familiar with all aspects of the technology and materials. However, he was not familiar with what it would mean to enact these materials in his classroom. None of us was! We were all rather uncertain about what Mr. K's experience would be as a teacher using WISE, and how this new format would affect his interactions with students.

Before a teacher can enact any new inquiry lesson, it must be integrated into his or her existing curriculum. This will typically require some redesign of the broader curriculum unit in which the new lesson will be situated (e.g., "biodiversity," or "forces and motion"). The typical science course in North America is made up of between two and four of these major units, each consisting of many individual lessons that address specific concepts. In the biodiversity unit, for example, there may be lessons on habitat, food chains, predator-prey relations, populations, invasive species, and so on. It is the teacher's job to make sure that the lessons within these curriculum units are coherent, gradually introducing new topics that build on previous ones.

Since WISE projects often address a mixture of topics that may previously have been introduced by the teacher across several lessons, this process of integration may be challenging. When should the WISE project occur within the unit? What prior knowledge must students have before they engage with the project? The teacher may have to make revisions to several preexisting lessons—shortening some, eliminating others, and even adding topics occasionally to make sure that the WISE project flows well within the science course. Unless such attention is given to embedding the WISE project within the wider curriculum unit, students may experience the project as being disconnected from the other lessons, and teachers may not feel that it fits well within their course.

Since Mr. K was a member of all the authoring partnerships that were creating the first WISE projects, he was able to work concurrently on integrating those projects into his 8th-grade (age 13) physical science course. Among the first WISE projects to run in his classroom were "Sunlight, SunHEAT" and "How Far Does Light Go?" Because these two projects addressed topics relating to Mr. K's energy unit, he revised that unit by removing some elements, reducing others, and creating short bridging activities. The bridging activities were designed to help students make connections from the previous topics that would lead into the WISE project. For example, to bridge into the "Sunlight, SunHEAT" project, Mr. K developed an activity where he asked students to discuss their experiences walking on black pavement or white sidewalks in the summertime. He asked why the black pavement was so much hotter than the white sidewalk and encouraged students to discuss their detailed ideas about the absorption of light. What happens when the light was absorbed? Why do you think dark colors absorb more light than light colors? These discussions also helped Mr. K get some insights into what his students were thinking, in relation to this topic.

Mr. K's classroom was a good setting for our first trials of WISE, as it was equipped with enough computers that students could work together in pairs. The physical space within the classroom was configured with tables set into clusters so that students faced one another, allowing a social atmosphere that contrasts with other configurations that serve to isolate students from peers (see Figure 7.1). Our group provided comprehensive technology support, diagnosing software or hardware problems, upgrading software, and making sure that all the computers and networks were running smoothly. The Web was still relatively new in 1997, and this level of intensive support was necessary in order to ensure that the only obstacles to Mr. K's enactment of WISE were pedagogical in nature.

Getting Started in the Classroom

When the day finally arrived for our first classroom trials of WISE, the first thing we noticed was the need for better login procedure for

Figure 7.1. Mr. K's Classroom. Students' desks are assembled into pods of four computer desks facing inward. Two students work at each desk, resulting in eight students per pod. Internet cables and power supplies are dropped from the ceiling at the center of each pod. This configuration supports an interactive teaching style and gives high visibility from all parts of the room.

students. In these preliminary trials, such matters of end-user interface were not urgent, because there were educational researchers on hand who could help get students registered and into the proper location on the WISE server. But it quickly became apparent that teachers would need very reliable registration systems and classroom management tools, and we began taking notes about the details of Mr K's experience. Based on such observations, we began designing a set of online supports and materials, which led us to the first versions of the WISE Teacher's Portal, described briefly in Chapter 2. We will provide more details about these teacher tools later in this chapter.

New Ways of Interacting with Students

As Mr. K got under way with WISE, one thing that we noticed right away was a dramatic increase in the time that was available for him to interact with students during class. Because the WISE project was helping to scaffold student activities, he had much more time to move around the classroom and engage in focused and often sustained discussions with small groups of students. Of course, it took Mr. K a while to find effective ways of using this time, and as he improved his techniques, we began to realize just how essential the teacher's role was in the enactment of a WISE project.

At first, we had interpreted the teacher's role as one of "guide on the side" who would monitor how students were progressing and respond to any confusion. However, we soon learned that WISE works best if the teacher acts as a "leader from within" who not only monitors students but actively engages them, helps them to synthesize their views, and maintains a dynamic process of exchange within the classroom. We began to recognize that WISE can provide scaffolding for more than just student activities. It can also help to scaffold teacher-student interactions.

With Mr. K's help, we began to study the kinds of interactions that were enabled between students and teachers within a technology-enhanced learning environment. We found that there were new opportunities for teachers to learn about student ideas. For example, in the WISE "Sunlight, SunHEAT" project, students use computer-based temperature probes to graph the temperature of two small cups—one painted black and one painted white—that are filled with water and placed directly under a bright lightbulb. Students are asked to graph their prediction of how the temperatures of the two cups will change over time using the WISE drawing tool. Mr. K was surprised that some students actually predicted that the temperatures of the water in the two cups would increase exponentially, approaching an infinite value, as shown in Figure 7.2.

Figure 7.2. "Sunlight SunHeat" Predictions. This figure illustrates an experiment that is used by students to measure the conversion of light energy to heat energy, as part of the WISE "Sunlight, SunHEAT" project. Thus, one of the features of WISE is that it can scaffold students in offline activities as well.

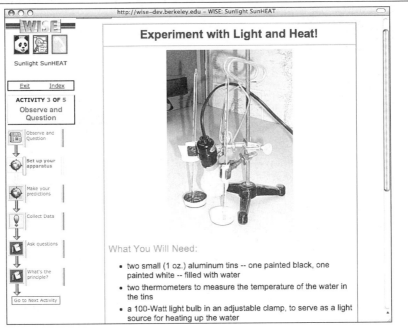

This example clearly illustrates how WISE can reveal student ideas to the teacher, who would be rightfully concerned about any such prediction.

Mr. K was quite good at learning from his students. When he encountered one pair of students who revealed some interesting ideas, such as those of the infinite temperature prediction, he would spend some time talking with them, in order to understand their reasoning, as well as to help them make progress (see Figure 7.3). For example, using the students' WISE drawing as a teaching tool, he might engage the students in discussing their predictions, asking: What would your graph predict for the temperature of the water after 40 minutes, 4 hours, or 4 days under the lightbulb?

If he noticed several groups of students making the same kind of prediction, Mr. K would interrupt the class to hold a more protracted discussion. After getting everyone's full attention, he would describe how he had noticed many students constructing their temperature graphs in an interesting way. He would then ask a series of probing questions to the whole class, encouraging discussions among peers. In

Figure 7.3. Mr. K Interacting with Students. WISE enables teachers to interact more deeply with students during class time, allowing them the time and space to walk around the room and providing visible evidence on students' computer screens that allows the teacher to learn more about how students are thinking.

this way, WISE offered Mr. K a tool that could help reveal his students' ideas and enable discourse about important topics. He would employ similar techniques to "slow the class down" as students progressed through WISE, pausing everyone occasionally to hold spontaneous whole-class discussions with the aim of making sure that students were seriously engaged with the ideas underlying the curriculum.

Because students' ideas are captured and made visible on their computer screens, WISE provides a means of formative assessment, allowing teachers to respond nimbly to student ideas and to change the flow of instruction accordingly. Formative assessment is one of the key challenges presented to teachers in their pre-service preparation courses, but it is very difficult for new teachers or even veteran ones to practice. WISE lends itself quite naturally to such assessment, allowing the teacher to become more of a tutor who works with students directly in helping them develop their ideas. This approach helps the teacher develop a much richer understanding of how students learn within the specific topic domain, and what kinds of misconceptions they may possess.

The capability of WISE to provide the teacher with "real-time feedback" about student ideas can also support new ways of engaging students in collaborations with their peers. For example, after viewing several students' work during one WISE activity, Mr. K would occasionally send one pair of students over to the workstation of another pair who had interpreted matters in a different fashion, so the two groups could exchange ideas. Of course, he would keep his eye on how this exchange progressed, in order to guide it forward productively. Without a high degree of general teaching experience and classroom savvy, Mr. K would have missed many such opportunities to engage with students and would not have been able to coordinate such impromptu interventions.

When WISE is used by the teacher as a means of creating an inquiry-oriented community within the classroom, it offers a valuable lens into student thinking and provides a source of powerful discussion topics related to pivotal cases or controversial evidence. If the teacher is not prepared to engage with WISE in this fashion, the knowledge integration processes that are at the heart of our curriculum designs will likely be lost.

The interactive style of teaching that characterizes a knowledge integration approach is quite intensive, compared with lecture or hands-on lab activities. After five or six consecutive periods of working intensively with students as they engaged with the WISE project, Mr. K would often comment on how challenging it was to teach with WISE. Even though he was tired at the end of the day, however, Mr. K would usually hold a final discussion with the educational researchers about how things had gone during the day, which materials had been successful, and what might be improved. During these reflections, the team would open students' work in the WISE Teacher Portal to get a sense of how students had responded to the materials. We would consider the next day's activities, trying to anticipate where students might be challenged, and what last-minute changes might help Mr. K respond to those challenges. These end-of-day reflections would invariably lead to improvements in the materials, as well as to Mr. K's abilities to help students gain the full benefits of the curriculum.

SUPPORTING TEACHERS WITH WISE TECHNOLOGY

The close collaboration with Mr. K in the early trials of WISE helped us begin to understand the role of the teacher in a knowledge integration curriculum. Based on what we learned, we developed a technology environment to help teachers who do not have Mr. K's experience with research partnerships or the level of technical and pedagogical support that he enjoyed in his classroom. Although technology tools are not sufficient in themselves to help teachers develop expertise in the knowledge integration approach, they provide important scaffolding for teachers as they try out new methods. Without a basic level of support, it is doubtful that any teacher could succeed in using WISE as a method of knowledge integration. The WISE Teacher's Portal, discussed next, was designed to provide this basic kind of support.

Supporting Classroom Management: The Teacher's Portal

The first set of tools that we created for the WISE Teacher's Portal were devoted to helping teachers manage their students before, during, and after they participate in a WISE project. We started by making an easy "Getting Started" document that provides the specific details about how to use WISE. One of the most vexing issues in using WISE is that a teacher's students needed to be linked to his or her account in the database. If students simply registered for WISE without linking to a specific teacher, they would not be able to know which project their teacher had set up for them to run. Nor would the teacher be able to find the project work from his or her students among the students of every other teacher who was using that project. Thus, we needed some way for students to find their teacher's name or identification number from among the many teacher accounts in WISE (currently more than 20,000). To achieve this, we decided on an approach called the "Student Registration Code," a unique alphanumeric "key" that teachers receive when they sign up for WISE. Teachers must provide this key to students when they are registering for WISE, and understanding this process can be a source of initial confusion.

Although a Student Registration Code was essential, it was nonetheless challenging for many teachers who were doubtful that they could remember the procedure of giving their students the Registration Code, guiding them through the login, and into the WISE Student Portal. We responded to this challenge by creating a Management area in the Teacher's Portal, shown in Figure 7.4. Here, teachers can quickly locate their Student Registration Code and follow a link to the Getting Started page, in case they can't recall some aspect of the procedure to get students logged in.

When students sign up for WISE, they are asked for their teacher's Student Registration Code. Once they enter this information and receive their accounts, the WISE portal links each student with the proper teacher and presents them with whichever WISE project their teacher had selected for use. Similarly, when teachers go to the assessment tool (described below) they will only see their own students' responses, drawings, and other data.

Another tool provided in the Management area of the WISE portal is the Setup Assistant, which allows teachers to login to every computer in their classroom or lab and confirm that it has sufficient software to

Figure 7.4. The Teacher's Portal includes several menus. The Management Menu (shown in the image) helps teachers manage class rosters and student accounts, set up WISE project runs, monitor how students are grouped together, detach students from classes, and change student passwords.

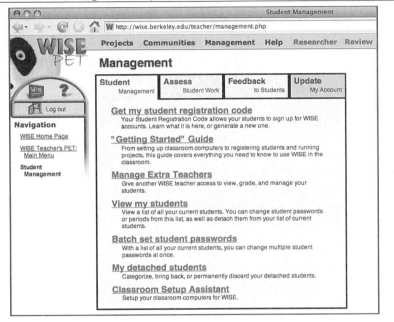

run WISE. Additionally, teachers can access a list of all their students, where they can change passwords, move students from one class period to another, or detach a student from their list altogether. Finally, teachers can add another teacher or mentor to their account, allowing that person permission to see their students' work, as well as all other management activities. These features of the WISE Management area provide detailed support for teachers who might otherwise not feel confident enough to risk enacting WISE in their classroom.

Supporting Assessment of Student Ideas

The next area that we designed for the WISE Teacher's Portal was aimed at supporting the assessment of student ideas. We needed to help teachers access students' reflection notes, drawings, arguments, concept maps, online discussions, and many other forms of work that occur within WISE projects. Teachers are extremely busy, and have limited time to spend examining this large volume of information. WISE must help them make the most out of whatever time they do have for assessment. Whether they are interested only in assigning grades, or if they want to scrutinize their students' ideas and send them feedback electronically, they must be enabled to easily access student data, assign marks, and give feedback.

In the Assessment area of the WISE portal, teachers can assign grading weights for each step in a WISE project, giving extra weight to steps that they feel are more important, or selecting a sampling of steps for grading (which may or may not be revealed beforehand to their students). To help engage teachers in reflecting about student ideas and knowledge integration, WISE makes it easy for them to view and respond to students' ideas. Teachers can choose to view all student work sorted either by student group (looking at all the data from a certain group of students) or by project step (viewing the work of all students for a specified step in the project). They can set the grading weights to each step and assign grades, as well as provide feedback on every grade. Figure 7.5 shows the WISE grading tool.

Supporting Feedback to Students

The third kind of technology support we developed for teachers was a Feedback area, which aimed to make the WISE portal a more interactive

Figure 7.5. WISE Grading Tool. The image shows a teacher's grading session for the WISE "Mitosis and Cell Processes" project.

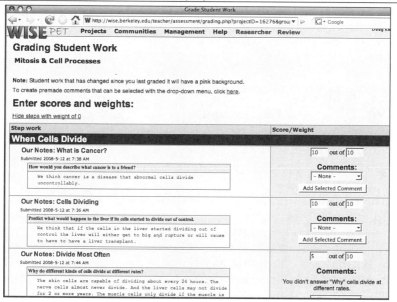

place for teachers and students. Although we have not yet implemented any functionality that enables students to interact with their peers in the portal, we have made some progress in helping teachers send feedback to their students. Figure 7.6 shows a screen capture of the WISE student feedback form, where the teacher is commenting on observations made about one group of students' work in the "Mitosis" project. The teacher notes that the students had only completed reflections about two of the three plants, and had not commented on the differences in the mitosis process among the three plants. In this example, the feedback form was used to encourage the students to complete a reflection on the third plant after they revisited their reflections about the first two. The students received this feedback when they logged in to WISE the next day.

The student feedback area helps the teacher provide formative assessments when the project is actually in use, ensuring that students get the most out of their experience. Receiving such immediate feedback keeps students motivated and reduces surprises at the end of the course. Typically, the teacher would follow up this feedback with face-to-face interaction the following day as the students were working on their project. In this way, the feedback process can also open the doors for productive exchanges between teacher and students during class time.

The process of providing formative assessments has always been a challenging one for teachers, and it is time-consuming by its nature. Technology environments like WISE can facilitate this process, allow-

Figure 7.6. Using the WISE Teacher Feedback Tool, teachers can send students timely messages about their progress within a project. Students receive these messages the next time they login to WISE.

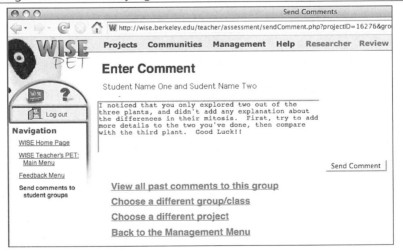

ing teachers to distribute their time efficiently, giving most students quick feedback and spending more time on those who really need it. Teachers often want to send quick notes to students that are not as detailed as the feedback in our example above, but that serve to convey that the teacher has reviewed student work. Examples of such feedback would be: "You're doing great!"; "Please give evidence for your reflections"; or even, "Try to explain the processes of mitosis in more detail." However, with 32 students (thus, 16 pairs) per period, for example, and five separate periods in the day, teachers may be faced with the prospect of giving feedback to 80 or more groups of students in a single evening! Even if the teacher spends only 2 minutes per student group in this example, that amounts to almost 3 hours just to review what students did that day and provide them with simple feedback.

In order to streamline the process of providing feedback and meet teacher needs, we created the WISE Pre-made Comments palette. This tool was developed in response to comments from several teachers who complained about typing similar comments to many students and worried about making typos. We developed a personal space where teachers create "pre-made" comments, proofread their spelling, and attach a digital sticker to reinforce the message (see Figure 7.7). Each teacher can create his or her own personalized palette of comments, drawing on a shared library of comments that was gathered from veteran WISE teachers such as Mr. K. The pre-made comments can help teachers communicate efficiently, increasing the time available to send more detailed feedback to those students who need it while reducing the overall time spent on this important task.

THE CHALLENGES OF ADOPTING WISE

Only the science teacher who is a member of the authoring partnership for a WISE project will be deeply familiar with that project when preparing to use it for the first time. All other teachers will be unfamiliar with the details of its design, and will not have any knowledge about how the project is supposed to succeed with students. For example, the WISE "Deformed Frogs" curriculum was quite successful in addressing topics of habitat, ecosystems, anatomy, and environmental science. The life science teachers who worked on the "Deformed Frogs" design team have restructured their courses to incorporate the WISE materials and continue to use the full sequence of "Deformed Frogs" curriculum in various configurations. However, for teachers who were not part of the design partnership, using the "Deformed Frogs" curriculum is not obvious. To many teachers, WISE curriculum projects

Figure 7.7. Most WISE teachers assess dozens of student groups each night. To reduce the amount of time required to send feedback and to eliminate the possibility of typos, we created the Pre-Made Comment palette. Teachers can create a menu of short comments, as shown in the image, from which they can select a relevant entry to send each particular student group.

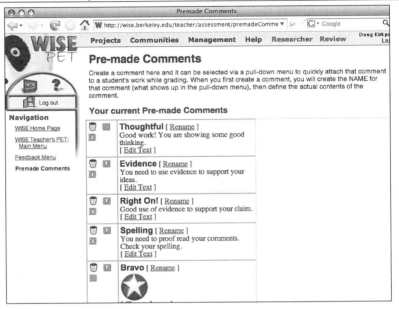

appear to require too much time that must be taken away from their regular instruction, and contain daunting new technology features. It is never easy for teachers to adopt new materials or methods—particularly those involving technology and complex pedagogical approaches. Below, we review some of the most significant challenges confronting teachers who wish to get started with WISE.

Curriculum Standards and Expectations: A Splintered Vision

Teachers receive mixed messages from different sources regarding changes to their instruction. While national standards and policy advisors may call for inquiry, many local school boards are calling for high-stakes accountability and a focus on basic skills. Although such "back to basics" movements are typically confined to the domains of mathematics and literacy, science teachers are nonetheless under constant pressure to "cover the standards." Most state or national science standards consist of an exhaustive list of every major topic within a discipline that was deemed relevant by some official committee.

Because science textbooks are often linked directly to the standards, this can result in the phenomenon of a "Splintered Vision," as revealed by the Third International Mathematics and Science Study (TIMSS). In analyzing results from that study, professor William Schmidt and his colleagues describe how the average number of topics addressed by middle school science textbooks in the United States was 65, compared with an average of 27 in all other nations studied and only 8 topics in the nation of Japan (Schmidt, Raisen, Britton, Bianchi, & Wolfe, 1997). This has led to a common description of the U.S. science curriculum as being "a mile wide and an inch deep," suggesting a serious challenge to science teachers who are asked on the one hand to cover the breadth of all the standards and on the other hand to focus on the depth of inquiry and technology methods.

Technology Access and Support

In addition to the challenge of covering the standards, teachers face additional obstacles regarding technology access and support. In order to make use of technology in a comprehensive fashion such as demanded by WISE, teachers must have access to sufficient resources for their whole class. For science teachers to employ a WISE project, they require access to one computer for every two students, with full-time access to those computers every day for at least 1 full week. In most schools, the technology resources are not reserved by teachers in such coherent blocks, but rather in small blocks of one or two periods on occasional days. The end result of such scheduling can be a very fragmented resource that makes it very difficult for teachers to reserve for a focused multiday lesson. Until technology becomes more universally available to teachers, it is unlikely that they will be able to make any deep commitment to technology-enhanced methods.

Finally, even when technology is available, it may still be too risky for teachers to rely upon. Every teacher knows that technology can be unreliable, which elevates the risk level if technology is a central component of a lesson or unit. It is one thing to show a videotape or use a CD-based adventure after an important lesson is completed, or to have students go to the computer lab to conduct supplemental Web searching. It is quite another to plan an entire lesson that relies on students being online or having access to working computers. Should the technology fail during such a lesson, important topics would not be addressed and the teacher would have to resort to a backup plan. Thus, another important challenge is that of reliability and support. Not only must teachers have access to sufficient technology, but they must be certain that is in good working condition, and there must be someone on hand who can respond to the inevitable problems.

Technology and Inquiry Methods: Risks and Expectations

As we described in Chapter 1, a great deal of educational research has demonstrated the benefits of inquiry activities where students collaborate with peers, manipulate visual representations of ideas, and develop a deep understanding of personally relevant problems. Researchers have explored a wide range of pedagogical approaches to implementing this kind of curriculum, such as encouraging students to develop their own designs or helping them hypothesize and experiment about real-world data. There is now little doubt within the research community that such engaging forms of learning and instruction are a more effective way to help students learn science than the traditional methods of lecture, rote memorization, and problem solving (Edelson, 2001; Quintana et al., 2004; Linn & Eylon, 2006). Inquiry-oriented curriculum is much more likely to inspire students to become lifelong science learners and to think critically about the complex issues they encounter in their lives.

There is also a wealth of support for the integration of technology into science classrooms. Researchers have employed technology tools and materials to provide powerful visualizations and developed software environments that scaffold inquiry learning. The research findings overwhelmingly support the notion of technology as a powerful mediator of learning. In a fortunate coincidence, national and local policymakers also continue to call for the integration of technology within all levels of education in order to help students develop new fluencies with computers and information technology. Moreover, students are quickly developing their own fluencies with such technologies outside the classroom through video and computer games or online social networking sites such as Facebook.

Students must certainly arrive at school expecting to see these kinds of technologies as part of the picture. And they must be disappointed, as educators have made very little progress in finding effective ways to integrate computers or the Internet (diSessa, 2000; Tyack & Cuban, 1995). At present, our schools are not generally successful in providing students the meaningful experience with technology that they expect and deserve, and teachers are justifiably cautious in undertaking the burden of solving this conundrum on their own.

Although positive endorsements of inquiry and technology may provide encouragement, they do not offer any insight into how teachers can develop a coherent approach to integrating such elements into their own classroom. Even WISE curriculum projects, which are carefully designed and highly scaffolded, require teachers to adopt new instructional practices. Most teachers develop their methods over years of successful practice, resulting in a deep pedagogical knowledge about how students learn within specific topics and age levels. Asking teachers to adopt an inquiry approach or infuse technology may well require them to step out of their comfort zone and risk taking their classroom into disarray. Thus, teachers are rightfully hesitant to take on new approaches that are not a close fit with their preexisting approaches.

Yet all teachers must be prepared to undertake some level of risk and experimentation if they wish to add new elements to their instruction. They may not need to develop totally new approaches, particularly if they choose to use a well-designed approach like WISE. But they must still be willing to test out new methods and materials and adapt them for their own students and courses. Indeed, a common message in pre-service instruction is that teachers must experiment with methods and continue to develop their teaching practices. It is also a fairly common expectation that teachers will engage in regular professional development, exploring new methods, reflecting on their practices, and designing new curriculum.

SUPPORTING TEACHERS IN KNOWLEDGE INTEGRATION

With the availability of the WISE Teacher's Portal, and a library of well-designed knowledge integration curriculum, the ingredients are in place for teachers to explore new forms of technology-enhanced instruction. WISE makes it possible for teachers to experiment with different strategies, including formative assessment and feedback, spontaneous interactions with students, and iterative refinement of curriculum based on evidence. Although these are the kinds of practices that teachers are encouraged to apply, it is very challenging to enact sophisticated methods in today's science classroom. A well-designed technology environment such as WISE can provide some scaffolding for everyone in the classroom, including the teacher, and thus support teachers as they undergo their own processes of knowledge integration with respect to the nature of learning and instruction.

Using WISE, teachers will be able to make the processes of knowledge integration more visible to themselves and their students. This will allow them to more easily add new ideas to their own repertoire:

When will it be most opportune to interrupt the class and hold mini-lectures or short discussions? What kind of student work provides the best example to discuss with students? How can students be supported in their collaborations so that they focus on one another's ideas about science? While WISE materials are designed to support such practices, only the teacher can enable them actually to occur. Thus, teachers must begin to sort out their own ideas, defining criteria for deciding which approach is most effective. WISE can also help teachers learn from their faculty peers and mentors, as it provides a clear reference for discussions of pedagogy and practice.

The tenets, processes, and patterns of knowledge integration were detailed in Chapters 3 and 4 of this volume, as they applied to student learning. They are just as relevant for teachers, as they engage in lifelong learning of their craft. We have observed many teachers as they use WISE for the first time. Many teachers use WISE cautiously at first, by extending their preexisting methods for small-group or lab activities. This is a very reasonable and effective strategy that allows teachers to connect new opportunities for instruction to their existing repertoire of ideas. Over time, teachers develop new methods of interacting with students that are directly connected to the WISE learning environment. They stop and chat with students as they work on WISE steps, occasionally asking them to click on a previous step in order to examine and discuss their ideas. They pose questions to extend thinking or challenge assumptions. Over time, teachers learn to anticipate places where students will need more time. They become familiar with dilemmas students face and identify ways to smooth the process of learning.

These are the kinds of practices that Mr. K discovered. These practices strengthen student learning. They illustrate the promise of WISE as a means to achieving an atmosphere of knowledge integration in the classroom. In order to arrive at a level of proficiency in such practices, teachers must be supported in a process of knowledge integration of their own, adding new ideas, sorting out their repertoire, and developing criteria for making effective decisions in the classroom.

The Need for Professional Development

How can we support teachers in the knowledge integration process described above? There are many challenges confronting teachers in their effort to adopt inquiry and technology methods: the pedagogical challenges of designing dramatic new ways for students to learn; the content challenges of adopting a depth of coverage approach within a breadth of coverage system; and the logistical challenges of gaining access to sufficient, reliable technology resources. These challenges provide the backdrop for our discussion of WISE professional development in the next chapter. We cannot expect teachers to adopt WISE if they have no access to computers. Nor can we expect them to address the difficult issues relating to standards and assessment without some contribution from school leadership. However, if the issues of access and support are suitably addressed, it is possible to support teachers as they develop confidence and expertise with new pedagogical approaches. To do so, we must provide professional development opportunities where teachers actively explore those methods, reflect on their experiences, and iteratively refine their practices over several successive trials.

By working closely with teachers like Mr. K as they integrated the earliest WISE projects into their courses, we developed a better understanding of the teacher's role before, during, and after a WISE project was enacted. We developed several areas within the WISE portal to help support teachers in the basic practices of classroom management, assessment, and feedback. Still, we recognize that such tools will only help teachers take the first steps with WISE. The tools reduce confusion, provide new opportunities to engage with students, and reduce the time burden for grading and providing feedback. But for teachers to make further progress in developing a knowledge integration approach to instruction, they require more than a Web site to help them get started. The next chapter explores our efforts to design various forms of professional development for teachers.

RECOMMENDED READINGS

Blumenfeld, P. C., Soloway, E., Marx, R. W., Krajcik, J. S., Guzdial, M., & Palincsar, A. (1992). Motivating project-based learning: Sustaining the doing, supporting the learning. *Educational Psychologist, 27*, 369–398.

  This research article discusses a large professional development program conducted by researchers at the University of Michigan. The program was aimed at enabling teachers to integrate an inquiry approach to science instruction. In this paper, the authors discuss their professional development efforts and evaluate their success.

Davis, E. A., & Varma, K. (2008). Supporting teachers in productive adaptation, in Y. Kali, M. C. Linn, M. Koppal, & J. E. Roseman (Eds.), *Designing coherent science education.* New York: Teachers College Press.

  In this chapter from a recent scholarly volume, Professors Betsy Davis (University of Michigan) and Keisha Varma (University of Minnesota) review two large-scale professional development programs that were associated with two different national centers. The authors seek common principles for designing professional development that allows teachers to adapt innovations for greater success in their own classrooms.

diSessa, A. (2000). *Changing minds: Computers, learning and literacy.* Cambridge, MA: MIT Press.

Andrea diSessa is a professor of cognition and human development at the University of California, Berkeley. In this book, he outlines the demands of a new technological society on students and citizens, and comments on the challenges confronting schools. He advocates a new form of literacy for students to become fluent with information technologies.

Songer, N. B. (2006). Curriculum-focused professional development: Addressing the barriers to inquiry pedagogy in urban classrooms. In R. Floden & E. Ashburn (Eds.), *Leadership for meaningful learning using technology: What educators need to know and do* (pp. 70–86). New York: Teachers College Press.

Nancy Songer, professor of education at the University of Michigan, provides this recent article describing the benefits of a curriculum-focused approach to professional development. Songer draws on her own research and offers synthesizing discussion for the field.

CHAPTER 8

WISE Professional Development

Implementing WISE in the classroom is not easy for teachers, particularly if they have not attempted anything like it before. Teachers require support as they embark on their journey with WISE, where students work in small groups at their own pace on inquiry projects. Not only must teachers enable all students in the class to conduct the inquiry activities, but they are critical to helping students engage with ideas and develop a coherent understanding. Thus, teaching with WISE is more than simply implementing a technology-based curriculum; it often entails adopting a new pedagogical approach with a focus on helping students engage with their ideas. Teachers need experiences that enable their own process of knowledge integration, as they add new ideas about learning and instruction, build coherence in their own repertoire, and develop autonomy with this new pedagogical approach. Ultimately, WISE can help teachers develop coherent understandings about how students learn science with WISE, leading to more effective practices with inquiry and technology.

Just as WISE presents new opportunities for students to engage with science topics, and new opportunities for teachers to engage with their students, it has also provided new opportunities for professional development. It helps make the teacher's ideas about instruction visible, which provides a source for reflection and discourse among peers and mentors. The kinds of interactions with students that were so evident when we observed Mr. K in his classroom were just as clearly missing in the classrooms of other teachers who were first-time users of WISE. This was to be expected, as Mr. K was a veteran teacher who had collaborated in every aspect of our design of the WISE technology environment and inquiry materials. He held frequent discussions with us about how to get the most out of WISE in the classroom, and led the way in evolving the most effective methods.

Even Mr. K was a novice with WISE when we began our first classroom trials. Based on his formative practices, we explored the pedagogical implications of WISE, and how it could be employed to help scaffold teachers as they explore this new form of pedagogy. Working with Mr. K as he developed his own expertise provided us with insight into the trajectory that teachers would need to follow in order to get the most out of their experience with WISE. We realized that professional development would be an important area for WISE research, and began a series of grant-funded projects in which we collaborated with various groups of teachers to help them begin using WISE. This chapter describes some of the lessons we have learned along the way.

Over the past 12 years, we have had a great deal of experience in working with science teachers to help them integrate WISE into their curriculum. Although some challenges, such as technology access, are not within our capacity to resolve, challenges that are related to the pedagogical or curricular dimensions of WISE can be addressed through various forms of professional development. The following sections delineate a typical trajectory for teachers using WISE. They highlight the supports that teachers need to succeed.

A good understanding of this trajectory can inform the designs of professional development programs, school- and district-wide communities of teachers, and new technology environments. We describe three distinct models that have been employed at various stages of the WISE research program, evaluating them in terms of the support they provide teachers and their implications for scaling and sustainable professional development.

THE CO-DESIGN MODEL: TEACHERS AS DESIGN PARTNERS

The most effective, but certainly the least scalable, model that we have found for conveying new pedagogical approaches and enabling teachers to integrate those elements deeply into their professional practice is that of co-design. This method is related to the notion of participatory design that is advocated within many disciplines, such as architecture, engineering, and urban planning. In participatory design, members of the community for which an innovation is to be designed are engaged throughout the design process (Spinuzzi, 2005). This method can be applied to a new building, a computer software application, or a school science curriculum. In the case of a new building, the architect would become deeply familiar with the community for which the building was intended, and the potential occupants of the building would participate in design meetings. At the design meetings, specific features and functions of the building would be determined. In the case of curriculum or assessments, this method has been advanced under the name of "co-design" (Roschelle, Penuel, & Shechtman, 2006), emphasizing the notion that teachers are essential members of the design team. Much more than just conveying the new ideas or approaches to a teacher, the co-design method involves a very deep level of participation by the teacher in planning and designing the new approaches.

In essence, we use this model in our WISE design partnerships (see Chapter 5). As described earlier, teachers in these partnerships are deeply engaged in every stage of the process, allowing them to become intimately familiar with the theoretical framework, the curriculum content, all the technology elements, and any ideas about classroom interactions that were discussed within the partnership meetings. Although the co-design approach would be too costly to serve as a scalable method of professional development, it does provide a useful way of understanding the trajectory of a teacher who learns to use WISE and adopt a pedagogical perspective of knowledge integration. By clarifying this trajectory, we can inform the development of a more practicable model that could support a wider audience of teachers.

One example of a teacher who engaged in co-design was Mr. W, the 5th-grade teacher who was a member of the "Space Plants" partnership introduced in Chapter 6. Mr. W made regular contributions to the development of curriculum materials and served as the voice of authority concerning how 5th-grade students learn science. The participation of Mr. W ensured that the group's final product would be well suited for students in his classroom and a good fit for his style of teaching. For example, Mr. W felt that his students respond better to a curriculum where small amounts of time are given each day to a mix of projects from the various major topics that he must address, including language, math, science, and humanities. He argued that his students would respond better if they engaged with WISE in smaller lessons that were interleaved with the rest of his curriculum. This resulted in a longer overall duration for the "Space Plants" projects, which he stretched over a 12-week span when the projects might ordinarily have required only 2 or 3 weeks if they had been delivered in a more intensive approach.

Thus, Mr. W's participation in the WISE authoring partnership was instrumental to the outcome of the "Space Plants" curriculum— but how did this co-design process provide him with professional development relating to the knowledge integration approach? Below, we examine three phases of the process that we feel are important to any teacher's trajectory in adopting the new pedagogical techniques that come with using WISE: first, planning, where the teacher makes important decisions relating to the way the WISE project will fit within his or her overall curriculum; second, enactment, where the teacher implements the plan, including productive reflections and formative assessments along the way; third, critical evaluation and revision, in which the teacher looks back on how the process went, how students were affected, and what might be improved to help better promote knowledge integration the next time. These three processes, which were also discussed in Chapter 5 (in relation to curriculum authoring) can offer a basic framework for the design and evaluation of many different professional development programs.

Planning

Before Mr. W ever tried out WISE in his classroom, he benefited from participating in the authoring process, discussing the flow of the activities and the way his own group of 5th-grade students would learn about the specific topic area of plant growth. During this time, he was learning about the WISE technology, including the WISE portal. On the first day of the lesson when he asked students to login to WISE, Mr. W was quite familiar with all aspects of the technology, the curriculum, and the theoretical basis of knowledge integration. His experience reflects the first aspect of teaching that we feel is important to a teacher's success with WISE: planning and preparation. Perhaps the single most important thing a teacher can do when trying to enact new methods or materials is to carefully plan and prepare the lesson.

The kind of preparation experienced by Mr. W goes a bit farther than just reviewing the materials in advance and making a lesson plan. He was also engaged in thinking about what ideas students would bring to class and how the various materials and activities within the project would connect with what students know and how they learn. This more challenging aspect of preparation benefits from collaborative discussions and planning with peers. Because planning time is a scarce commodity for most teachers, particularly once the school year is under way, WISE professional development must help teachers make the most out of any time they do commit to this phase.

Enactment

Once a teacher begins enacting the WISE lesson, he or she is in a position to learn a great deal about how students think about the science topics. As we saw in the case of Mr. K, the teacher is free to move about the room and interact with students who are engaged with WISE. The challenge is to know what to look for in such interactions, and to develop some expertise in interacting with students. Of course, some teachers are quite good at conducting such exchanges with students because of the teachers' prior experiences with inquiry methods, hands-on labs, and other engaging forms of curriculum. Others are less familiar with these kinds of deep interactions in their classroom, and may not gather as many insights, initially, from their time walking the classroom floor. Because the knowledge integration framework applies to teachers' learning as well as students', we acknowledge the importance of providing teachers with authentic interactions with their own peers or mentors where they can sort out their own ideas about pedagogy and practice. Ideally, such exchanges would occur in the classroom during the use of WISE, allowing immediate reflections at the end of the class period or even during the class, as time allows.

As an elementary school teacher, Mr. W already embraced a dynamic, interactive style in his classroom and was naturally inclined toward the kinds of deep interactions with students that Mr. K had demonstrated. Even so, he benefited from the opportunities to reflect about his experiences and observations that came from interactions with the other members of the "Space Plants" partnership. The educational researcher, Michelle Williams, was often present in his classroom during the times when he was using WISE. This allowed the two of them to reconcile their insights about the effectiveness of various curriculum elements and the responses of students to certain ideas. Experience and insight gained through feedback from students and reflective discussions with peers or mentors is a valuable aspect of WISE professional development.

Critical Evaluation and Revision

Critical evaluation and revision is a third dimension of WISE teaching practice, where the teacher reviews student achievements and experiences, reflects about the effectiveness of specific features or materials, refines the curriculum for the next set of students, and (ideally) repeats the process over several consecutive offerings of their course in order to evaluate whether the revisions resulted in improved performance or experiences for students. In this way, teachers become active researchers within their own classroom, gradually improving the curriculum and, in the process, learning about how their students learn and how to get the most out of WISE.

Of course, reflection and revision of curriculum is a goal held by most teachers, and is encouraged by pre-service instruction that advocates "action research," evidence-based curriculum (where student achievement provides a source of evidence for teachers' subsequent decisions), and formative assessment. However, this kind of active, iterative investigation of curriculum is quite difficult for teachers to attempt, as they must contend with the many constraints of today's classrooms. The WISE technology environment can facilitate the process by capturing all student responses, making those responses readily available for critical evaluation, and supporting revisions to the curriculum within the authoring tool.

Even with the technology scaffolds provided by WISE, critical evaluation and refinement requires a substantial commitment from teachers, who will need to gain some experience in these practices before they become adept. Mr. W was fortunate to have the ongoing collaboration with the WISE researcher, Michelle Williams, who was also a veteran elementary school teacher. Michelle was present within Mr. W's classroom during all of the WISE activities, which allowed the two of them to discuss the curriculum as it transpired. Most important, this allowed them to jointly identify which elements within the WISE project would be the most important or diagnostic of student ideas (Williams et al., 2004). After class, the two would login to the WISE Teacher's Portal and examine student responses, and were often surprised by what they found there. Several times, it was evident that the WISE materials had not been well understood by students and needed to be revised.

Other WISE components, such as the reflection journal, revealed that students were thinking about the topics in ways that had not been anticipated—even by these two veteran teachers! For example, in several cases, it was revealed that when prompted by reflection notes about the topic of plant growth, many students possessed an anthropomorphic view where plants are attributed human traits such as volition, desire, and other emotional states. These student ideas were surprising to both the teacher and the mentor, and WISE was able to reveal their presence in the classroom. Thus, WISE exposed student thinking to the teachers, challenging some of their assumptions about the ideas that students are bringing into the curriculum. As a result of examining his students' responses within WISE, Mr. W began to develop a better sense of how his students thought about science topics related to plant growth, such as light, photosynthesis, and osmosis. Thus, the process of critical evaluation and revision led to improvements in the WISE materials, as well as in how teachers prepared for and delivered the curriculum.

THE WORKSHOP MODEL:
TEACHERS AS CURRICULUM CUSTOMIZERS

Although the sustained, intensive experience of the co-design model certainly results in professional development for those few teachers who are able to participate in that fashion, this approach was not suitable for reaching a larger audience of teachers. The WISE research group would not have the time and resources to replicate the co-design model in more than a handful of cases. Nor would most science teachers have the significant amount of time to invest in the authoring partnership model, with so many planning and design meetings. Ideally, we wanted to offer WISE to science teachers as a fairly straightforward resource for adding inquiry and technology to their classrooms.

Over the years, more than 20,000 teachers have registered for WISE (see Figure 8.1), and while many have managed to enact a WISE project (see the student data in Figure 8.1), it is not clear how well these teachers have succeeded in the knowledge integration approach. We would like to determine effective ways of supporting teachers from a range of different backgrounds and settings in a knowledge integration approach to professional development.

Certainly, our goal in developing WISE was to offer it to a large number of teachers, but how could we enable those teachers to engage with WISE in the manner of Mr. K or Mr. W? Our earlier partnerships taught us about the opportunities that can be gained from working with WISE, and the reflective processes required for teachers to establish an atmosphere of knowledge integration in their classrooms. We want to design WISE professional development approaches that help any teacher follow such a trajectory, including the basic elements of planning and preparation, feedback and reflection, and critical evaluation.

Ideally, we can arrive at a more condensed format than that of a co-design partnership. Indeed, the protracted effort of the design

Figure 8.1. An Increasing Number of WISE Teachers and Students. In the initial years of WISE, most usage was restricted to our partnerships with teachers like Mr. K and Mr. W. Later, we began running teacher workshops and school partnerships, and ultimately we began collaborating with school districts. Throughout this time, many teachers simply found WISE on their own.

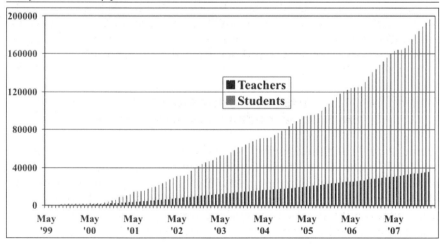

partnership would not seem to be necessary for teachers who simply wanted to adopt an existing WISE project, such as "Sunlight, SunHEAT," "Deformed Frogs," "Wolves in Your Backyard," or "Space Plants." After all, the authoring partnerships have already completed the time-intensive process of designing those projects, testing them in classrooms and refining them based on student evidence. New teachers would only need to understand the material, integrate it into their courses, and learn how to enact WISE. Thus, we began experimenting with a more focused workshop model that would engage teachers in a short, intensive professional development experience that emphasizes planning and preparation, and hopes to provide teachers with their own knowledge integration experience.

Since 1997, we have conducted dozens of WISE teacher workshops, working with diverse groups of teachers who joined these events for a variety of reasons: a common interest in a science topic such as frogs or wolves, an association with a professional meeting like the National Science Teachers Association, or because they were from the same school district that was hosting a professional development event. Several different workshop formats have been developed, with overall durations ranging from several hours to several days. In all of these events, we maintained a focus on replicating the basic professional development model that was identified in our co-design partnerships and engaging teachers in a process of knowledge integration.

We interpreted the process of teacher professional development in terms of the four tenets of the knowledge integration framework: Teachers must be provided with accessible materials that are personally relevant, the materials must make ideas visible to teachers, activities should be collaborative so that teachers learn from their peers, and the workshop should foster a perspective of autonomous lifelong learning. Below, we describe how WISE workshops implemented these tenets of knowledge integration in a generalized version of the workshop, where we assume a one-day format (8 hours, including lunch).

WISE teacher workshops are typically held at national conferences, or during the summer in conjunction with another organization or one of our own grant-funded projects. Because they are held during a time when class is not generally in session, the workshops are inherently focused on planning and preparation. Teachers vary widely in their prior experiences with technology and inquiry, although most have had no experience with WISE. Thus, before we can engage the teachers in preparing to run a WISE project, we must begin with an introduction to our theoretical perspectives and pedagogical approaches, as well as the basic technology systems.

The WISE workshop begins with teachers organizing into small groups according to the grade level and science discipline they teach, such as middle school physical science or high school chemistry. In their small groups, we ask them to discuss the most challenging topics in their courses, including any surprising ideas they have observed in their students. Then we ask all teachers to browse the library of WISE projects and select one that could potentially fit within their existing curriculum. For example, the middle school life science teachers might choose the "Deformed Frogs" project or "Healthy Creeks" (a project where students evaluate the health of a local waterway). It is desirable for all teachers to have their own computers, although we have occasionally conducted workshops with teachers working in pairs at computers.

Making Teachers' Ideas Visible

To help make teachers' ideas visible (the first tenet of knowledge integration), we rely on the WISE student learning environment and authoring system. We begin by asking teachers to work through their chosen WISE project as if they are students (specifically, their own students), which helps them build on the earlier discussion about their students' ideas. Using WISE as if they were students, teachers add reflection notes, draw concept maps, configure models, and build graphs and data tables. Of course, it is not possible for teachers to experience the full depth of activities that would be undertaken by students, as this would require several hours, including possible hands-on or collaborative activities that are not practical for a short workshop. Still, this process helps teachers become familiar with the project, identify the challenges their students would confront, and plan what elements they would like to customize.

Making WISE Relevant and Accessible to Teachers

After exploring their chosen project and thinking about the ideas that students will encounter there, teachers usually identify some aspects of its design that are not a perfect fit to their existing curriculum or to the students in their school. Helping teachers adapt existing projects so that they fit within their courses serves as the main emphasis of the workshop and provides an excellent opportunity to help make the materials more accessible and relevant to teachers (the second tenet of knowledge integration). We engage teachers in discussions about how their students will respond to the ideas and activities within the project, and how the project can be adapted or "customized" to provide a better fit to their overall curriculum, including any local characteristics of their geographical location, their school, or student populations. For example, in customizing the "Healthy Creeks" project, a teacher might want to change the materials so that they refer to a local creek with which the students are familiar. This could include more than just changing the name of the creek that appears within the project. Perhaps there are specific issues that are relevant to the students in that teacher's school, such as agricultural fertilizers that are a common problem in rural areas, or the dirty water that flows from paved surfaces that surround many urban waterways.

By engaging teachers in the process of making these projects more accessible to their students, we hope to make WISE more accessible to the teachers as well. It is important to note that we do not encourage substantial editing of the WISE materials within these workshops, as teachers are new to WISE and might make changes that are inconsistent with the intended pedagogical design. Small customizations are supported, though, as they give teachers an opportunity to build a personal connection to the materials and to think about their students' process of knowledge integration.

Helping Teachers Collaborate with Peers and Mentors

As often as possible within the workshop, we design opportunities for teachers to engage in discussions, reflections, and critical exchanges with peers or workshop leaders (the third tenet of knowledge integration). For example, teachers work closely with a WISE researcher or mentor to develop a customized lesson plan for using the project. Often, teachers recognize that a project would fit better within their curriculum if they made certain changes in the sequencing within their broader course outline, or added a preliminary lesson in a certain topic. For example, a teacher might choose the "Wolves in Your Backyard" project because it offers a good treatment of topics in biodiversity and the role of the top predator, but after looking through the project, the teacher might decide that she would need to revise her existing lesson about food chains and ecosystems, which would immediately precede her use of the "Wolves" project. The workshop was designed to help teachers create such a customized plan for using a WISE project, providing a reflective process for them to deeply consider the ideas within the project and how their students may respond.

Encouraging Teachers' Autonomy

The overall goal of the workshop is to help teachers develop a detailed lesson plan for implementing their WISE project, which includes notes about where students may experience difficulties, and how certain features of the project should be assessed. In a final session, there are demonstrations of how to use WISE on the first day of class, such as helping students sign up for WISE accounts, opening the WISE project in the student portal, and using the assessment tool. The workshop is designed so that every teacher works autonomously (the fourth tenet of knowledge integration) with a focus on developing skills with the technology and familiarity with the curriculum materials. After a full day of such activities, teachers often feel that they are still not fully prepared, but at least they are familiar with the WISE project they want to use, and they have a lesson plan with detailed notes and links to important parts of WISE.

Sustaining Contact After the Workshop

Once a workshop is completed, there is ideally some follow-up contact with WISE researchers or mentors. This is common whenever the workshop was part of a grant-funded project or a larger professional development program, but teachers who are not members of such ongoing programs will receive very little support as they move into the stages of enacting their WISE project and reflecting on their experience. When left to their own devices, teachers often experience difficulties engaging with WISE, and many of them never manage to fully enact their projects, despite the planning they conducted at the workshop.

The reasons that many teachers from these workshops do not implement their WISE lesson plans are closely related to the challenges outlined at the beginning of this chapter. The first reason is lack of access to technology, such as being able to reserve a computer lab for 1 full week of exclusive use. The second is lack of sufficient curriculum time, where the number of days required by the WISE lesson plan is simply too great an investment for teachers who are feeling challenged to cover all the standards in the limited amount of available time. A third challenge that is more relevant to our models of professional development is the lack of support and contact with mentors. The confidence that teachers gained during the workshop may fade by the time they are ready to enact a project, and they may have difficulty remembering all the details about how to use WISE. In contrast, teachers in the WISE authoring partnerships benefited from close collaboration with the educational researcher throughout the preparation, enactment, and revision phases. This was clearly an important factor in those teachers' professional development, and it was just as clearly missing from the experience of our workshop teachers.

Although there is not much that our research group could do to provide teachers with better technology access or more time within their curriculum, it might be possible for us to improve the contact and communication they receive once they are back at school. We have considered various ways of improving our contact and support for new WISE teachers who are not working in close partnership with our group. One interesting possibility is concerned with the use of online communities and peer support networks. In some WISE workshops, the participants were teachers from the same school or school districts, who knew one another and would be in close contact throughout the next school year. We began to think about ways of working with these school communities to establish a more coherent, ongoing relationship. The next section describes a model that can offer sustained support to all the teachers within a school and help them develop as an autonomous professional development community.

THE WISE MENTOR MODEL:
SUPPORTING SCHOOL AND DISTRICT PARTNERSHIPS

A more intensive model of professional development that provides an added level of support for teachers throughout their adoption of WISE is that of the school partnership, where the WISE research group commits to ongoing support of all the science teachers within a certain school. In return, those teachers commit to performing the required steps of planning, enactment, and reflection, and to working closely with a WISE mentor. We have explored this model in conjunction with various funded research projects that required a group of teachers who would implement WISE projects over a period of several years and reflect on their practices. For example, one grant sought to explore the process of teacher customization in greater detail, examining teachers' success with customized projects and how they revised their projects from one year to the next based on student evidence. Another grant investigated the kinds of interactions that occur between new WISE teachers and a mentor from the research group.

Just as in our workshop model, the WISE school partnership model has developed out of previous experiences with schools, and even a few school districts. Some of our partnerships have included only a few teachers from the school, and some have been more comprehensive, involving all science teachers as well as librarians, technology staff, and school principals. Here, we describe a generic model of a school partnership, drawing on an example of an early partnership where Mr. K served as the mentor and every science teacher adopted and enacted a WISE project over a period of several years.

Establishing the Partnership

An effective school partnership typically builds upon a preexisting foundation that began with earlier collaborations or professional connections between the researcher and one or more members of the school community. For example, perhaps the researchers had worked with a science teacher or administrator from the school in a previous project. Or perhaps a single teacher from the school had participated in an authoring partnership or used WISE within a research study. We build on this prior connection, introducing members of our research team to all the science teachers at the school and presenting our proposed partnership at a science department meeting. These early meetings help to define the broad agenda of the partnership and address the concerns of science teachers and administrators. Only after all science teachers and school administrators are in agreement can an effective partnership begin within the school.

One example of a school partnership is that of Frontier Middle School (fictitious name), a suburban school with approximately 1,100 students and three science courses taught by six teachers, with two for each course: Earth science, taught in the 6th grade (age 11); life science, taught in the 7th grade (age 12); and physical science, taught to 8th graders (age 13). Every day, teachers instructed five class periods, each with approximately 30 students, and had one preparation period that varied in what time of the day it occurred (depending on the school's master schedule).

We had been working with one of the Frontier teachers for several years in conjunction with a previous research project. So, when a new research project came up that required the participation of a group of teachers, our teacher collaborator helped us propose the idea to the science department chair and the school principal. We wished to study how Frontier teachers would integrate WISE into their curriculum, reflect on their enactment of WISE projects, and revise their lesson plans based on critical evaluation of how the lesson had gone, including assessments of student understanding.

Once all the members of the science department and administration were in agreement, we began a communication process among all members of the partnership, the teachers as well as the educational researchers. We discussed the goals for science instruction at the school, the ways in which students seem to learn best, and the current state of technology. We outlined the kinds of supports that could be provided by the research group and the level of activity that would be required of the teachers. We also discussed the impact of WISE on the science curriculum, how teachers would address the content standards, and whether a knowledge integration perspective was something they would like to bring into their instruction. We planned to start with a workshop, much like the one described in the previous section, where we would help each science teacher choose a WISE project and develop a lesson plan, as well as to orient teachers to learn about the WISE portal and student learning environment.

Planning

The most important feature of this model is the addition of a mentor, who is essentially a workshop leader who stays in contact with teachers after the workshop, visiting their classrooms before and during their enactment of the lesson, and supporting their participation in all phases of professional development. We recognized that the relationship developed between the mentor and teachers during the workshop would provide an ideal basis upon which to build subsequent contacts, as the mentor would already be familiar with the teacher's lesson plan and everyone could build on the rapport they had already established. The introductory workshop for this partnership, while quite similar to that of previous workshop models, was therefore modified to include new opportunities for mentors and teachers to plan future contacts.

In the Frontier school partnership, we began as usual by introducing the WISE curriculum library to teachers, helping them find the WISE project that best fit with their existing courses. Because there were three science courses taught in the school with two teachers for each, it was decided that the two teachers from each grade would collaborate on making a single lesson plan, as this would allow all students to experience the same curriculum. The 6th-grade teachers decided to use the WISE "Healthy Creeks" project, where students study a local creek and critique different possible sources of pollution. The 7th-grade teachers chose the "Cycles of Malaria," which engages students in debating the most effective approaches to controlling malaria worldwide: vaccine research, pesticides, or social programs. Finally, the 8th-grade teachers selected the "How Far Does Light Go?" project, where students create their own arguments about whether light goes forever or dies out, drawing on various sources of evidence. The two teachers from each grade worked in pairs while the mentor circulated among the three groups, helping in the design of a customized lesson plan.

Because we were working with a small group of teachers who were committed to an ongoing partnership, we were able to organize an initial workshop that was 2 full days in length. This allowed us to spend more time in the planning and preparation and hold detailed discussions about how the selected WISE projects would promote knowledge integration in the classroom. The workshop also included an activity where teachers reflected on WISE assessments by identifying specific steps within their chosen WISE project that would be most challenging for students and thus most productive as a source of feedback and discussion. We helped teachers create a customized set of grading weights for the project and worked on a rubric for how grades would be assigned. Teachers also created a set of comments for their custom feedback palette, which was a helpful exercise in trying to anticipate the comments they might offer students (knowing that this set of comments would be revised with practice).

We spent some time during the final hours of the workshop discussing how the mentor would be involved, which was an important matter for planning and preparation. The Frontier teachers had never worked with a mentor who came into their classroom to help them reflect on instruction. Thus, they had few prior experiences or ideas upon which to build an understanding of how to collaborate productively with the mentor, and most of the teachers were somewhat nervous about being observed. It was important to characterize the role of the mentor as someone who was an expert with WISE but whose goal was to try to understand how each teacher would integrate WISE in his or her classroom. This led to a collaborative relationship where the teacher and the mentor were jointly responsible for developing a successful enactment of WISE and made sure that the mentor was not seen as "an expert coming in from the research group."

The planning and preparation workshop ended with a scheduling activity, as the prospect of six teachers all using the school computer lab for 1 week was a serious challenge for the school's technology resources. Teachers left the workshop with a fairly good idea of how WISE functions, a solid start on their lesson plans, and a sense of confidence that the mentor would be there to help. Every teacher was expected to revisit their lesson plan before classes began and then meet once more with the mentor to set up a detailed plan for the first day of the lesson. For most of the teachers, the lesson included at least one day of preliminary instruction where they would address some topics that they felt were prerequisites for students to fully understand the materials in the WISE project. The mentor made arrangements to visit the teacher's classroom during the day before students would use WISE, so that introductions could be made between the mentor and the students.

Enactment

When the first day of the WISE lesson finally arrived, the teacher introduced the mentor to students as a special expert who would be helping them use a new kind of learning tool. The mentor then spoke briefly about WISE, providing the students with some context: This was a new system that came from research concerned with how to use the World Wide Web in science class. This message made sense to students, who expect the Internet to be a factor in their learning. The mentor then encouraged students to ask questions about WISE and about the specific topic to be addressed by the WISE project they would conduct, thereby demonstrating an interactive style for the teacher.

The mentor actually helped lead the very first class period of the first day, in order to model for the teacher the best way to get students logged in and under way efficiently. The mentor also modeled a style of teaching where he circulated through the room checking in with many groups of students, talking with them about their ideas and occasionally interrupting the whole class in order to give short mini-lectures that were concerned with either the curriculum or logistics of using WISE. There were five class periods that would each go through the same routine, giving the teacher plenty of time to practice in the remaining portion of the day. The mentor remained in the computer lab with the teacher for the entire day, gradually fading his involvement until the teacher was leading the entire process in the final period of the day.

It turned out to be a favorable characteristic of the school day that each science teacher taught five identical periods of the same course, as this arrangement allowed teachers to gradually take more control over each successive class period as the day progressed. Because each new day of class involved new activities in the WISE project, this pattern was repeated, allowing the mentor to model how he helped students interact with WISE and reflect about their ideas. Meanwhile, the teacher circulated among the students as well, trying out new techniques of interacting with students, and learning about how they engage with WISE. Overall, the teachers experienced a greatly reduced level of workload and stress because of the presence of the mentor in the classroom, allowing greater confidence as they experimented with the teaching methods.

During breaks between class periods (approximately 10 minutes) and over lunch, the mentor would check in with the teacher about how things were going, whether there were any questions, and so on.

This ensured a fairly continuous level of dialogue about the WISE curriculum and pedagogy, and helped make sure that any confusion was addressed promptly. At the end of each day, the mentor and teacher would sit down together to quickly review students' performance in that day's WISE activities. They would examine a few student data files in order to get a sense of how students had responded to certain reflection notes, and would look at the work of a few students that they remembered from earlier that day as being either exemplary or problematic. This process allowed the mentor to help the teacher develop a comfort level in working with student materials in the WISE portal as well as to develop a sense of the range of student ideas that appear within the project.

The Frontier teachers varied in how they interacted with students during the WISE instruction. Jim Slotta worked as an educational researcher within this partnership and Mr. K served as the mentor. Slotta (2004) compared the various teachers in terms of their instructional styles. He found that some teachers interacted much more deeply with students, engaging them in discussions about their ideas, while others kept their interactions with students on a surface level, such as by checking that they were not confused and were keeping up with the rest of the class. Slotta observed that some teachers were more experienced than others in the use of hands-on labs, which were oriented toward student investigations and collaborations. Those teachers who were more experienced in the use of such inquiry-oriented labs were also the most comfortable in adopting the interactive style with students during their use of WISE.

Slotta (2004) found that these differences in teaching style resulted in measurable differences in the quality of student contributions, underscoring the importance of the knowledge integration approach in helping WISE curriculum achieve its full potential. However, Slotta also made an even more important observation that the combination of WISE and the mentor was sufficient to ensure the success of all teachers, despite any differences in their initial teaching style. For those with a less interactive teaching style, WISE scaffolded their students with prompts and hints, and the mentor helped model the interactions with students. For those who were less experienced with technology, WISE made sure that their students could easily navigate and receive clearly defined tasks throughout the project, and the mentor helped the teacher become more comfortable with WISE tools and features.

Because the Frontier teachers had entered the partnership with different levels of experience, they responded differently to their first encounter with WISE. Some loved it, while others were more critical. Some teachers treated WISE as "just another lesson," while others felt that it could help them transform their entire curriculum. All the teachers were able to succeed, however, and all felt that WISE was a valuable experience for their students and themselves. The goal of this school partnership was to help all the science teachers mature in their use of inquiry and technology, which would clearly involve different trajectories for different individuals. The next phase of the model where teachers were engaged in reflecting about their experience and revising their lesson plans would prove to be the most important aspect of the model, in terms of the professional development of the participating teachers.

Critical Evaluation and Revision

In the school partnership model, the mentor maintains communication with all participating teachers for the duration of their involvement. One aspect of this communication has to do with supporting teachers' reflections once the WISE project is completed: Was the project a success, in their judgment? Did their students perform well on the relevant portions of any summative assessments, such as the final exam for the course? More important, how did WISE help reveal student ideas that might not otherwise have been seen? Not long after a teacher had finished with the chosen WISE project, the mentor would visit once more to discuss such questions in an interview format. The mentor would also help the teacher identify aspects of the lesson plan that could be revised in the following summer, before the next school year.

An important part of the WISE mentor model is a recurring summer workshop, where teachers come together for 2 days each summer to reflect on their experience in the preceding year and to revisit their curriculum designs. If they are pleased with how WISE worked in their course, teachers might consider further changes to the course design that promote knowledge integration. Perhaps they could resequence some lessons to help students capitalize on learning opportunities, or remove some elements in order to give students more time to think deeply about topics. The specific goal of this annual workshop is to help teachers revise their lesson plan, perhaps adding another WISE project or customizing the first one.

The summer workshop helps teachers plan and prepare their curriculum, informing their revisions with an analysis of student ideas from the previous year. We begin the workshop by presenting teachers with printed excerpts from their students' activities within WISE, chosen carefully by the mentor to reveal interesting student ideas. Teachers collaborate with a peer to reflect on those excerpts, comparing them against their expectations and reflecting on how they might have responded differently during class to help students make better progress.

The workshop also provides an opportunity for teachers to engage in their own knowledge integration regarding how they can use WISE to help students develop an understanding of science topics. Mentors and teachers are reunited, deepening their relationship and preparing for the following school year. They identify some key activities within their WISE project that they will closely observe during the enactment in the coming year, and make a plan to reflect on those activities immediately afterward. Teachers leave the workshop with an improved lesson plan and an expanded vision for their overall curriculum. The annual cycle of planning, enactment, and revision helps them develop a more engaging, rewarding style of instruction and participate in reflective practices.

The Frontier science teachers continued in such a cycle for 3 years, which was the duration of the research study that provided the funding for a mentor. During that time, one science teacher left the department and another was hired, who joined in the process. This partnership succeeded in the sense that all teachers used WISE effectively and showed improvement in their abilities to support knowledge integration among their students. By the end of the first year, the two 6th-grade teachers were working with the mentor to develop a new version of the "Healthy Creeks" project that engaged their students in a data collection activity where they collected and analyzed creek water samples. The 7th-grade teachers had expanded from "Cycles of Malaria," their initial selection of projects, and added a second major lesson that was designed around the "Deformed Frogs" sequence. The 8th-grade teachers continued using "How Far Does Light Go?", but adopted a new curriculum unit on scientific controversy, based on the WISE "Malaria DDT Debate," where students debated evidence about the use of DDT to control malaria worldwide and created an argument to either support or oppose a proposed global ban on the pesticide.

All six Frontier teachers made progress in their interactions with students, and the mentor gradually faded his presence within the school. In the third year, he visited each teacher's classroom only twice: once on the first day of their WISE project to discuss the learning goals of the lesson and introduce WISE to students, and once again just after the lesson was complete to capture their reflections. Interestingly, as this partnership progressed, the students in the school became more comfortable with WISE, just as their teachers did. In the third year of the partnership, the 8th-grade students had already seen WISE in their sixth and seventh year. Slotta (2004) reported on the aggregated effect of students and teachers gaining experience with WISE in a school partnership.

A final summer workshop was held in the third year, where teachers discussed their goals moving forward as a department. Would they continue to use WISE without the support of the research group and the encouragement of the mentor? Over the past 7 years since this partnership officially ended, the school has remained involved with WISE. One of the original partner teachers has retired and another moved away, but currently four of the six science teachers remain actively engaged with WISE. They have run various projects during this time, and some have participated in co-design partnerships. Overall, the science department has become more reflective about student learning as a result of this experience, and the level of engagement and reflection within classrooms is outstanding.

Measuring the Progress of Teachers in Adopting a Knowledge Integration Approach

To document the effects of WISE on teacher practice, we have interviewed teachers and connected their responses to our classroom observations and workshop experiences. These interviews support our observation that, with increased use of WISE, teachers are able to ask more effective inquiry questions. For example, one teacher with whom we worked in a research partnership became very adept at generating new inquiry questions for his class, and even contributed to our own understanding about effective knowledge integration prompts.

Teachers also develop effective techniques for using visualizations. For example, teachers using the mitosis visualization report that they now interrupt the class when students arrive at the point in the WISE project where they encounter that visualization, in order to make sure that everyone understands how to start and stop the animation and interact with it. While this intervention is rather mundane, in the sense that it is concerned only with the procedural aspects of using the visualization, it nonetheless demonstrates an important insight that students will not make good progress in their understanding if they are confused about controlling the visualization.

Teachers also report that they develop insight into the science content related to the WISE projects they are teaching. For example, one teacher recounted that he had deepened his own understanding of the topic through the process of analyzing how his students had come to their own diverse understandings. Through the process of teaching with WISE, teachers develop new practices and new ways of interacting with students, as detailed in Chapter 7. Through classroom observations, teacher interviews, and professional development workshops, we are able to capture teachers' stories, allowing us to tailor our technology tools and professional programs to meet their needs.

IMPLICATIONS AND FUTURE DIRECTIONS

Clearly, the mentored school partnership supports the professional development of participating teachers. It is also a much more intensive, sustained process than the basic workshop model, and involves a substantial investment of time from both teachers and mentors. But as long as the teachers within such a partnership are committed to exploring a knowledge integration approach, this model succeeds in providing the support that teachers require in order to try out new practices and reflect on their experience.

Initially, the mentor model was informed by our observations of teachers working within the co-design partnerships, who received the highest level of support and reflection throughout their experience with WISE. This high level of support and continuous contact is necessary for teachers to feel confident in trying out new practices and reflecting on their students' knowledge integration. But equally necessary is the teacher's own commitment to professional development. One characteristic that is common to all of the co-design teachers is their interest and enthusiasm for the project, which translates directly into engaged and reflective participation in the three phases of professional development. Thus, it is not enough simply to establish a partnership with a school science department, recruit a mentor, and trust that this will lead to professional development of science teachers in the school. Indeed, our research team has experienced other school partnerships where the teachers were not as committed as those of Frontier, and in such cases, the results have been less rewarding.

Because this model involves all or most of the science teachers working within a school, it also reinforces a sense of community among the teachers, who feel that they are "all in this together." Teachers enter into the partnership with varying levels of experience in their prior use of inquiry and technology methods. Some teachers start out with a high confidence level, and are comfortable with an interactive style where students work autonomously. Others are more nervous, as they have tended toward the traditional methods of lecture and scripted labs. Just as science students need to experience opportunities to sort out their ideas about science, teachers need opportunities to develop a rich understanding about how students learn within their topic domain.

WISE has taken some strides in researching these models of professional development, but there is much work remaining. We are investigating the possible benefits of giving teachers more targeted feedback during class, as well as between classes, extending the capabilities that have been provided by the mentor. We are also interested in the potential benefits of establishing online communities of teachers and researchers that employ social networking and the latest in real-time communications (e.g., chat and video or audio connections) to provide support and a sense of identity for members of the community. For example, we hope to establish dynamic curriculum communities where teachers share versions of materials, reflect on best practices, and develop the most effective assessments within specific topic areas. These approaches will build on the models described above, in hopes of establishing professional development communities where teachers develop reflective practices and build deeper social connections among their peers.

Our current projects, described in the next chapter, are aimed at achieving better and more streamlined levels of support and feedback for teachers during their use of technology-enhanced inquiry activities. For example, we have established the center for Technology Enhanced Learning in Science (TELS), which includes several grant-funded projects and more than a dozen researchers who are using WISE in a variety of investigations. This large-scale effort has resulted in several replications of the mentor model, with efforts to reduce the role of the mentor and increase the coherence of teachers working within a school. In the next chapter, we describe several new directions that are emerging from our current work, including new opportunities for teacher supports and professional development.

RECOMMENDED READINGS

Fishman, B., Marx, R., Best, S., & Tal, R. (2003). Linking teacher and student learning to improve professional development in systemic reform. *Teaching and Teacher Education, 19*(6), 643–658.

> This research paper presents a study of teacher professional development, measuring progress in terms of teacher and student learning and making connections to an analytic framework. The study employed a range of measures including teacher reflections, classroom observations, and measures of student achievement.

Penuel, W., Fishman, B., Yamaguchi, R., & Gallagher, L. (2007). What makes profession-al development effective? Strategies that foster curriculum implementation. *American Educational Research Journal, 44*(4), 921–958.

This paper reports on a large research study of 454 teachers who participated in an inquiry science program. It investigates the various factors that are required for teachers to succeed in professional development, with an emphasis on teachers' prior knowledge, the coherence of their professional development, and the amount of time they spend in planning and preparation.

Slotta, J. D. (2004). The Web-based Inquiry Science Environment (WISE): Scaffolding knowledge integration in the science classroom. In M. C. Linn, P. Bell, & E. Davis (Eds). *Internet environments for science education* (pp. 203–232). Mahwah, NJ: Lawrence Erlbaum.

This chapter presents an overview of WISE, and details the research study reported above in Frontier Middle School. It describes two teachers in particular who differed in their initial uses of WISE, and for whom the mentor provided different kinds of support.

CHAPTER 9

Toward the Classroom of the Future

As WISE has progressed along the trajectory described in previous chapters, it has done so against a background of more general development within the world of technology and information science. This chapter summarizes the major dimensions of achievement within WISE, the overall trajectory of the Internet, and how our current research is responding to new opportunities while building on prior achievements.

As more schools and classrooms become connected to the Internet, science teachers find themselves with improved capacity to integrate technology into their courses. And science students are spending an increasing amount of time and creative energy on the Internet before and after class (see Figure 9.1), most certainly wondering when they will encounter such technologies in the classroom. Over a 10-year span, the WISE curriculum and technology have gone from the cutting edge of Web applications to being somewhat outdated in terms of their functionality for classrooms. As innovators who are driven

Figure 9.1. Students' Use of Internet. Graph showing how students are becoming increasingly connected to the Internet and to their peers and are regularly using the Internet, cell phones, and text messaging.

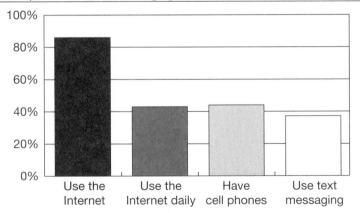

by the goal of promoting knowledge integration (which will never become outdated!), we are eager to keep pace with the evolution of computers and information technologies.

We are currently creating new technology frameworks and learning environments that capitalize on recent developments in how the Internet can be used by educational communities. Our new generation of WISE technology and curriculum extends our previous ideas and approaches. We build on several dimensions of WISE success, including the capability of technology to help scaffold student activities, the capability to provide real-time feedback and reflection opportunities for teachers, and the capability of supporting communities of curriculum or technology developers.

WISE CONTRIBUTIONS TO LEARNING TECHNOLOGIES

WISE has contributed to our knowledge about technology, curriculum, and instruction. The sections below review these contributions, which may be useful to other research or development projects, and which continue to guide our new designs.

Scaffolding Inquiry Curriculum

WISE has made a general contribution to scaffolding students and teachers as they conduct inquiry science activities. When it is used to deliver activities and materials that are designed according to the knowledge integration framework, WISE scaffolds the entire classroom to become a learning community. Students collaborate with peers, teachers engage deeply with students, ideas are exchanged in open discussion and electronically. Not only do students receive carefully designed or selected materials with strategic timing, but they are guided to reflect, create new ideas, and critically review the work of peers. WISE can also provide instructions for setting up experimental apparatus, collecting data, making field observations, or holding a classroom debate.

In addition to scaffolding student activities, WISE is able to help teachers adopt a knowledge integration approach by drawing attention to student ideas, providing time for deep interactions with students and allowing flexibility for holding spontaneous whole-class discussions. When combined with some guidance from a mentor, WISE can help teachers reflect on the progress of their students and the usefulness of classroom activities. Teachers can use the information about student ideas to make decisions about when to provide feedback and how to structure a class discussion.

We are continuing to investigate the most effective patterns for inquiry curriculum and matching them to appropriate learning goals. For instance, a debate pattern lends itself to the treatment of socioscientific issues such as global climate change. We are also adding new technology features to WISE (discussed in detail below) that allow a wider range of curriculum designs. For example, we are expanding the available features for collaborations and peer exchange on the WISE student portal, which will allow curriculum that includes brainstorming activities, wiki pages, collaborative concept maps, and peer review galleries. New capabilities for logging student activities will allow WISE to provide more information to teachers, allowing them to select the information that they need. We can also use the logging of student contributions within WISE to allow for new forms of feedback to students. For example, students could receive automatic feedback on their choice of settings for a scientific model, or they could be directed into a certain discussion group based on their responses to previous assessment items. Such tools and features will be a focus of our own continuing research on the most effective forms of inquiry curriculum and assessments.

Integrating Technologies

WISE has also made substantial contributions in the domain of technology integration. The initial goal of WISE was to embed Web materials within rich inquiry projects in order to make them more relevant and engaging for students. Recently, WISE has achieved even greater levels of interdependency and interoperability among its component technologies. For example, WISE reflection notes typically depend upon the context in which they appear. The graphing tool can be automatically loaded with data from student observations. And embedded assessment items called Challenge Questions can be programmed to redirect students automatically to certain points within the project depending on their response.

Recently, we have enabled the integration of powerful visualization tools such as Molecular Workbench into WISE inquiry projects (Linn, Husic, Slotta, & Tinker, 2006). Visualizations of unseen processes such as molecular motion, rapid events such as collisions, or large-scale phenomena such as global climate change can now be explored, including guidance from WISE and linked reflection prompts. Embedding such visualizations within a WISE project can enable students to make sense of highly complex phenomena by directing their attention to important elements and allowing them to test out their ideas. Many research groups have claimed that visualizations are too difficult for students to follow, but including scaffolding and guidance allows us to make visualizations accessible to students in such a way that they contribute to an integrated understanding.

Another good example of technology integration within WISE is seen in our incorporation of handheld computers. Tim Zimmerman (2005) investigated the use of these mobile devices (in his case, Palm Pilots) to support students during a field trip to a local aquarium. He formed a partnership with educators from the aquarium who were concerned that students were not engaging deeply with the science content of their exhibits. The partners decided to create a WISE project that would provide a rich inquiry context relating to issues of habitat destruction, seafood harvest, and global climate change. They created the WISE "Adaptation and Marine Conservation" project, which helped students anticipate issues of habitat destruction and marine conservation in advance of their aquarium visit, collect meaningful observations during the visit itself, and then work with those observations as data in a culminating activity once they returned to the classroom. Zimmerman introduced a special use of Palm Pilots to support student observations during the aquarium visit. He developed WISE "Palm Forms," which could be downloaded to the handheld computers, completed by students, and then uploaded back to the WISE server (see Figure 9.2). The data from all student observations could then be aggregated on the server, resulting in a "class data set" that could be viewed and manipulated during later activities within the project.

The integration of handheld technology into WISE using the Palm Forms tool illustrates the general goal of technology integration, and the contributions that WISE has made in this dimension. Ultimately, science classrooms should include a wide array of different technologies that are integrated, including Web applications, local software applications running on student computers (e.g., rich simulations or probeware), handheld devices and applications, and various forms of displays and interfaces.

Finally, the WISE portal is itself a major achievement of technology integration, managing a complex network of sharing and permissions, connecting student data with the appropriate teacher and allowing the original author of a curriculum project to share permissions with other teachers or authors. The authoring tool integrates a variety of technologies, supporting the design of new WISE project with wizards and allowing the creation of an arbitrary sequence of activities and steps that are made up from any of a large selection of technology tools. In the WISE Teacher's Portal, we see a high level of integration between the curriculum, the database of student responses, and the assessment tool. In the world of educational technologies, WISE was the first platform to support such a substantive array of interdependent functions.

Figure 9.2. WISE pioneered the integration of handheld devices with Web-based activities. As early as 1999, we created the WISE Palm Form, which students downloaded onto their Palm Pilots and used to collect observation data. This allowed WISE researchers to investigate how they could enrich students' activities and observations during field trips by connecting them with ongoing classroom-based curriculum.

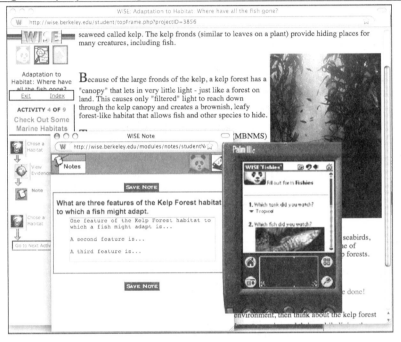

WISE has taken important strides in technology integration, with many well-integrated tools and the incorporation of some other devices and software platforms. But much more remains to be done to improve the level of integration among WISE steps, as well as the access of student data by teachers. Meanwhile, the entire fabric of technology continues to evolve in every sector of society. Sections below discuss some recent trends in the evolution of the Internet and computer technologies, as well as some recent developments in our own designs.

Supporting Educational Communities

A third area where WISE has made important contributions is that of communities and partnerships. As described in Chapter 5, the process of designing, developing, testing, and revising a WISE curriculum project provides a natural context for a multidisciplinary partnership, whose members work closely together over a span of months or even years. These partnerships sometimes develop two or more WISE projects to create themes or sequences, such as "Space Plants" or "Deformed Frogs." To support partnerships and other groups, we added the WISE Community tool to the portal.

Overall, the WISE curriculum library illustrates an important contribution to the notion of a global curriculum community. We launched WISE in 1997 with the aim of developing a small public library of inquiry curriculum projects. At first, our goal was to provide that library to a wide audience of teachers, maintaining the projects, fixing any broken Web links and updating the science content as new development occurred. For example, as new evidence emerges in the deformed frogs debate or new arguments are developed around global climate change, the authoring partnerships continue to update those curriculum projects. WISE has achieved this goal, serving an active network of science teachers that extends well beyond our research partnerships.

Over the past 8 years, the number of teachers running projects and the total number of runs has grown rapidly (see Figure 9.3). These are

Figure 9.3. Although WISE has registered 40,000 teacher accounts, the number of teachers actively running WISE projects is relatively small. Even so, it is remarkable that several hundred teaches per year are now running WISE inquiry projects and that this number appears to be rising notably.

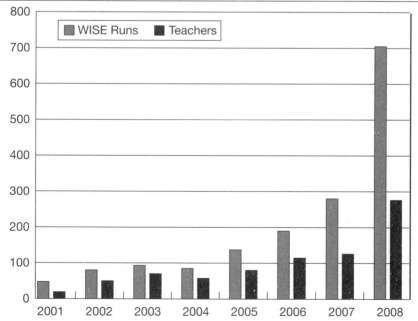

teachers who use a WISE project in their classroom as opposed to simply registering for a WISE account. The number of teachers is clearly increasing over the last 3 years of this span, and the ratio of project runs per teacher is climbing as well. In 2008, almost 300 teachers ran WISE projects, with an average of more than two projects per teacher. Because many teachers only ran a single WISE project, this means that many others ran as many as three or four during the school year.

Of course, a curriculum library does not really constitute a community. Teachers who access WISE projects from the portal do not generally make contact with peers or mentors there. However, most teachers who use WISE regularly do interact with some community, such as an authoring partnership, professional development partnership, school district initiative, or other research project. Indeed, one of the important findings from our professional development research is that most teachers cannot simply adopt prepackaged curriculum materials without performing some kind of customization or adaptation. Less than half of the project runs depicted in Figure 9.3 used WISE projects from the public library (those projects listed for any user in the portal). Approximately 60% of the time, teachers instead used some adapted version of the library project that was developed as part of a professional development program or research partnership. These various partnerships and programs can interact using the WISE portal. These users form a kind of dynamic, interactive community with many different special interests and subgroups.

Thus, WISE has stimulated a new form of community for the development and exchange of inquiry curriculum. A variety of content developers have employed WISE in creating curriculum that meets their professional agenda. For example, as described in the previous section, the Monterey Bay Aquarium (Monterey, California) has co-authored a WISE curriculum concerned with habitat adaptation of marine species. The American Physiology Society has created several inquiry projects on health-related topics (e.g., physiology of fitness and organic foods). The U.S. Forestry Service has sponsored the design and development of a forest fire project that helps students debate whether the construction of new homes should be permitted next to national forests.

One community of designers and customizers has grown around the topic of wolf management. Wolves are a vital "top predator" in many North American wilderness areas, and a valuable example of the role of such animals in promoting biodiversity. A team of environmental educators working in the International Wolf Center (Ely, Minnesota) used the WISE authoring system to design and develop an inquiry-oriented curriculum concerned with wolf management. This project has now been used by dozens of teachers in several states, and has been translated into three different languages. More importantly, any teacher who runs the wolf project can edit the content, delete steps, add new webpages, or change the discussion topics. Such customizations are fairly common, and to date, there are more than 20 distinct versions of the wolf project. One group used the basic structure of the project while changing all of its contents to address the issue of salmon preservation.

WISE has demonstrated the potential of a technology platform to foster and sustain real communities of designers and developers, including exchange and adaptation of curriculum by teachers. We have also seen the emergence of a community of researchers who have found that they could adapt existing WISE materials or create new ones for the purposes of their investigations, then conduct their classroom trials using the WISE platform. Professor Frank Fischer and his group have translated the WISE "Deformed Frogs" and "How Far Does Light Go?" projects into German and used them as the basis for a series of well-regarded investigations on the nature of student argumentation (Fischer & Slotta, 2002; Kollar, Fischer, & Slotta, 2007). Professor Janice Gobert (2005) added the WISE Show-and-Tell environment to the existing "Plate Tectonics" project to enable her research of students' peer review. She ran a fascinating experiment where students in a California classroom critiqued the models of Earth processes drawn by students in Massachusetts (on the opposite side of the United States) and vice versa. Several other researchers have staked their careers on WISE as a suitable research platform, and we are committed to supporting this community. Indeed, we feel that we have only begun in this dimension of community, and seek new ways of engaging our colleagues in the co-design of new features for WISE.

Ironically, although many researchers investigate the power and promise of technology and even online communities for learning and instruction, there are very few examples of online communities where such researchers, their graduate students, or the wider public can access or exchange resources, demos, information, or expertise. There is great potential for online communities that mirror the needs and practices of existing offline collaborations and exchange communities.

Research is needed to determine the most effective design for such communities. Although many have created digital libraries, few find these repositories useful. Researchers and graduate students would like to be able to go to a single location and easily access demos of successful innovations (such as WISE). Many who instruct courses in educational technologies would like to access other functional demos or electronic versions of papers for their students. And many researchers would like to offer their innovations for wider use. Yet most repositories are poorly curated, difficult to search, or inadequately annotated. In addition, most potential users complain that the available resources are too disorganized for them to benefit.

Ideally, an online community for educators would become a dynamic source of new ideas, new materials, and new collaborations. WISE has been able to provide a fairly flexible curriculum development environment to the research community, but it has not been very easy for researchers to add new technologies into WISE or to change the user interface of the overall system. Ultimately, we hope to promote a more robust technology exchange community where educational researchers are able to collaboratively develop new applications for WISE, new kinds of interfaces, and new extensions of the technology. Rather than relying on the WISE team to create and maintain a common resource for the field, we hope that our collaborators will begin to contribute new resources and extend existing ones. Perhaps multiple versions of WISE could evolve, or extensions of WISE that run on mobile devices or within virtual worlds.

In summary, WISE has contributed to the corpus of learning technologies by creating scaffolds for inquiry learning, developing interoperable resources, and creating a place for communities to be formed and sustained. In the next section, we describe how recent developments in computer and information technologies will help promote such a community, including a new open source version of the WISE curriculum and learning environment.

EVOLVING TECHNOLOGIES, PHILOSOPHIES, AND PARADIGMS

When we began developing WISE in the mid-1990s, the Web was mainly employed for sending information from Web servers (large computers whose purpose was to store and retrieve files) to Web browsers (software applications that run on a Web user's local computer and request files from Web servers). Within just a few years, however, the Internet had matured to include an increasingly large spectrum of Web applications, where people direct their browsers to a certain location where they can perform valuable tasks such as banking, shopping, travel arrangements, or email. Indeed, WISE was an early example of such a Web application, as teachers and students went to the WISE location in order to access the wealth of functionality that it provided. The next two sections define areas of tremendous growth over the past several years that hold promise for a new generation of technology-enhanced learning environments—including the next version of WISE.

Open Source, Open Content, and Social Networks

One phenomenon that continues to grow in its importance and its relevance to education is the open source software movement, exemplified and catalyzed by the cooperative development of the Linux operating system. Linux was a variation of a popular Web server operating system called Unix that was written with the express purposes of being "opened" to the wider community of software developers. Because they all needed a highly flexible operating system that would run on their servers and host their Web applications, it was in everyone's best interest to cooperatively develop this common resource. Even dot-com companies that were actually in competition with one another saw the advantages of participating in the Linux community. The fantastic success of Linux demonstrated to technophiles and philosophers of science around the world that the connectivity of the Internet had enabled a new form of very complex cooperation.

At the turn of the millennium, a new era of open source development had sprung up, with developers everywhere seeking economic and technical advantage by jointly creating portions of their software. For example, programmers in the gaming industry freely share code that is arduous to develop but commonly needed, such as graphics algorithms for representing animated characters and the worlds in which they live. Search algorithms, Web browsers, and even multiuser virtual environments have been offered for co-development as open source projects. Indeed, Sourceforge.net, one of the most prominent Web sites for hosting and supporting such open source projects, now has more than 200,000 software projects registered with almost 2 million users.

By "open sourcing" such common code elements, the community ensures that everyone has access, which results in the emergence of norms and standards. The economic arguments for open source are solid, as the combined human resources of all participating groups are maximized through the joint development of software elements that are commonly needed by all members. This allows programmers to focus less time on developing basic software infrastructure such as operating systems or graphics subroutines, and more of their time on the specific details of their end products.

Inspired in part by the startling productivity and spirit of cooperation that were experienced by those who were developing materials for the Internet, new philosophies of "openness" and online community began to emerge. Through their participation in or observations of open source software communities, people began to realize that their own connectedness was the key to an entire new dimension of the Internet. Computer programmers, content developers, and professionals from all walks of life soon recognized that by connecting themselves with extended peer groups online they could gain leverage in matters of common interest, from developing software algorithms to sharing music preferences to forming political action groups. Although this chapter cannot begin to review all of the activities and groups that characterize this movement, it is important to point out that the Internet has become a social phenomenon.

No longer is the Web just a place where files are served to browsers, it is now a true web that interconnects people and activities. Web applications have followed this trend, becoming increasingly devoted to functionality that can only be realized by connecting large numbers of people. For example, many young people first experienced the power of such social applications through Napster, a music sharing community that exploded to include more than 25 million users by 2001. Logging on to Napster, a member was immediately connected to all of the music files belonging to all other members, allowing a shared universal library of songs from every genre of music. Of course, there were many issues of copyright and licensing, and several lawsuits from the music industry eventually brought Napster to an end. Still, Napster and many other file sharing communities that followed have solidified the role of online sharing applications.

Many other popular social applications have emerged, including eBay, Craigslist, TripAdvisor, and online spaces for every imaginable interest group. More recently, applications such as MySpace, LinkedIn, and Facebook have offered ways for people to build and maintain their social relationships. These applications boast tens of millions of members and are extremely valuable business commodities (current estimates place the value of MySpace at several billion U.S. dollars). All of this value is based solely on the power derived from social connections, with various business models (such as advertising or private member services) designed to capitalize on those networks. A new era of social networking, sometimes referred to as "Web 2.0" has begun.

Collaborative Editing, Shared Repositories, and Semantic Metadata

The idea of aggregating resources across a wide membership, popularized in part by Napster, has matured into several new forms of shared storage and collaborative creativity. Whereas Web servers (such as the WISE server) are dedicated to the use of specific groups, new universally accessible spaces are emerging, such as Wikipedia, YouTube, or Google.

Wikis are a very promising new form of collaborative knowledge construction. Depending on how the authoring permissions are configured (Wikipedia can be authored by anyone), users simply direct their Web browser or follow links to a certain page, where they can read about the topic, and then—somewhat surprisingly—add their own edits, additions, or deletions. In this way, the contents of the page actually represent the combined contributions of many visitors, who tend to learn from one another's ideas and improve the overall content of the page. Wikipedia is by far the best example of this form, with more than 2.5 million articles contributed solely by volunteers. There is no single authoritative source of information, and almost all Wikipedia pages are written collaboratively. Simply by virtue of the sheer number of visitors and their shared value for keeping information current and accurate, these pages are becoming an authoritative reference. The checks and balances to keep information current and accurate are not yet resolved, but the tremendous interest and depth of coverage is motivating widespread participation.

Many new applications of wikis have emerged, and many software platforms exist (some of which are available as open source) that make it easy for any individual or group to install a wiki of their own. It is now common for businesses, research projects, sporting clubs, or any other group to host their own private wikis where members can aggregate their knowledge about strategic product development, upcoming events, or even the best hotels in certain cities. Academic groups such as our WISE research team maintain wikis to track all of our design ideas and resources. More recently, more advanced technologies are emerging where a group of users can collaboratively edit a document at the same time. This is different from wikis, where only one user at a time can edit the page. In Google Docs, for example, many users can observe a page in "real time" as it grows and changes while multiple people work on editing it simultaneously. These are very new forms of collaboration, but they illustrate a changing nature of documents, from static objects that are kept closely on a Web server to public documents that grow and change over time in relation to who is using them for what purposes.

Another new, socially oriented technology is that of peer-to-peer networking and multi-user environments, in which users connect with one another "synchronously," meaning that each person sees what the other is doing, "in real time." In real-time chats, for example, each member of the chat session sees what every other member is typing in a constant stream of comments that are usually not saved or recorded, similar to spoken conversation. In virtual network connections (VNC), users can connect through the Internet to a single, common computer, which they can all observe, and take turns operating from a distance. In virtual environments such as Second Life or World of Warcraft, many thousands of users can interact with one another in the form of "avatars" or animated representations that they create for themselves. Both Second Life and World of Warcraft offer users highly engaging, "immersive" experiences, and both are highly successful, each with more than 10 million registered users and tens of thousands logged in at any moment in time.

Another exciting new form of socially oriented software is that of online repositories of user-generated content. These are online exchanges, commonly referred to as "communities" because their users share a common database. One example is YouTube, where 80 million users (in 2008) have contributed more than 2 billion video clips. The Wikipedia article about YouTube says that more than 2.5 billion "views" of videos occurred just in the month of June 2008. Early television shows such as *America's Funniest Home Videos* demonstrated that people love to watch amateur home videos. But how can you find the good ones? Online social spaces are the perfect setting for establishing such popularity. With 80 million viewers, the best videos can easily be determined as those that are rated the highest, forwarded to friends, and simply viewed the most often. Many other repositories have been established, notably Flickr, an online community for sharing photos among friends, in private networks, and with the whole world.

An interesting challenge is how to find certain videos or photos amid 2 billion candidates (the number of items boasted by both Flickr and YouTube). If a member of the community is seeking items in a specific topic area, such as skydiving or how to build a fence, there must surely be some way to help narrow the search. Repository communities like Flickr and YouTube are addressing this challenge in two ways. The first is through the use of social tagging, where the individual who submits the photo or video "tags" the object with keywords that describe it. Anyone that finds and uses that item can add new tags to it, resulting in a growing set of tags that provide a semantic description. The patterns of probability that describe the co-occurrence of tags are referred to as "tag clouds" and can be used to predict new items that might match a person's query. For example, if many items that include a "skydiving" tag also include a "basejumping" tag, the developers of the repository might use that information to suggest images or videos with one of those tags when people search for the other.

Social tags are one example of semantic metadata, which is a broad category that refers to any data that serves to capture the semantic content of a media object. While regular metadata might refer to the author or submitter of the content, its file type, size, and so on, semantic metadata is meant to capture the meaning and context of its contents. Is it suitable for 6th graders? Is it about space travel? Is it highly rated? The wide use of semantic metadata as a means of searching and filtering information is an exciting new dimension of the Internet. One interesting pattern of metadata has to do with co-occurrence of use or preference. Most of us are familiar with the uncanny ability of online shopping sites like Amazon to recommend a book that we would like, based on our prior selection. This is achieved by examining the selections of others with whom we shared some common prior selections. When sufficient numbers of people are included in such analysis, the results can be very effective.

The emergence of socially oriented software has indeed signaled a new era of Internet-based applications, and may indeed be a more suitable use of the Internet than the previous generation of Web applications. Marshall McLuhan (1964) famously observed that whenever a new medium emerges, we tend first to employ it in ways that recapitulate those of previous media. Thus, when motion pictures arrived on the scene, the very first films simply captured live theatrical performances. It took some years for producers to realize that the audio and video streams could be separated, and that the narrative flow could be creatively and productively fragmented and intertwined. Even now, the medium of television is evolving to include reality formats and audience participation via telephone. Similarly, the new medium of the Internet was first employed essentially as a file server, because that was the kind of application that came naturally to developers. We required a decade or so of experience with the Internet before we could begin to draw on its true affordances, which can be found within the social and semantic realms.

THE ROLE OF THE NEW INTERNET IN EDUCATION

What are the implications of Web 2.0 and the other emerging technologies for education? These new forms of Internet applications could be particularly engaging for students if combined with new hardware devices such as multitouch screens (allowing for zooming, swiping, or rotating, such as employed by the Apple iPhone), gestural interfaces, such as the Nintendo Wii and open source, immersive environments, such as the Croquet engine for developing virtual worlds.

But these new collaborative and social technologies must be incorporated into educational research and refined for purposes of learning and instruction. Just as WISE investigated effective uses of Web technologies within inquiry-oriented instruction, new research is required to understand how Web 2.0 technologies can be added to science classrooms.

Clearly, these recent developments are relevant to our future endeavors in WISE—particularly the three dimensions that were detailed in the beginning of this chapter: scaffolding curriculum, technology integration, and online community. With powerful new technology mechanisms such as peer-to-peer networks, social tagging, and virtual network connections, our technology framework can be expanded to scaffold more intricate patterns of inquiry and collaboration in the classroom. By adopting the latest software development strategies that advocate rich media environments with Internet connectivity, we can improve the integration of our various technologies. And by implementing an open source approach and enhancing our cooperative environments with semantic metadata, we can advance our support of educational communities. The next section describes our latest efforts in developing a new generation of technology and research.

NEW TECHNOLOGY AND RESEARCH
FOR KNOWLEDGE INTEGRATION

In the mid-1990s, WISE was at the forefront in its technology designs. During more than a decade of research, however, we have observed the evolution of the Internet and other computer technologies, and often discussed how we would change or improve WISE to take advantage of this trajectory. Even within our own partnerships, we began to feel the need to expand in the areas of scaffolding frameworks, technology integration, and online communities. This section describes our recent efforts to expand the capacity of WISE in order to better serve the purposes of our own research and that of our collaborators, and to support a richer level of community and open source development.

Technology Enhanced Learning in Science (TELS)

Because WISE is a Web application, its functionality occurs within a Web browser, with no other software to install on student computers. With the click of a URL, anyone with a computer and the Internet can be up and running with a WISE project in no time. Indeed, this is what makes Web applications so powerful, and what was so compelling to our own team as we sought a platform that would be accessible to a wide audience of science teachers in various technology settings. Using Java applets, it has even been possible for WISE to develop highly functional tools for drawing, concept-mapping, argumentation, and other kinds of inquiry activities.

However, there are many other forms of technology-enhanced learning that cannot occur within a webpage, but are still attractive as knowledge integration resources for science inquiry. Computer-based probes are one such technology, which typically have software that is installed on a local computer that allows students to work with the probe software (for reading temperatures, forces, light intensity, and so on). Simulations and animations are another important form of learning technology, and are often used by science teachers to supplement lectures. Many kinds of simulations are programmed using a Web-based technology called Flash, which can be delivered via the Web browser. However, more sophisticated visualizations can require significant computation on the end-user's computer, with sizeable software libraries and dedicated learning environment of their own. These are functional models, meaning that their visual elements are not simply drawn and animated by an artist, but are instead generated dynamically by an underlying computational engine. The result is a highly interactive visualization that helps students investigate scientific concepts.

Two examples of functional models are Genscope and Molecular Workbench, shown in Figure 9.4. Genscope is an interactive biology

Figure 9.4. Genscope (top) and Molecular Workbench (bottom). Recent advances in highly interactive modeling tools offer a new kind of learning experience for students. They also challenge curriculum designers to embed such activities into meaningful inquiry contexts.

model designed to allow students to manipulate the genetics of fictitious species, such as the dragons depicted in the figure. Students can manipulate the processes of genetic inheritance on six levels: DNA, chromosome, cell, organism, pedigree, and population, allowing them to observe and manipulate processes at one biological level that affect life at another level. For instance, they can zoom into the chromosome level and alter the gene that codes for a specific trait, such as "having wings," then observe the effects of this alteration at all the other levels. Molecular Workbench offers a rich visualization of atomic-level processes, including chemical reactions, changes of phase, bonding and energy levels, as well as all physical parameters of the model elements (mass and bonding characteristics of individual atoms, ionic states, initial energy levels, and so forth). Students can experiment with these models, setting initial conditions, changing temperatures of the system, adding new reactants, and comparing different conditions.

Genscope and Molecular Workbench are developed by researchers at the Concord Consortium, a private developer of science education and technology materials located in Concord, Massachusetts. All products from the Concord Consortium are open source and available to the public free of charge. They are built upon sophisticated computational models that offer a true advantage over artistic animations, in terms of scientific validity. For example, atoms and molecules within the Molecular Workbench experience gravitational and even nuclear interactions, as well as hydrogen bonding, in addition to the typical electrical forces. Just as in nature, these other types of forces are most often negligible, but in some cases, they are very important. Solid water would not float if it weren't for hydrogen bonding, which would make for a very different planet Earth!

As discussed in Chapter 3, students can be deeply engaged by the science within such models, although the more complex the model, the more active must be the teacher's engagement in helping students make sense of what is happening. It occurred to us that the powerful visualizations developed by Concord would be well suited for knowledge integration, and that WISE could provide scaffolding for students and teachers, as well as an important inquiry context to help make student investigations of these models more personally relevant. We began a new authoring partnership, including researchers from WISE as well as Concord, to develop a series of WISE projects that would integrate Genscope and Molecular Workbench into WISE. The Molecular Workbench model of hydrogen gases, for example, would be integrated within a new WISE project called "Explosions!" New activities for Genscope would be developed to complement a WISE project on genetic inheritance and disease.

Because the Concord materials consisted of sophisticated computational modeling environments that included large software libraries and local software that required installation on student computers, this presented a technical challenge. How could WISE, which runs within whatever Web browser the student happens to be using, interact deeply with Concord software running on the student's local computer? Thanks to a new software tool called Java Webstart, it was indeed possible to "launch" a Concord model from within WISE. However, once students were engaged with the Concord software, they were outside the Web browser, and there could be no linked scaffolds (such as reflection notes) from WISE. Further, WISE was not capable of collecting any data or log files from student interactions with the Concord models. Thus, our technology integration was limited, and the Web browser in particular was beginning to show its fundamental limitations.

In 2003, WISE and Concord began a much more substantive collaboration, co-founding a new research center that would be dedicated to the study of inquiry curriculum that employs complex visualizations, as well as to the development of a new technology architecture for interactive curriculum materials. We had conducted grant-funded partnerships with the scientists and educators at Concord before, but this time we had something more ambitious in mind. Working together, we created a new proposal to establish a national center for teaching and learning, known as TELS: Technology Enhanced Learning in Science. TELS was funded by the U.S. National Science Foundation with 5 years of initial funding. In addition to researchers from the University of California, Berkeley, and from Concord, TELS involves scholars from several other universities in the United States, Israel, and Canada. It also includes teachers from a dozen middle and high schools, several full-time teacher mentors, and a sizeable technology team. The center is ongoing, with several million dollars of new funding received at the time of this writing.

TELS seeks to advance along the three dimensions that were enumerated above: scaffolding frameworks, educational communities, and technology integration. First, we have advanced our scaffolding framework by adding rich new modeling activities and investigating new designs of inquiry patterns. This effort has required us to develop more than a dozen new WISE projects that allow the deep interconnections between students' experimentation with the models and an overarching inquiry theme. To undertake such a major curriculum design effort, we established six new authoring partnerships: middle school Earth science, life science, and physical science, and high school chemistry, biology, and physics. Each of these partnerships implemented the design process that was detailed in Chapter 6, first identifying suitable inquiry themes, then designing knowledge integration activities that were iteratively refined over a period of several years. Figure 9.5 shows the TELS curriculum, which has been added to the WISE library. Each of these projects includes links to one or more Concord models and targets a science topic that was identified by our teacher partners as being difficult for students to understand.

The second dimension targeted by TELS is that of educational communities. WISE engaged many different kinds of communities, including our authoring partnerships, school partnerships, and online curriculum communities. TELS has made progress in how it supports these groups, with new online supports and a greater emphasis on establishing ongoing authoring and school partnerships. From the outset, we established school partnerships where the teachers were deeply engaged in the process of critically reviewing curriculum, creating customized lesson plans, enacting, and reflecting about TELS assessments. These school partnerships strengthen the experience of teachers and offer an excellent resource for TELS authoring partnerships.

Each summer, we have convened all members of the center—typically between 30 and 50 participants—at a retreat where we review our progress along various dimensions, plan new curriculum, and critique technology designs. The retreat provides an invaluable opportunity for all the different voices within the center to listen to one another. We have also made progress in developing new features for the WISE portal, including improved features for mentors to interact with teachers. Online community is currently an emphasis within the center as we add Web 2.0 functionality into our new technology designs, as discussed in the next section. In essence, TELS has helped WISE itself develop into a stronger community, which serves to strengthen the many educational communities that intersect with the center.

A third dimension of progress is that of technology integration. As discussed above, WISE offers a fair degree of interoperability among its various tools and within its own portal. However, it is not very well suited for integration with other tools or environments, and cannot be easily adapted by our collaborators for their own research purposes. For example, one collaborator wished to extend the functionality of WISE online discussions by adding a feature where students would be placed within a different discussion group depending on their responses to a particular assessment item. WISE was unable to be programmed in that way. Ideally, we would share the software source code with such collaborators, offering it under an open source license. However, WISE was not well suited to be developed as an open source project as the various software libraries were old and intertwined, and

Figure 9.5. TELS Curriculum. Since 2003, The Technology Enhanced Learning in Science (TELS) center has been developing powerful new WISE curriculum projects aimed at every major science topic and grade level. TELS began by asking science teachers at all levels what the most challenging topics were, then created new WISE curriculum to help students develop deep understanding of those topics. The two parts of the Figure show Middle School and High School curriculum projects, respectively.

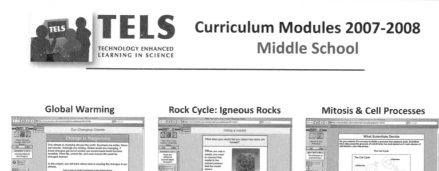

Curriculum Modules 2007-2008
Middle School

Global Warming

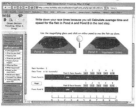

Rock Cycle: Igneous Rocks

Mitosis & Cell Processes

Ocean Bottom Trawling

Simple Inheritance

Heat & Temperature

Hydrogen Fuel Cell Cars

Hanging with Friends: Velocity

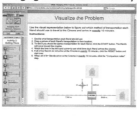

Wolf Ecology & Population

http://TELSCenter.org

Figure 9.5. (cont'd)

TELS
TECHNOLOGY ENHANCED LEARNING IN SCIENCE

Curriculum Modules 2007-2008
High School

Your Community: Asthma

Birds of a Feather Evolve Together

Meiosis: Diversity for Survival

Chemical Reactions

Hydrogen Fuel Cell Cars

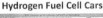

Phases of Matter

Recycling Old Tires   **Airbags: Too Fast, Too Furious?**   **Modeling Static Electricity**

http://TELSCenter.org

lacked the modularity that would be required for a wide community of developers to use it productively.

Moreover, WISE is limited in its ability to share data with other software programs that are running on the student's local computer. This is an intentional limitation designed into the basic architecture of Web browsers that is meant to reduce the prospect of virulent Web applications that can access the data from a user's computer files. However, it means that it is difficult or impossible for an application like WISE to read data directly from a Microsoft Excel spreadsheet, a probeware application, or any other locally running software. Thus, while it was possible to launch Molecular Workbench from within WISE, it was not possible to capture any information from the students' use of the models during the project. This limitation had serious implications for TELS, as the researchers wished to access the student data logs from Concord models within their WISE curriculum. For example, Kevin McElhaney was the researcher on the TELS airbag project. He wanted to design WISE scaffolds for students' experimentation with a Concord model of the relative movements of the airbag and driver. Ideally, the WISE software would be able to know how many times students had run the model, and whether they were ever able to set the parameters so that the airbag deployed safely. Because of the fundamental separation of Web browsers from all other applications, this was not possible.

Right from the start, TELS sought to completely redesign the technology framework in such a way that would allow new tools and scaffolds to be developed, and existing software projects like the Concord models to be deeply integrated. We also recognized the opportunity to providing new supports for teachers, such as real-time updates on student progress or the capability to freeze all student machines with the click of a mouse. We set out to design a new platform for learning technologies that would support educational researchers as they continued developing such innovations and would make our innovative methods and materials more accessible to the wider learning sciences community.

The Scalable Architecture for Interactive Learning (SAIL)

We convened a team of educational researchers, computer scientists, and technology developers from several universities who have worked for 5 years to design and developed the Scalable Architecture for Interactive Learning (SAIL). This new open source technology framework will underlie all future tools and materials developed within our research community and hopefully will support a much wider community of software and curriculum developers.

The SAIL architecture is a specification for Java-based learning objects that are interactive in nature: curriculum materials that respond to user inputs, capture user data, support groups of users who collaborate, and dynamically call other objects, depending on user inputs. SAIL is thus concerned with the basic technology architectures and ontologies of the various tools and features that will make up our new technology environment. By carefully designing the "genetics" of digital content and functionality, we can enable the development of technology-enhanced learning environments that support much more powerful kinds of learning, with more scalable, sustainable software. From the outset, SAIL has been designed to leverage the power of open source development, offering a common, open architecture that will support a wide array of richly interactive learning technologies. SAIL will serve as a resource to an international community of designers and developers from diverse projects, leading to interoperability of technology tools, flexibility of interfaces, reusability of content, and greater longevity and sustainability for our innovations.

The SAIL design team evaluated many possible development strategies, including the use of new platforms such as Flash, or the development of plug-ins for Web browsers. Ultimately, they settled on the Java platform, because it is supported by many industry standards, is flexible and scalable, and is used widely by software developers. Java also lends itself quite well to the kind of modularity and interoperability that we wished to support, and is well suited to structured open source code projects. To implement student learning environments in Java, however, means letting go of the convenience and accessibility of the Web browser. Because the previous version of WISE required only a Web browser, any move to a richer software infrastructure would inevitably render the process more complex for teachers, and hence, our decision was not taken lightly. However, it will open the door for much more sophisticated learning environments, highly integrated learning technologies, and open source exchange communities. And we have emphasized in our design that we must come close to the ease of use enjoyed with the previous version of WISE.

WISE 3.0

Once we had developed SAIL, our first order of business was to implement a new version of WISE that would respond to the various technical obstacles described above. All of the TELS researchers as well as our various collaborators required a continuity of the WISE functionality in order to continue with their work. However, they were excited about the expanded capabilities for scaffolding and the interoperability with Concord models that SAIL would provide. We also wished to address the very real issue that all WISE content was "endangered" as a result of its universal dependence on the single WISE server and software code base. We wanted to enable other researchers who had previously used WISE to install and develop their own version of the software. Expanding the number of distinct code installations would help ensure the survival of WISE and begin the slow but important process of evolving its form. Because the new version of WISE was based on the SAIL architecture, our collaborators could begin to share the load of software development, as well as the ownership.

In 2008, we released version 3.0 of WISE as an open source project (see Figure 9.6). Although it is no longer a Web application, it is still very much an Internet application. Students still direct their Web browsers to a portal where their teacher has set up a project for them to run. They select that project and it is downloaded to their local machine as a fairly large (approximately 10–20 megabyte), interactive Java application. If they had already downloaded it in a previous session, it will not download again unless there have been changes in the master version that must be updated. The new Java version of WISE is a more modern, interactive application than the previous Web version, whose interface was essentially one of hyperlinks that could occasionally result in sluggish response times. This was particularly true whenever WISE steps had to download large Java applets like WISE-Draw or even larger Java applications like Concord models. Although the new Java format does require substantial download times initially, once the students begin working on the project, the performance of all steps is immediate, providing a satisfactory user experience that students have come to expect from software.

Figure 9.6. Though WISE 3.0 runs in Java, the Internet is still used as a means of accessing curriculum and saving all student work into a database for assessment. This approach allows for new kinds of functionality within the WISE curriculum, such as embedded models like Molecular Workbench (as shown). It also will allow interesting new forms of interaction between students and teachers. All materials are currently offered under an open source license, with an active community of technology developers across many academic institutions.

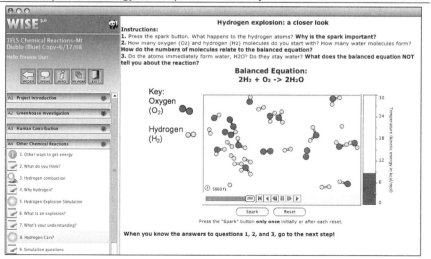

WISE 3.0 has now replaced WISE 2 in our research projects, but not in every classroom or school partnership. Some teachers still prefer the simplicity and accessibility of the Web-based version, perhaps because their school computer lab is of an older vintage. Other teachers have trouble gaining permission to download any software (including WISE) to school computers, making it troublesome to engage with the new version of WISE. We expected such challenges, and are continuing to serve WISE 2 for the next few years in parallel to the new SAIL-based version. Indeed, at the time of this writing, we are still in the early stages of classroom trials of WISE 3.0. This project holds significant promise of new forms of scaffolding, greater levels of technology integration, and better performance for students and teachers, as well as further advances through the open source community. New technology development is an essential aspect of our research, and we are not strangers to the cutting edge.

FUTURE DIRECTIONS

Technology is coming to students' pockets, their notebooks, their classroom walls, and their furniture. Students will be wirelessly connected to the Internet, to one another, and to their teachers at school, on the playground, and at home. They will come to expect technology to play a meaningful role in their learning, and they will very likely be rewarded. Teachers are increasingly ambitious about what they attempt with technology, and schools are increasingly supportive.

Although educational research is only beginning to develop solid recommendations for how such technologies should be applied in support of deep learning, there is plenty of room for optimism. While it is difficult to foresee where our own research will go in the next decade, we are beginning to develop some exciting new directions within the TELS center, and in our extended collaborations. Our current funded projects are aiming to achieve a higher level of collaboration among students, with rich scaffolding approaches that allow students to work autonomously on complex projects.

The SAIL framework allows a much greater flexibility in the control of the flow of activities, permitting us to design special tools where teachers can pause students' computers for discussion, send the class to an interesting Web site, or take stock of how students are doing. We are investigating new ways to provide feedback to teachers, before, after, and even during class, such as graphical displays of student progress and samples of their work. We are also making progress in the development of a powerful new portal that capitalizes on the latest developments of social networking and semantic metadata. In general, it is safe to assume that WISE curriculum will begin to take on a higher degree of collaboration, and a richer array of interactive materials, including probeware, models, and even multi-user environments.

Finally, the theoretical foundation of knowledge integration will never be retired by the emergence of new technologies or software paradigms. The goal of establishing an atmosphere of inquiry and reflection in the classroom and of encouraging the teacher to develop expertise in this form of pedagogy is an enduring one. The curriculum patterns and design principles that we have identified over the course of 2 decades in the CLP, KIE, and WISE projects will serve us well in designing any new form of technology-enhanced learning. We are looking forward to building on this legacy, and welcome the ever-changing landscape in which we will conduct our continuing research.

RECOMMENDED READINGS

Kolbitsch, J., & Maurer, H. (2006). The transformation of the Web: How emerging communities shape the information we consume. *Journal of Universal Computer Science, 12*(2), 187–213.

> This article provides an accessible and comprehensive summary of the various new dimensions of the Web. It summarizes and discusses features such as blogs, wikis, podcasts, file sharing, and online communities.

Slotta, J. D. (in press). Evolving the classrooms of the future: The interplay of pedagogy, technology and community. To appear in F. Fischer and P. Dillenbourg (Eds.), *Kaleidoscope Volume on Classrooms of the Future*. New York: Springer.

> This book chapter outlines some new directions for technology-enhanced research to promote more elaborate forms of collaborative learning in the science classroom. It offers a discussion of new types of computer interfaces, handheld devices, and the rich use of semantic metadata. It also discusses the potential value of open source and open content communities for education.

Virtual community. (2008, September 21). Retrieved September 22, 2008, from http://en.wikipedia.org/w/index.php?title=Virtual_community&oldid=239946672; http://en.wikipedia.org/wiki/Online_communities

> With such rapidly evolving topics as social networks and online communities, readers are referred to this highly authoritative and up-to-date source for summaries and links. Indeed, Wikipedia exemplifies many aspects of the socially oriented nature of Web 2.0, as its content is aggregated from the contributions of millions of people.

Recommendations and Next Steps

We have been fortunate to carry out a sustained research and development effort with input from a community of enthusiastic users, researchers, and reviewers. What have we learned and what are the next steps?

We are enthusiastic about the opportunities technology offers for improving science education, but we are also daunted by the perils of misusing this important resource. This book has emphasized and illustrated the importance of weaving together the ways that students integrate and sort out their ideas with the design of instruction. The least effective uses of technology are often those that neglect the process of knowledge integration.

We realize that technology remains a scarce resource for many schools. It is therefore important that technology be used where it can do the most good, namely in helping students integrate their ideas about complex science topics and enabling them to become lifelong learners. Our collaborations with hundreds of teachers in schools around the world have demonstrated the complexity of science teaching and the importance of inquiry learning. The use of technology to support inquiry is consistent with the findings of a wide range of research and literature in the learning sciences. Technology can streamline inquiry activities by scaffolding students' learning and resolving logistical issues in the classroom so that teachers can focus on supporting conceptual understanding.

Our work over the past decade suggests some promising directions for policy decisions by school districts and government education panels, as well as some important lessons for educators, curriculum and assessment designers, and professional developers.

WHAT ARE THE TAKE-HOME LESSONS?

First, WISE demonstrates that technology can enable new forms of learning and instruction in the classroom. New teachers are constantly encouraged to apply a constructivist approach to learning, emphasize inquiry, and become a "guide on the side" instead of a "sage on the stage." But this is very difficult to put into practice, especially in a domain like science where standards often call for covering an extensive list of challenging concepts. Scaffolding technologies like WISE can help teachers transform their classes by allowing students to work autonomously, interact with rich learning materials, collaborate with peers, and independently develop a deep understanding of topics.

Second, technology environments like WISE can incorporate assessment into instruction as a learning opportunity that also informs refinement of the curriculum. When teachers enact new forms of learning and new patterns of interaction, they need new forms of assessment that tap progress and reveal the limitations of instruction. Technology tools can help collect students' ideas and make them visible to teachers. This information can inform spontaneous, formative adjustments of instruction. For example, a teacher may notice that many students are interpreting an interactive model without exploring all the variables, or that they are setting up their axes in a graphing tool without considering the experiment they will conduct. Because students are engaged in working with the technology and inquiry materials, teachers can observe these events and respond by interrupting the class with spontaneous mini-lectures, discussions, or reminders for students. Teachers can make even more thoughtful appraisals of student work when they survey them from one class to the next. They can use embedded notes and drawings to develop a deep understanding of what students are thinking and to explore areas where students might be facing conceptual difficulties. Technology tools can help teachers stay aware of their students' learning trajectory and stay involved in guiding its progression. In this way, assessment becomes less a means of grading students' achievement and more a means of helping teachers monitor students' progress and adjust their instruction accordingly.

Third, innovative, technology-enhanced curricula can serve as a means of teacher professional development. Teachers emerge from certification programs with enthusiasm for establishing an atmosphere of inquiry and collaboration in their classrooms. Unfortunately, the limited experience they receive with such approaches during their preparation programs rarely prepares them to use complex pedagogical activities such as collaborative projects. Many teachers find themselves relying on lectures with supplemental labs, resulting in their continued approach of delivering authoritative messages in a didactic fashion. Even though educational research has established that these traditional approaches are not effective for most students, they are much easier to implement and do not have the same sort of risks that often accompany the use of technology.

Teachers benefit from well-planned science lessons where students work autonomously at computers for a week of curriculum time. WISE demonstrates how carefully designed materials can help teachers learn to use inquiry practices. Adding a rich technology environment such as WISE allows teachers to experiment with new ways of teaching and learning in their classroom. This presents a superb context for professional development programs, which are most effective when they are connected with teachers' actual practice and the outcomes of student learning.

Fourth, the most effective curriculum innovations are those that combine technology advances with insights about learning and instruction from educational research. For example, new technologies like on-line discussions, drawing and graphing tools, and interactive visualizations are all well suited to the kinds of rich inquiry learning described in this book, but only if they are used in conjunction with insight from educational research. The patterns of interaction emerging from our own research of knowledge integration show how theories of learning can guide the design of effective curriculum. In general, the synergies between learning theories and technology can promote the design of materials that are both motivating and effective.

WHAT ARE THE IMPLICATIONS?

There are several implications from WISE that can inform the decision-making within schools, districts, and governmental departments of education. First, schools should promote substantive uses of technology over fragmented, supplemental ones. Schools often have limited technology resources, such as computer labs, that are scheduled in piecemeal fashion by many teachers for supplemental activities. Such fragmented scheduling makes it difficult to achieve the kind of learning and instruction we describe in this book. Instead, teachers need to plan sustained investigations that have learning consequences for students even when they can only access technology for a few days at a time. Furthermore, teachers who begin developing or adopting innovative technology-enhanced curriculum need to be able to refine their practice over time. Thus, priority should be given to teachers who present a clear plan for integrating the technology deeply into their instruction and who are committed to regular use of this approach. Such a plan should incorporate assessments, student homework, and long-term projects emphasizing inquiry and peer collaborations.

Second, technology requires support. Even with extensive access to computer resources, teachers will rightfully be hesitant to plan for any deep integration of such resources unless they are certain that they will be up and running. And without the availability of support staff, it is simply impossible to ensure that all computers and software will always be up and running. Because such staff are much more costly than the computer equipment, this is a major issue that must be addressed within any school or district. As long as it remains a possibility that computers will not be working properly on any given school day, teachers will not commit to using them in any meaningful fashion.

Third, curriculum partnerships are an effective and efficient way of creating new science materials. The goals and interests of technology developers, science interest groups, and educators are distinct, but often complementary. Many science disciplinary groups are actively engaged in developing rich materials for classrooms, but have little experience with technology and little opportunity to consider educational research. These include governmental and non-governmental agencies (e.g., NASA, the National Geographic Society, or local departments of forestry or natural resources), as well as museums, conservation groups, and even private citizens. Curriculum designers should draw on the wealth of science knowledge within this community, ensuring that materials are accurate and current, and enabling connections between students and the scientists where possible. Such partnerships benefit all members, who gain pedagogical perspective and work together to define an effective intersection of specific technologies, learning goals, and science content domains.

HOW CAN YOU GET INVOLVED?

The efforts of all the designers, educators, and researchers in the WISE project have aimed to provide an open, sustained, and well-supported resource for science educators around the world. WISE is free to all users and can be translated into any language. It is available to any researcher as a platform for developing materials, delivering them to classrooms, and collecting student data. Moreover, the collection of WISE curriculum projects are maintained as a Web-based library for public access by all science teachers, who can even make their own customized copies. Teachers can sign up their students to use any project and then save their work on the WISE public server. Because this basic functionality is also important to our research, we do not anticipate any interruption in the service in the foreseeable future. Any teacher, researcher, or curriculum developer can access the WISE materials at our project Web site: *http://wise.berkeley.edu.*

The new generation of WISE software is portable and open-source, allowing researchers or technology developers to make their own copy and develop the tools or materials as they see fit. We have established a community of users and developers—including many former WISE PhD students, who are now conducting their own programs of research, and other individuals who share a common pedagogical perspective, but who may have different research goals and approaches. Already, the technology community is growing, and we expect many wonderful new features and environments in the coming years. Anyone interested in accessing this community can find contact information on the WISE Web site.

School district administrators or teacher educators can get involved in WISE by supporting its use among teachers. School administrators can provide access, support, and encouragement to teachers who are interested in using technology in science.

This book can be used by pre-service or in-service teachers who want to understand a knowledge integration approach to instruction. It is designed for use in pre-service courses or in-service workshops on topics of technology integration, curriculum customization, or science teaching.

Policymakers can use this book as a source of evidence to support their planning or decisions about technology. Our experiences in WISE illustrate the benefit of coherent programs of technology, support, and teacher professional development.

The WISE Web site provides information about our various research projects, both past and present. We also recommend the book *Designing Coherent Science Education* (Kali , Linn, & Roseman, 2008), that synthesizes the research findings from two major research programs funded by the U.S. National Science Foundation (WISE and IQWST).

We invite anyone who is interested in science education and eager to prepare the leaders of the future to test our ideas, add new insights, and continue to build a coherent and generative community of innovation. As a field, we have a promising trajectory, with exciting innovations on the horizon and a stunning potential for transforming learning in 21st-century classrooms.

References

Anderson, R. C., Nguyen-Jahiel, K., McNurlen, B., Archodidou, A., Kim, S.-Y., Reznits-kaya, A., Tillmanns, M., & Gilbert, L. (2001). The snowball phenomenon: Spread of ways of talking and ways of thinking across groups of children. *Cognition and Instruction, 19*, 1–46.

Becker, H. J., & Ravitz, J. L. (1999, Summer). The influence of computer and internet use on teachers' pedagogical practices and perceptions. *Journal of Research on Computing in Education., 31*(4), 356–384.

Bell, P. (2004). The educational opportunities of contemporary controversies in science. In M. C. Linn, E. A. Davis, & P. Bell (Eds.), *Internet environments for science education* (pp. 233–260). Mahwah, NJ: Lawrence Erlbaum.

Bell, P., Davis, E., & Linn, M. C. (1995). The knowledge integration environment: Theory and design. In T. Koschmann (Ed.), *Proceedings of the Computer Support for Collaborative Learning 1995 Conference* (CSCL'95, Bloomington, IN). Mahwah, NJ: Lawrence Erlbaum.

Bloom, B. (1956). *Taxonomy of educational objectives: The classification of educational goals. (Handbook 1: Cognitive domain).* New York: David McKay.

Chang, H.-Y. (2008). *Review of research on dynamic visualizations in science learning.* Proceedings of the 8th International Conference of the Learning Sciences, pp. 3-226–3-227. Utrecht, The Netherlands: International Society of the Learning Sciences.

Chi, M. T. H. (2005). Common sense conceptions of emergent processes: Why some misconceptions are robust. *Journal of the Learning Sciences, 14*, 161–199.

Chi, M. T. H., Bassok, M., Lewis, M., Reimann, P., & Glaser, R. (1989). Self-explanations: How students study and use examples in learning to solve problems. *Cognitive Science, 13*, 145–182.

Clark, D. B. (2004). Hands-on investigation in Internet environments: Teaching thermal equilibrium. In M. C. Linn, E. A. Davis., & P. Bell (Eds.), Internet environments for science education (pp. 175–200). Mahwah, NJ: Lawrence Erlbaum.

Clark, D., & Linn, M. C. (2003). Designing for knowledge integration: The impact of instructional time. *The Journal of the Learning Sciences, 12*(4), 451–494.

Cuban, L. (2001). *Oversold and underused: Computers in the classroom.* Cambridge, MA: Harvard University Press.

Cuthbert, A., & Slotta, J. D. (2004). Fostering lifelong learning skills on the World Wide Web: Critiquing, questioning, and searching for evidence. *The International Journal of Science Education, 27*(7), 881–844.

Davis, E. (1998). *Scaffolding students' reflection for science learning.* Unpublished doctoral dissertation. University of California, Berkeley.

Davis, E. A. (2004). Knowledge integration in science teaching: Analyzing teachers' knowledge development. *Research in Science Education, 34*(1), 21–53.

Davis, E. A., Linn, M. C., & Clancy, M. J. (1995). Learning to use parentheses and quotes in LISP. *Computer Science Education, 6*(1), 15–31.

Davis, E. A., Linn, M. C., Mann, L. M., & Clancy, M. J. (1993). Mind your Ps and Qs: Using parentheses and quotes in LISP. In C. R. Cook, J. C. Scholtz, & J. C. Spohrer

(Eds.), *Empirical studies of programmers: Fifth workshop, Palo Alto, CA* (pp. 62–85). Norwood, NJ: Ablex.

diSessa, A. (1993). Toward an epistemology of physics. *Cognition and Instruction, 10*(2/3), 105–225.

diSessa, A. (2000). *Changing minds: Computers, learning, and literacy.* Cambridge, MA: MIT Press.

Edelson, D. C. (2001). Learning-for-use: A framework for the design of technology-supported inquiry activities. *Journal of Research in Science Teaching, 38*(3), 355–385.

Eylon, B. S., & Linn, M. C. (1988). Learning and instruction: An examination of four research perspectives in science education. *Review of Educational Research, 58*(3), 251–301.

Fischer, F., & Slotta, J. D. (2002). Online-controversen in WISE. Wie das Internet genutzt werden kann, um naturwissenschaftliches Denken zugänglich zu machen. *Computer und Unterricht, 11*, 27–29.

Gerard, L. F., Bowyer, J. B., & Linn, M. C. (2008). Principal leadership for technology-enhanced science. *Journal of Science Education and Technology, 17*(1), 1–18.

Gobert, J. (2004). What's on your plate? Exemplary science unit highlighted in *Essential Science for Teachers: Earth and Space Science.* Harvard-Smithsonian Center for Astrophysics, Science Media Group, Annenberg/CPB Project.

Gobert, J. (2005). The effects of different learning tasks on conceptual understanding in science: teasing out representational modality of diagramming versus explaining. *Journal of Geoscience Education, 53(4),* 444–455.

Gobert, J., Slotta, J., & Pallant, A. (2002). Collaborative model-building and peer critique via the Internet. In P. Bell, R. Stevens, & T. Satwicz (Eds.), *Keeping learning complex: The proceedings of the Fifth International Conference of the Learning Sciences (ICLS)* (pp. 536–537). Mahwah, NJ: Lawrence Erlbaum.

Hoadley, C. (1999). *Scaffolding scientific discussion using socially relevant representations in networked multimedia.* Unpublished Ph.D. Dissertation, University of California, Berkeley, CA.

Hoadley, C. M., & Linn, M. C. (2000). Teaching science through online peer discussions: SpeakEasy in the knowledge integration environment. *International Journal of Science Education, 22*(8), 839–857.

Hsi, S., & Hoadley, C. M. (1997). Productive discussion in science: Gender equity through electronic discourse. *Journal of Science Education and Technology, 6*(1), 23–36.

Hyde, J. S., Lindberg, S. M., Linn, M. C., Ellis, A. B., & Williams, C. C. (2008). Gender similarities characterize math performance. *Science, 321*(5888), 494–495.

Kollar, I., Fischer, F., & Slotta, J. D. (2007). Internal and external scripts in computer-supported collaborative learning. *Learning & Instruction, 17*(6), 708–721.

Kolodner, J. L., Crismond, D., Fasse, B. B., Gray, J. T., Holbrook, J., Ryan, M., & Puntambekar, S. (2003). Problem-based learning meets case-based reasoning in the middle-school science classroom: Putting a Learning-by-Design curriculum into practice. *Journal of the Learning Sciences, 12*(4), 495–548.

Lewis, E., Stern, J., & Linn, M. C. (1993). The effect of computer simulations on introductory thermodynamic understanding. *Educational Technology,* Research Section, *33*, 45–58.

Lewis, E. L., & Linn, M. C. (1994). Heat energy and temperature concepts of adolescents, naïve adults, and experts: Implications for curricular improvements. *Journal of Research in Science Teaching, 31*, 657–677.

Linn, M. C. (1995). Designing computer learning environments for engineering and computer science: The scaffolded knowledge integration framework. *Journal of Science Education and Technology, 4* (2), 103–126.

Linn, M. C. (2006). The knowledge integration perspective on learning and instruction. In R. K. Sawyer (Ed.), *The Cambridge handbook of the learning sciences* (pp. 243–264). New York: Cambridge University Press.

Linn, M. C., Davis, E. A., Bell, P. (2004). *Internet environments for science education.* Mahwah, NJ: Lawrence Erlbaum.

Linn, M. C., & Eylon, B.-S. (2006). Science education: Integrating views of learning and instruction. In P. A. Alexander & P. H. Winne (Eds.), *Handbook of Educational Psychology* (2nd ed., pp. 511–544). Mahwah, NJ: Lawrence Erlbaum.

Linn, M. C., & Hsi, S. (2000). *Computers, teachers, peers: Science learning partners.* Mahwah, NJ: Lawrence Erlbaum.

Linn, M. C., Husic, F., Slotta, J. D., & Tinker, R. (2006). Technology enhanced learning in science (TELS): Research programs. *Educational Technology, 46*(3), 54–68.

Linn, M. C., Lee, H-S., Tinker, R., Husic, F., & Chiu, J. (2006). Teaching and assessing knowledge integration in science. *Science,* 313, pp. 1049–1050.

Linn, M. C., Shear, L., Bell, P., & Slotta, J. D. (1999). Organizing principles for science education partnerships: Case studies of students' learning about "Rats in Space" and "Deformed Frogs." *Educational Technology Research & Development, 47*(2), 61–84.

Linn, M. C., & Slotta, J. D. (2006). Enabling participants in online forums to learn from each other. In A. O'Donnell, C. E. Hemelo-Silver, & G. Erkens (Eds.), *Collaborative Learning, Reasoning, and Technology* (pp. 61–98). Mahwah, NJ: Lawrence Erlbaum.

Linn, M. C., & Songer, N. B. (1991). Teaching thermodynamics to middle school students: What are appropriate cognitive demands? *Journal of Research in Science Teaching, 28*(10), 885–918.

Liu, O. L., Lee, H.-S., Hofstetter, C., & Linn, M. C. (2008). Assessing knowledge integration in science: Construct, measures and evidence. *Educational Assessment, 13*(1), 33–55.

McCluhan, M. (1964). *Understanding media: The extensions of man.* New York: Routledge.

McElhaney, K. W., & Linn, M. C. (2008). *Impacts of students' experimentation using a dynamic visualization on their understanding of motion. International perspectives in the learning sciences: Creating a learning world.* Proceedings of the 8th International Conference of the Learning Sciences. Utrecht, The Netherlands: International Society of the Learning Sciences, Inc.

National Research Council (2002). *Improving learning with information technology* (G. E. Pritchard, Ed.). Washington DC: National Academy Press.

Palinscar, A. S., & Brown, A. L. (1984). Reciprocal teaching of comprehension-monitoring and comprehension-fostering activities. *Cognition and Instruction, 2,* 117–175.

Penuel, W. R., Fishman, R., Yamaguchi, R., & Gallagher, L. (2007). What makes professional development effective? Strategies that foster curriculum implementation. *American Educational Research Journal, 44*(4), 921–958.

Quintana, C., Reiser, B. J., Davis, E. A., Krajcik, J., Fretz, E., Duncan, R. G., Kyza, E., Edelson, D., & Soloway, E. (2004). A scaffolding design framework for software to support science inquiry. *The Journal of the Learning Sciences, 13*(3), 337–386.

Reiner, M., Slotta, J. D., Chi, M. T. H., & Resnick, L. B. (2000). Naive physics reasoning: A commitment to substance-based conceptions. *Cognition and Instruction, 18*(1), 1–35.

Reiser, B. J., Tabak, I., Sandoval, W. A., Smith, B. K., Steinmuller, F., & Leone, A. J. (2001). BGuILE: Strategic and conceptual scaffolds for scientific inquiry in biology classrooms. In S. M. Carver & D. Klahr (Eds.), *Cognition and instruction: Twenty-five years of progress* (pp. 263–305). Mahwah, NJ: Lawrence Erlbaum.

Roschelle, J., Pea, R., Hoadley, C., Gordin, D., & Means, B. (2001). Changing how and what children learn in school with computer-based technologies. *The Future of Children, 10*(2), 76–101.

Scardamalia, M. (2002). Collective cognitive responsibility for the advancement of knowledge. In B. Smith (Ed.), *Liberal education in a knowledge society* (pp. 67–98). Chicago: Open Court.

Schmidt, W. H., Raisen, S. A., Britton, E. D., Bianchi, L. J., & Wolfe, R. G. (1997). *Many visions, many aims: A cross-national investigation of curricular intentions in school science.* Dordrecht/Boston/London: Kluwer Academic Publishers.

Slotta, J. D. (in press). Evolving the classrooms of the future: The interplay of pedagogy, technology and community. In F. Fischer & P. Dillenbourg (Eds.), *Kaleidoscope Volume on Classrooms of the Future*. Hillsdale, NJ: Springer.

Slotta, J. D. (2004). The Web-based Inquiry Science Environment (WISE): Scaffolding knowledge integration in the science classroom. In M. C. Linn, P. Bell, & E. Davis (Eds.), *Internet environments for science education* (pp. 203–232). Mahwah, NJ: Lawrence Erlbaum.

Slotta, J. D., Chi, M. T. H., & Joram, E. (1995). Assessing the ontological nature of conceptual physics: A contrast of experts and novices. *Cognition and Instruction, 13*(3), 373–400.

Slotta, J., & Linn, M. C. (2000). How do students make sense of Internet resources in the science classroom? In M. J. Jacobson & R. Kozma (Eds.), *Learning the sciences of the 21st century*. Hillsdale, NJ: Lawrence Erlbaum.

Songer, N., & Linn, M. C. (1991). How do students' views of science influence knowledge integration? *Journal of Research in Science Teaching, 28*(9), 761–784.

Spinuzzi, C. (2005). The methodology of participatory design. *Technical communication, 52*(2), 163–174.

Tinker, R., & Wilensky, U. (2007). *NetLogo climate change model*. Retrieved February 18, 2009, from http://ccl.northwestern.edu/netlogo/models/ClimateChange. Evanston, IL: Center for Connected Learning and Computer-Based Modeling.

Tyack, D., & Cuban, L. (1995). *Tinkering toward utopia: A century of public school reform*. Cambridge, MA: Harvard University Press.

Vygotsky, L. S. (1962). *Thought and language* (E. Hanfmann & G. Vaker, Trans.). Cambridge, MA: MIT Press.

Vygotsky, L. S. (1978). *Mind in society*. Cambridge, MA: Harvard University Press.

White, B. Y., & Frederiksen, J. R. (1998). Inquiry, modeling, and metacognition: Making science accessible to students. *Cognition and Instruction, 16*, 3–118.

White, B., & Frederiksen, J. (2000). Technological tools and instructional approaches for making scientific inquiry accessible to all. In M. Jacobson & R. Kozma (Eds.), *Innovations in science and mathematics education: advanced designs for technologies of learning* (pp. 321–359). Mahwah, NJ: Lawrence Erlbaum.

Wilensky, U. (1999). NetLogo. *http://ccl.northwestern.edu/netlogo*. Center for Connected Learning and Computer-Based Modeling. Northwestern University, Evanston, IL.

Wilensky, U., & Resnick, M. (1999). Thinking in levels: A dynamic systems approach to making sense of the world. *Journal of Science Education and Technology 8*(1), 3–19.

Williams, M., & Linn, M. C. (2003). WISE inquiry in fifth-grade biology. *Research in Science Education, 32*(4), 415–436.

Williams, M., Linn, M. C., Ammon, P., & Gearhart, M. (2004). Learning to teach inquiry science in a technology-based environment: A case study. *Journal of Science Education and Technology, 13*(2), 189–206.

Zhang, H. (2008). Using drawings to support learning from dynamic visualizations. Proceedings of the 8th International Conference on Learning Sciences, Utrecht, The Netherlands: International Society of the Learning Sciences, Inc.

Zimmerman, T. (2005). *Promoting knowledge integration of scientific principles and environmental stewardship: Assessing an issue-based approach to teaching evolution and marine conservation*. Unpublished doctoral thesis. University of California, Berkeley.

Index

About the Authors

Jim Slotta is a cognitive scientist and Associate Professor of Education at the Ontario Institute for Studies in Education (OISE) at the University of Toronto. In 2006, he was named Canada Research Chair in the area of Education and Technology. He also received the 2006 World Technology Award in the category of education. Professor Slotta's current research explores new models of technology-enhanced learning for "smart classrooms." His designs employ cutting edge technologies such as peer-to-peer networks, geographic information systems, multi-user virtual environments, probeware, and cell phone systems in order to scaffold complex curriculum structures and patterns of interactions between students. In order to deliver on the promise of open source and open content materials for education, he has helped to organize a dynamic international community of researchers and technologists who are designing common technology frameworks and exchanging tools and materials. Slotta has published and presented widely concerning the opportunities, challenges, and limitations of technology-based environments.

Marcia C. Linn is professor of development and cognition specializing in education in mathematics, science, and technology in the Graduate School of Education at the University of California, Berkeley. She is a member of the National Academy of Education and a fellow of the American Association for the Advancement of Science, the American Psychological Association, and Association for Psychological Science. She directs the NSF-funded Technology-Enhanced Learning in Science (TELS) center. Board service includes the American Association for the Advancement of Science, the Graduate Record Examination Board of the Educational Testing Service, the McDonnell Foundation Cognitive Studies in Education Practice, and the Education and Human Resources Directorate at the National Science Foundation. She has twice been a fellow at the Center for Advanced Study in Behavioral Sciences. Her books include *Computers, Teachers, Peers* (2000) and *Internet Environments for Science Education* (2004). She has received the National Association for Research in Science Teaching Award for Lifelong Distinguished Contributions to Science Education and the Council of Scientific Society Presidents first award for Excellence in Educational Research.